ScottForesman

SPELLING

Authors

James Beers

Ronald L. Cramer

W. Dorsey Hammond

 ScottForesman

A Division of HarperCollins*Publishers*

Editorial Offices: Glenview, Illinois
Regional Offices: Sunnyvale, California • Tucker, Georgia
Glenview, Illinois • Oakland, New Jersey • Dallas, Texas

ACKNOWLEDGMENTS

TEXT

p. 133: Untitled haiku by Kikaku from *Word Works* by Cathryn Berger Kaye; illustrated by Martha Weston. Copyright © 1985 by the Yolla Bolly Press. By permission of Little, Brown and Company.

ILLUSTRATIONS

pp. 12-33: Susan Swan; **pp. 12, 38, 64, 81, 90, 116, 129, 132:** Marla Rubin; **pp. 23, 24, 28:** Linda Kinnaman; **pp. 38-59:** Mary Grand Pre; **pp. 60-62, 86-89, 112-115, 138-141, 164, 165, 167, 184-187, 189, 195, 197, 199, 201, 205-207, 210-213, 215, 219-221, 225-227:** Beth Herman Design Associates; **pp. 60, 63, 88, 210, 211:** Slug Signorino; **pp. 61, 89:** Patti Green; **pp. 62, 113, 166:** Fran Lee; **pp. 63, 86, 87, 89, 115, 139, 165, 204, 207-209, 220, 221:** B.J. Johnson; **pp. 64-85:** Kathy Petrauskas; **pp. 87, 114, 140, 141, 202, 203:** Donna Reynolds; **pp. 90-111:** Marianne Wallace; **pp. 113-115, 139, 167, 184, 185, 222, 223:** Linda Kelen; **pp. 115, 138, 166, 192, 193, 214:** Carl Kock; **pp. 116-137:** Darryl Goudreau; **pp. 140, 193, 195, 209, 224, 225, 227:** Tom Herzberg; **pp. 142-163:** Linda Helton; **pp. 189, 200, 201:** Leon Bishop; **pp. 190, 191:** David Uhl; **pp. 194, 195, 198, 199, 216, 217, 228, 229:** Jacque Auger.

PHOTOGRAPHS

pp. 16, 42, 84, 162: Marilyn Meyerhofer; **pp. 77Top Left, Bottom Right, 246Bottom, 261Top:** Hans Reinhard/Bruce Coleman, Inc.; **p. 77Top Right:** Michael & Patricia Fogden; **p. 77Bottom Left:** Belinda Wright/DRK Photo; **p. 109Left:** Grant Heilman/Grant Heilman Photography, Inc.; **p. 109Right:** Jane Grushow/Grant Heilman Photography, Inc.; **p. 131:** Connie Geocaris/Tony Stone Images; **pp. 153, 271T:** Lawrence Migdale; **pp. 167T, 256B:** Don & Pat Valenti; **p. 167Center:** "Life On The Prairie, The Buffalo Hunt" by Currier & Ives, 1862, Library of Congress; **p. 182TR:** Steve McCutcheon; **p. 182TL:** Fred Bruemmer; **p. 182BL:** François Gohier/Photo Researchers; **pp. 182BR, 183 TL, 183Top Center, 183 TR:** Johnny Johnson/AlaskaStock; **p. 183BR:** Chris Arend/AlaskaStock; **p. 201:** Dwight R. Kuhn/DRK Photo; **p. 203:** Library of Congress; **p. 210:** Vic Thomasson/Tony Stone Images; **p. 211:** Chris Haigh/Tony Stone Images; **p. 211:** Editions Houvet; **p. 213:** R. Maiman/Sygma; **p. 225L:** Ray Amati/Focus On Sports; **p. 225Center Left:** Focus On Sports; **p. 225Center Right:** J. Daniel/ALLSPORT USA; **p. 225R:** Stephen Dunn/ALLSPORT USA; **p. 247:** Dr. Ralph Buchbaum/Department of Zoology, University of Chicago; **pp. 248T, 274:** Courtesy NASA; **p. 250T:** James L. Ballard/ScottForesman & Co.; **p. 252T:** Robert B. Tolchin/ScottForesman & Co.; **p. 252B:** Michael & Patricia Fogden; **p. 256T:** J. Pickerell/The Image Works; **p. 260:** Miami Seaquarium; **p. 266B:** Cy Furlan; **p. 268B:** J.C. Stevenson/Animals, Animals; **p. 270T:** Florida Division of Tourism; **p. 270B:** GemMedia; **p. 273T:** Belinda Wright/DRK Photo; **p. 277:** M. Austerman/Animals, Animals; **p. 278:** Raymond Schoder; **p. 280B:** Arizona State Museum, University of Arizona, Helga Teiwes, Photographer; **p. 284T:** Jurg Klages; **p. 284B:** Camermann International, Ltd.; **p. 286B:** Lorraine Rorke/The Image Works; **p. 287:** Geo. T. Hillman; **p. 290T:** Daniel L. Feicht; **p. 291:** Carmen Morrison/ScottForesman & Co.; **p. 292:** American Museum of Natural History, New York; **p. 293:** Michael Heron

All photographs not specifically credited are ScottForesman photographs.

UNIT 1

■ CONTENTS

4

UNIT 3

■ CONTENTS

UNIT 5

■ CONTENTS

Cross-Curricular Lessons

✋ SOCIAL STUDIES

🍎 HEALTH

💡 SCIENCE

■ CONTENTS

▼ READING

✂ MATHEMATICS

✏ WORK AND PLAY

REFERENCE TOOLS

Commonly Misspelled Words

Do you know what this symbol ♲ means? It means that something is used over and over again—it is recycled. Most students your age use the same words over and over when they write, and they often misspell some of those words.

Look through your spelling book. Some of the words have the recycled symbol next to them. These are the words you need to give special attention. They are the words most frequently misspelled by students your age.*

too	where	first
a lot	caught	watch
because	chocolate	people
there	friend	always
their	into	took
favorite	everybody	everyone
that's	off	morning
our	through	school
when	friends	something
really	swimming	with
they're	want	would
were	you're	are
it's *its*	another	enough
know	beautiful	except
finally	I'm	friend's
again	let's	probably
they	then	upon
Christmas	believe	vacation
went	cousin	brought
until	especially	house
outside	happened	might
said	heard	myself
we're	I	basketball
sometimes	whole	hospital
different	didn't	opened

***Research in Action** is a research project conducted in 1990-1993.
The misspelled word list is one result of an analysis of 18,599 unedited compositions. Words are listed in the order of their frequency of misspelling.

STRATEGY WORKSHOP

Steps for Spelling Problem Parts

REVIEW THE STEPS FOR SPELLING Here is the spelling strategy you should use when learning to spell a new word. Read it over step by step.

1. **Look** at the word. **Say** it and listen to the sounds.
2. **Spell** the word aloud.
3. **Think** about the spelling. Do you notice anything special that you need to remember?
4. **Picture** the word with your eyes shut.
5. **Look** at the word and **write** it.
6. **Cover** the word and picture it. **Write** the word again and **check** its spelling.

DISCOVER THE PROBLEM PARTS STRATEGY If some words are still hard for you to spell, try the problem-parts strategy.

Think

Which part of the word gives me a problem?

Underline your problem part.

wrong
trick

Picture the word.

"wrong" "trick"

TRY IT OUT Practice the problem-parts strategy with words that gave another writer problems. Follow the directions on the next page.

Work with a partner or group. Find the four misspelled words in the description below and write them correctly. Underline the part of each word that gave the writer problems. Use a dictionary if you need help.

I was down on one nee picking up mangoes when the squrrel saw me. It wiggled its nose at me. I bit into a mango and lafed. It turned and ran throgh the trees.

1. _____
2. _____
3. _____
4. _____

Now practice the Problem Parts Strategy with your own personal words.

List four words you sometimes misspell. Be sure to spell them right. Underline the part of each word that gives you a problem. Picture the words. Focus on the problem parts.

Have a partner quiz you on your words. Then check the results. How did you do?

5. _____
6. _____
7. _____
8. _____

LOOK AHEAD   Look at the next five lessons. Write four list words that look hard to spell. Underline the part of each word that you think might give you a problem.

1. _____
2. _____
3. _____
4. _____

13

Words with thr, scr, str, squ

■ **FOCUS** Look at each word and read the meaning phrase. Find the **thr, scr, str,** or **squ** in each word.

scrub	**scrub** the floor
street	driving down the **street**
threat	the **threat** of war
skyscraper	62-story **skyscraper**
thrown	**thrown** from a horse
square	a **square** box
scream	a **scream** for help
throat	have a sore **throat**
strawberry	bite a juicy **strawberry**
squeal	the **squeal** of a pig
thrill	the **thrill** of a roller-coaster ride
screen	a hole in the window **screen**
strength	the **strength** of a weight lifter
squeeze	**squeeze** a lemon to get juice
through ♻	strolling **through** the park
strike	two balls and a **strike**
squirm	**squirm** in someone's grasp
scratch	**scratch** an itchy leg
strange	a **strange** pig with long tusks
squirt	**squirt** water at someone

1. _____
2. _____
3. _____
4. _____
5. _____
6. _____
7. _____
8. _____
9. _____
10. _____
11. _____
12. _____
13. _____
14. _____
15. _____
16. _____
17. _____
18. _____
19. _____
20. _____

■ **DISCOVER** Letter combinations like the **scr** in **scrub** are called **blends**. What blends do you see in **street, square,** and **throat**? To spell words with blends correctly, be sure to include every letter in the blend.

■ **WRITE**
- five words with **thr**
- five words with **scr**
- five words with **str**
- five words with **squ**

CHALLENGE!

instrument
astronaut
arthritis
squeezable
description

14

DRAW YOUR OWN CONCLUSION   Write the list word that matches each clue.

1. You might clear this when you begin to speak.
2. A piglet might make this sound if you chase it.
3. Never cross this without looking both ways.
4. A box often has this shape.
5. This is a delicious red fruit.
6. You do this to a match when starting a fire.
7. This is what you might call something odd or unusual.
8. An elevator is necessary if you live or work here.
9. Using soap, do this to get a floor clean.
10. If you have poison ivy, you'll feel the urge to do this.
11. Do this loudly if you are frightened and need help.
12. Sledding down a steep hill may give you this.
13. Little children may do this if they have to sit quietly.
14. An elephant might do this with the water in its trunk.
15. This keeps bugs from flying through an open window.

WORDS IN CONTEXT   Write the list word that is missing from each animal's statement.

16. **Monkey:** I swing ___ the jungle from tree to tree.
17. **Zebra:** I was ___ to the ground by a lion, but I escaped.
18. **Gorilla:** I have the ___ of ten men.
19. **Boa:** I wrap around my prey and ___ very hard.
20. **Mongoose:** I'm so quick, even a cobra is no ___ to me.

1. _____
2. _____
3. _____
4. _____
5. _____
6. _____
7. _____
8. _____
9. _____
10. _____
11. _____
12. _____
13. _____
14. _____
15. _____
16. _____
17. _____
18. _____
19. _____
20. _____

STRATEGIC SPELLING

Using the Problem Parts Strategy

Study the problem parts of words. Write two list words that are hard for you. Underline the part of each word that gives you the problem and study it extra hard.

21. _____   22. _____

Take a Hint
This sentence may help you remember the difference between *throne* and *thrown.*
The king was thr**own**
from the throne he once **own**ed.

≡	Make a capital.
/	Make a small letter.
∧	Add something.
ℯ	Take out something.
⊙	Add a period.
⁋	New paragraph

PROOFREAD A SIGN Find the misspelled word in the photograph below. Why do you think it is misspelled in this particular way? Write the word correctly.

PROOFREADING TIP
When you create a sign, watch for spelling errors. You don't want people laughing at your message.

THE GYROS STAND
FROZEN CUSTARD
STRAWBERY
OPEN

Word List

scrub	thrill
street	screen
threat	strength
skyscraper	squeeze
thrown	through
square	strike
scream	squirm
throat	scratch
strawberry	strange
squeal	squirt

Personal Words

1. _____

2. _____

CREATE A SIGN
Now it's your turn to try to get a message across. Imagine you own The Gyros Stand and want customers to try your exciting new dessert. Use list words to create a sign with a short, sweet message.

EXPLORING LANGUAGE: HINK-PINKS Have you ever played the rhyming game called *Hink-Pink?* Now is your chance. First, you read a question. Then, you answer it with two rhyming words. Here's an example:

Q: What do you call an oven that is very odd?

A: a strange range!

Now try to answer the questions below. Hint: one of the words is always a list word.

1. **Q:** What do you call an avenue covered with candy?

   A: a _____ _____

2. **Q:** When you clean the place you bathe in, what are you giving it?

   A: a _____ _____

3. **Q:** What do you call it when kids refuse to ride bicycles?

   A: a _____ _____

4. **Q:** If a pig cries during dinner, what is it having?

   A: a _____ _____

ENRICHMENT Pick one.

Picture Hink Pinks
Think of a *Hink-Pink* question and answer. Write the question and then draw a picture that shows the answer.

Hink-Pink Two-Do
Work in pairs to ask and answer Hink-Pinks. One of you asks the question and the other answers. Then you switch.

CHALLENGE!
Make lists of rhyming words, such as *scream/dream* and *screen/green*. Try turning them into Hink-Pinks.

Words with kn, gn, wr, mb

■ **FOCUS** Say each word and read the meaning phrase. Notice which consonants you don't hear.

wrist	a bracelet on one's **wrist**
know ♻	**know** the answer to a question
thumb	a baby sucking his **thumb**
sign	wait at a stop **sign**
unknown	a painting by an **unknown** artist
wreck	a rusty old **wreck** of a car
limb	a tree **limb**
wrench	tightening bolts with a **wrench**
knit	**knit** a sweater
comb	**comb** one's hair
wreath	a holiday **wreath** on the door
assign	**assign** a task to someone
knot	a **knot** in my shoelace
lamb	a woolly **lamb**
design	wallpaper with a striped **design**
knob	the **knob** on a cabinet door
wren	a chirping **wren** in the tree
writing	**writing** a novel
climb	**climb** a tree
kneel	**kneel** in prayer

1. _____
2. _____
3. _____
4. _____
5. _____
6. _____
7. _____
8. _____
9. _____
10. _____
11. _____
12. _____
13. _____
14. _____
15. _____
16. _____
17. _____
18. _____
19. _____
20. _____

■ **DISCOVER** Sometimes two consonants together have only one sound. In **knot** you hear only the **n**, not the **k**. Which letters are silent in **thumb, wrist,** and **sign?**

■ **WRITE** Sort the words by writing
- six words with **kn**
- three words with **gn**
- six words with **wr**
- five words with **mb**

CHALLENGE!

bologna
lasagna
align
wrestler
cologne

RHYME TIME   Write the list word that rhymes with each word below.

1. teeth
2. snow
3. biting
4. hum
5. rim
6. bench

7. list
8. clam
9. roam
10. peel
11. when
12. deck

DEFINING WORDS   Write the list word that means the same as the underlined words.

13. The explorers traveled to a land that was <u>not familiar</u> to them.
14. I like to <u>make clothing by looping yarn</u>.
15. We had to <u>use hands and feet to go over</u> the fence to get into our yard.
16. Please <u>tie the ends of</u> this rope tightly.
17. I caught my coat on the <u>handle on a door</u>.

STRATEGIC SPELLING

Seeing Meaning Connections

Write the list word that completes each sentence. The underlined word is a clue.

18. The <u>designer</u> will _____ a dress for her.

19. Please don't _____ another <u>assignment</u>.

20. Write the list word that both of the words you wrote above are related to: _____.

1. _____
2. _____
3. _____
4. _____
5. _____
6. _____
7. _____
8. _____
9. _____
10. _____
11. _____
12. _____
13. _____
14. _____
15. _____
16. _____
17. _____

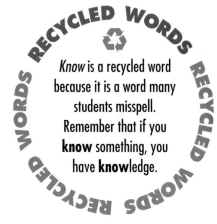

RECYCLED WORDS RECYCLED WORDS RECYCLED WORDS RECYCLED WORDS

Know is a recycled word because it is a word many students misspell. Remember that if you **know** something, you have **know**ledge.

☰	Make a capital.
/	Make a small letter.
∧	Add something.
ℓ	Take out something.
⊙	Add a period.
⁋	New paragraph.

PROOFREAD A NOTE Read the thank-you note that Pat wrote her aunt. Find three misspelled words and three capitalization errors. Write them correctly

PROOFREADING TIP

Pat is guilty of three "Capital Crimes"—mistakes with capital letters. Did you find them? If not, check the beginnings of sentences, the names of people, and the opening and closing of her note.

October 10, 1995

Dear aunt Sally,

Thank you for the sweater. I love the desine, especially the lamb on the pocket. did you knitt it yourself? I no I will wear it a lot.

love,

Pat

ANSWER THE NOTE Imagine that you are Pat's aunt. Answer the note above. Use some of your spelling words and personal words in your reply.

Word List

wrist	wreath
know	assign
thumb	knot
sign	lamb
unknown	design
wreck	knob
limb	wren
wrench	writing
knit	climb
comb	kneel

Personal Words

1. _____

2. _____

DICTIONARY: GUIDE WORDS At the top of each dictionary page are two guide words in dark type. The first guide word is the first entry word on the page. The second guide word is the last entry word on the page. All the words between these guide words are listed in alphabetical order.

When words begin with the same letter, use the second letter, the third letter, and so on to alphabetize them. Write the words in this tongue twister in alphabetical order.

Kindly King Kinton knit knights' knickers.

1. _____

2. _____

3. _____

4. _____

5. _____

6. _____

Now, use the guide words below to help you locate the words in the tongue twister. Write each word under the set of guide words they would come between in the dictionary.

**knew	knob**	**kilt	kiss**
7. _____	10. _____
8. _____	11. _____
9. _____	12. _____

ENRICHMENT Pick one.

Jungle A B C
Look up the following animals in the Spelling Dictionary: *hippopotamus, ocelot, iguana,* and *anaconda.* Be sure to use the guide words. Draw a picture of one of the animals.

Orderly Alphabet
Get together with five or six classmates. Line up alphabetically by last name. Invite classmates to join in based on their placement between the others.

CHALLENGE!
Write *Guide Word Travel* on your paper. Label three columns: **Australia | Korea Luxembourg | Spain Sweden | Zaire** List your classmates' last names alphabetically under the guide words.

Consonant Sounds /k/ and /f/

■ **FOCUS** Say each word and phrase. Find the letters that stand for the consonant sounds /k/ and /f/.

care	**care** about a friend
snack	ate an after-school **snack**
attack	**attack** the weeds in a garden
cover	**cover** a baby with a blanket
pocket	a hole in my **pocket**
Kansas	the state of **Kansas**
brake	using the **brake** to stop
track	trains running on a **track**
because ♻	**because** she said so
record	play a phonograph **record**
stiff	a **stiff**, lacy collar
dolphin	a sleek, wet **dolphin**
rough	a **rough**, bumpy road
elephant	the big, gray **elephant**
muffin	bit into a blueberry **muffin**
enough ♻	had **enough** to eat
photo	a **photo** of the family
laughed	**laughed** at the joke
alphabet	the **alphabet** from *a* to *z*
giraffe	a long-necked **giraffe**

1. _____

2. _____

3. _____

4. _____

5. _____

6. _____

7. _____

8. _____

9. _____

10. _____

11. _____

12. _____

13. _____

14. _____

15. _____

16. _____

17. _____

18. _____

19. _____

20. _____

■ **DISCOVER** The sound /k/ is spelled **c** in **care** and **ck** in **snack**. How is it spelled in **Kansas?** The sound /f/ is spelled **gh** in **rough** and **ph** in **dolphin**. How is it spelled in **stiff?**

■ **WRITE**
- four words with /k/ spelled **c**
- six words with /k/ spelled **k** or **ck**
- six words with /f/ spelled **ff** or **gh**
- four words with /f/ spelled **ph**

CHALLENGE!
freckles
sheriff
autograph
headphones
cuckoo clock

POETRY IN MOTION Complete the poem by writing list words.

Sitting by the TV eating a (1).
Watching a train smoking down the (2).
Energetic engineer pulling on the (3).
The gear is (4), so it doesn't take.
I (5) at his antics, sure enough.
Stopping that train was going to be (6).
Cow on the track without a (7).
Train finally stopped without a second to spare.

CLASSIFYING Write the list word that fits in each group.

8. snapshot, picture, ___
9. Iowa, Nebraska, ___
10. pouch, clothes, ___
11. tape, CD, ___
12. letters, *a* to *z*, ___

13. set upon, fight, ___
14. roll, cupcake, ___
15. since, on account of, ___
16. plenty, full, ___

WHO AM I? Write the list word naming each speaker.

17. "I love to swim and dive. I'm a _____."

18. "My sore throats are endless. I'm a _____."

19. "I fill my trunk with water. I'm an _____."

| 1. _____ |
| 2. _____ |
| 3. _____ |
| 4. _____ |
| 5. _____ |
| 6. _____ |
| 7. _____ |
| 8. _____ |
| 9. _____ |
| 10. _____ |
| 11. _____ |
| 12. _____ |
| 13. _____ |
| 14. _____ |
| 15. _____ |
| 16. _____ |

STRATEGIC SPELLING

Seeing Meaning Connections

recover
discover
coverlet

20. Write a list word that is related to the words in the box. _____

Write words from the box that fit the definitions.

21. to find out

_____

22. to get back a lost item

_____

23. a covering for a bed

_____

Take a Hint
Is it *break* or *brake*?
Just remember to
brake at the **lake**.

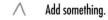
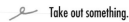

≡	Make a capital.
/	Make a small letter.
∧	Add something.
ℰ	Take out something.
⊙	Add a period.
¶	New paragraph

PROOFREAD A SELF-PORTRAIT

Julio's class is drawing self-portraits and writing short descriptions of them. Find four misspelled words and one incorrect pronoun in Julio's writing. Correct them.

PROOFREADING TIP

Would you ever say "Me go to the zoo"? Well, that's really what Julio did in his sentence. Drop "Mom and ..." to be sure the personal pronoun is correct.

Here I am at the zoo. Mom and me go a lot beacause we like the dofin show. An elefant and a girafe are behind me.

CREATE A SELF-PORTRAIT
Draw a picture of yourself doing something you enjoy. Write a description of where you are and what you're doing. Use some of your list words.

Word List

care	stiff
snack	dolphin
attack	rough
cover	elephant
pocket	muffin
Kansas	enough
brake	photo
track	laughed
because	alphabet
record	giraffe

Personal Words

1. _____

2. _____

MULTICULTURAL CONNECTION: LANGUAGES

Julio and his mother saw these signs at the zoo. Each animal is named in English, Swahili, Spanish, and Japanese. Julio had fun saying all the names.

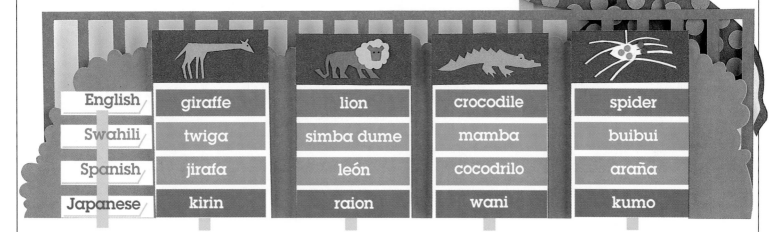

English	giraffe	lion	crocodile	spider
Swahili	twiga	simba dume	mamba	buibui
Spanish	jirafa	león	cocodrilo	araña
Japanese	kirin	raion	wani	kumo

Complete each sentence. Write the missing word in a different language each time.

1. Count the eight legs of the ___.
2. Can you tell the difference between an alligator and a ___?
3. The roaring of the ___ scared the baby.
4. The ___ can reach the treetop.

1. _____
2. _____
3. _____
4. _____

ENRICHMENT Pick one.

CHALLENGE!

Say It This Way
Write a sentence about each of the animals mentioned above. In each sentence, write the animal's name in a different language.

Interview
With a partner, plan how you would interview someone who speaks another language. What questions would you ask about the language?

The dollar is the basic unit of money in the United States. Use an encyclopedia to find the names of the basic units of money in Ecuador, Japan, Kenya, and France. Make a list.

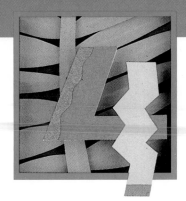

Adding -ed and -ing

1. _____

2. _____

3. _____

4. _____

5. _____

6. _____

7. _____

8. _____

9. _____

10. _____

11. _____

12. _____

13. _____

14. _____

15. _____

16. _____

17. _____

18. _____

19. _____

20. _____

■ **FOCUS** Look at each base word. Notice whether the spelling changes when **-ed** and **-ing** are added.

open	opened ♻	opening
happen	happened ♻	happening
chase	chased	chasing
dance	danced	dancing
worry	worried	worrying
study	studied	studying
dry	dried	drying
stop	stopped	stopping
slip	slipped	slipping
rob	robbed	robbing

■ **DISCOVER** Many base words do not change when adding **-ed** and **-ing:**

open, opened, opening.

- In words that end with **consonant-e,** the **e** is dropped when adding **-ed** and **-ing:**

chase, chased, chasing.

- In words that end in **y,** the **y** is changed to **i** when adding **-ed** but kept when adding **-ing:**

worry, worried, worrying.

- In one-syllable words that end with **consonant-vowel-consonant,** the final consonant is doubled when adding **-ed** and **-ing:**

stop, stopped, stopping.

■ **WRITE** Sort the list words by writing
- four words in which the final **e** is dropped
- seven words with no spelling changes
- six words in which the final consonant is doubled
- three words in which **y** changes to **i**

CHALLENGE!

occurred	occurring
argued	arguing
skied	skiing

26

CONTEXT CLUES Use list words to finish the sentences.

1. The party-goers were _____ to the music.

2. The thief _____ the man of his wallet.

3. Is she _____ her present now?

4. Dad was very _____ when I was late.

5. The clown _____ on a banana peel.

6. We washed and _____ the dishes.

7. I was _____ for my history test all night.

8. The lion _____ the monkey up a tree.

9. What _____ to the injured ape?

10. We _____ talking to listen to the bird sing.

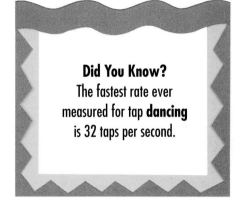

Did You Know?
The fastest rate ever measured for tap **dancing** is 32 taps per second.

ADD ENDINGS Complete each group with a list word.

11. worry, worried, ___
12. rob, robbed, ___
13. slip, slipped, ___
14. chase, chased, ___
15. open, ___, opening

16. study, ___, studying
17. dry, dried, ___
18. happen, happened, ___
19. stop, stopped, ___
20. dance, ___, dancing

11. _____
12. _____
13. _____
14. _____
15. _____
16. _____
17. _____
18. _____
19. _____
20. _____

STRATEGIC SPELLING

Building New Words

Use the rules you learned to complete the chart.

Base word	Add -ed	Add -ing
21. scrub	_____	_____
22. cause	_____	_____
23. cry	_____	_____

≡	Make a capital.
/	Make a small letter.
∧	Add something.
ℯ	Take out something.
⊙	Add a period.
⸿	New paragraph

PROOFREAD A BLURB A **blurb** is a short, favorable description written on the jacket of a book or album. The blurbs below were written about the book *Night of the Twisters*. Find four misspellings and two handwriting errors and write them correctly.

PROOFREADING TIP

Jodie knows how to spell the words, but her handwriting looks as though she doesn't. Not closing letters like **d** and **o** will really frustrate your reader.

"From the moment I opend this book I never stopt reading it!" – Jodie

"Frightening things kept hapeneng. I woried about Dan and Art." – Dana

WRITE A BLURB Write blurbs about two of the following: a favorite book, an enjoyable movie, or a good record album or tape. Try to use your list words.

Word List

opened	opening
happened	happening
chased	chasing
danced	dancing
worried	worrying
studied	studying
dried	drying
stopped	stopping
slipped	slipping
robbed	robbing

Personal Words

1. _____

2. _____

_____

_____

_____

_____

_____

_____

ANTONYMS Words that have opposite meanings are called **antonyms.** There are many different ways to write them. You might:

Use different words: *opened* and *closed.*

Add a prefix such as un-: *opened* and *unopened.*

Complete the second sentence in each pair with an antonym of the underlined word.

1. *Fortunately,* my family <u>won</u> a trip to the Amazon.
   Unfortunately, we ___ our luggage on the way.

2. *Fortunately,* we were able to <u>buy</u> T-shirts.
   Unfortunately, we had to ___ our watches.

3. *Fortunately,* the weather was <u>dry</u> and warm.
   Unfortunately, we got very ___ in the rain forest.

4. *Fortunately,* we were <u>happy</u> camping.
   Unfortunately, we were ___ when we had to leave.

1. _____

2. _____

3. _____

4. _____

ENRICHMENT Pick one.

Good News/Bad News
Write a "good news/bad news" letter to a friend. For every sentence that begins "The good news is...," write another that begins "The bad news is...." Try to use antonyms.

Draw the Words
Write adjectives with the prefix *un-* on ten index cards. Ask a partner to write the name of a thing that can easily be drawn on each of ten other cards. Pick one card from each pile. Take turns drawing pictures of the combinations.

CHALLENGE!
Make up a Fortunately/Unfortunately story about one of these things:
■ an unpainted fence
■ an unbeaten team
■ an uneaten meal
■ an unwanted pet
Tell the story to your class.

Adding -er and -est

1. _____

2. _____

3. _____

4. _____

5. _____

6. _____

7. _____

8. _____

9. _____

10. _____

11. _____

12. _____

13. _____

14. _____

15. _____

16. _____

17. _____

18. _____

19. _____

20. _____

■ **FOCUS** Look at each base word. Notice whether the spelling changes when **-er** and **-est** are added.

deep	*deeper*	*deepest*
small	*smaller*	*smallest*
close	*closer*	*closest*
large	*larger*	*largest*
scary	*scarier*	*scariest*
funny	*funnier*	*funniest*
happy	*happier*	*happiest*
hot	*hotter*	*hottest*
fat	*fatter*	*fattest*
sad	*sadder*	*saddest*

■ **DISCOVER** The endings **-er** and **-est** are added to words to make comparisons. Many base words do not change when adding **-er** and **-est**:

      deep, deeper, deepest.

■ In words that end with **consonant-e,** the **e** is dropped when adding **-er** and **-est**:

      close, closer, closest.

■ In words that end in **y,** the **y** is changed to **i** when adding **-er** and **-est**:

      scary, scarier, scariest.

■ In words of one syllable that end with **consonant-vowel-consonant,** the final consonant is doubled when adding **-er** and **-est**:

      hot, hotter, hottest.

■ **WRITE** Sort the list words by writing
■ four words in which the final **e** is dropped
■ four words in which the base word does not change
■ six words in which the final consonant is doubled
■ six words in which **y** changes to **i**

CHALLENGE!

gentler	gentlest
weirder	weirdest
angrier	angriest

ANTONYM ALERT Write the list word that means the opposite of each word below.

1. larger
2. skinnier
3. smallest
4. colder
5. shallower
6. saddest
7. coldest
8. largest
9. farther
10. happiest
11. skinniest

1. _____
2. _____
3. _____
4. _____
5. _____
6. _____
7. _____
8. _____
9. _____
10. _____
11. _____

HAPPY ENDINGS Add an ending to each word in parentheses to form a list word that completes the sentence.

12. (scary) This is the _____ thriller I've read.

13. (funny) Your skit was _____ than mine.

14. (deep) Pike Lake is the _____ lake around.

15. (close) Morgan is my very _____ friend.

16. (sad) Was *Sounder* _____ than *Old Yeller*?

17. (large) A gorilla is _____ than a gibbon.

18. (funny) Ribsy is the _____ dog of all time.

19. (happy) Al was _____ with the gift than Di.

20. (scary) I think snakes are _____ than lizards.

STRATEGIC SPELLING
Building New Words

Did You Know?
The **smallest** horse ever recorded, Little Pumpkin, stood only fourteen inches tall and weighed twenty pounds.

Write the words that complete the chart. Remember what you learned.

Base word	Add -er	Add -est
21. busy	_____	_____
22. big	_____	_____
23. strange	_____	_____

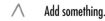	Make a capital.
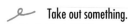	Make a small letter.
∧	Add something.
	Take out something.
⊙	Add a period.
	New paragraph

PROOFREAD AN INVITATION Lizzy is having a party. Below is the first draft of her invitation. Correct three misspellings and one incorrect comparison.

PROOFREADING TIP

Remember to use **-er** when you compare two things. Use **-est** when comparing more than two.

COME TO A HALLOWEEN PARTY!!!

PLACE: *Lizzy's house —202 Lake St.*

TIME: *October 31 from 3:00 to 6:00 P.M.*

Wear your scaryest costume. We'll carve the fatest pumpkins and drink the hotest cider. I'll be the sadder ghoul in town unless you come!

WRITE AN INVITATION What kind of party would you like to give? Write an invitation for it. Use list words.

Word List

deeper	deepest
smaller	smallest
closer	closest
larger	largest
scarier	scariest
funnier	funniest
happier	happiest
hotter	hottest
fatter	fattest
sadder	saddest

Personal Words

1. _____

2. _____

COME TO A _____ PARTY!!!

PLACE: _____

TIME: _____

_____

_____

_____

_____

EXPLORING LANGUAGE: EXAGGERATION Lizzy once read a book in which a character "had eyes as large and brown as a coconut." She liked this exaggerated wording, and was eager to try it out herself. Exaggeration is often used to emphasize, amuse, or surprise.

Lizzie practiced using exaggeration in her diary, but left a few words out. Choose list words to finish each sentence.

October 31   My party was the (1) I've ever given—spilling over into five states. People came in costumes that were (2) than a barrel of comedians. One tiny kid dressed as a peanut, and was (3) than one too! We drank cocoa that was (4) than an oven, and ate so much we felt (5) than an overweight elephant. Then we told stories that were (6) than a haunted hotel. It was the (7) time of my life!

1. _____
2. _____
3. _____
4. _____
5. _____
6. _____
7. _____

ENRICHMENT Pick one.

You Exaggerate!
Use exaggerated wording to describe one of the following people or animals:

- a very hungry person
- a person working hard in 108-degree weather
- a girl trying to convince her parents to let her have a snake
- a very swift animal

Top This One
Get together with a friend and try to outdo one another using exaggeration. Choose a topic such as "I'm so tired ...."

CHALLENGE!
Write a story based on an event in your life. Use as much exaggerated language as you can think of.

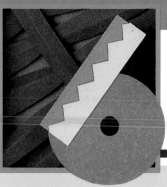

Review

Look back at the word lists in Lessons 1–5 and think about how you are doing in spelling.

1. The hardest words for me to spell were

_____   _____   _____

2. I learned to spell a hard word by
   ☐ picturing the word in my mind.   ☐ connecting it to a word I already knew.
   ☐ saying it as I wrote it.   ☐ working on the part of the word that is a problem for me.

3. The most interesting word that I've learned to spell is _____

_____

4. When I spell a word from my spelling book,
   I usually spell it correctly in my writing.   Yes   No   Sometimes

5. I try to use words I am learning to spell in my writing.   Yes   No   Sometimes

6. When a word doesn't look correct, I usually _____

BAKERY SPECIALS

Complete the newspaper advertisement using list words.

| strawberry |
| scratch |
| snack |
| worrying |
| alphabet |

1. _____
2. _____
3. _____
4. _____
5. _____

BELLA'S BAKERY

Every batch is made from (1).

SPECIALS OF THE WEEK:

Monday Fruit pies on sale today! Try (2) or apple.

Tuesday Stop (3) about your next party. Let Bella bake the cake.

Wednesday Children love chewing an initial with our (4) cookies.

Thursday Choose Bella's oatmeal bars for your after-school (5).

get out and have fun

Where do you usually ride your bike? Do you ride all _____ town or just on the _____ you live on? Do you _____ hills or bounce along on _____ trails? Maybe your town has a racing _____. No matter where you ride, you should remember these two tips. ❶ Always wear a helmet. ❷ Keep your bike in good repair, especially the _____ system. Good brakes make _____ safe. Take good _____ of your bike, and it will take good care of you.

Bret writes articles about outdoor activities for the class news bulletin. Use each list word once to complete this article.

| stopping | care | rough | brake | track | through | street | climb |

Fairy Tales

Lindy doesn't like fairy tales, but she had to read one. Use the list words to complete her book review.

know
scrub
scariest
danced
wren
scream
kneel
because
knit

1. _____
2. _____
3. _____
4. _____
5. _____
6. _____
7. _____
8. _____
9. _____

The Sweetest Princess
A Book Review by Lindy Grach

This is another one of those stories about a sweet princess and the (1) old queen you could ever imagine. The princess has to (2) the hard marble floor until it shines every day. Not a day goes by that the queen doesn't (3) at the princess for some little thing, and the queen demands that the princess curtsey and (4) before her friends. The queen wants the princess to marry a neighboring king (5) he is rich. You probably (6) who the princess wants to marry. Right! A poor young man she (7) with at the fair. The only surprise in the book is that there is no fairy godmother, just a troll who asks the princess to (8) him a sweater from her golden hair. In return, he turns the queen into a (9), and the princess locks her safely in a bird cage. The princess marries the young man, and lives . . . well, you know the rest.

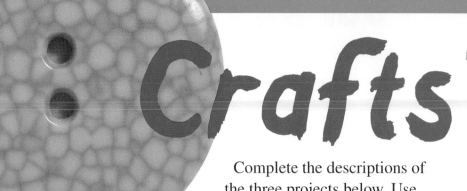

Crafts

Complete the descriptions of the three projects below. Use each list word once.

I. Make an outline picture of a city in winter. Cut squares and rectangles out of newspapers and make a (1) and other such buildings. Glue the buildings along the bottom of a piece of black construction paper. For snow, fill a spray bottle with water and white paint and (2) your paper. Then, (3) your name to your art work.

II. Shape grapevines into a ring to make a festive (4) for your front door. Decorate it with bunches of (5) flowers.

III. Make a picture frame in the shape of a (6). Collect buttons of all sizes and colors. Make sure there are (7) buttons to cover the frame. Arrange them in an interesting (8) and then glue them on the frame.

sign
dried
design
square
squirt
skyscraper
wreath
enough

1. _____
2. _____
3. _____
4. _____
5. _____
6. _____
7. _____
8. _____

Pairing Things and Places

Write the list word that relates to each shape.

1. _____
2. _____
3. _____
4. _____
5. _____

Kansas   **pocket**   **dolphin**   **wrench**   **elephant**

1   2   3   4   5

WATER PARK

Complete the announcement below.
Use each list word once.

opening
squeal
cover
thrill
assign
worried
photo

1. _____
2. _____
3. _____
4. _____
5. _____
6. _____
7. _____

Hey Scouts!

Troop #116 is going to the grand (1) of Rocky Valley Water Park on Saturday, August 10. Imagine us as we holler and (2), sliding down the new water slide! Included will be a souvenir (3) of our group for us to take home. So, get ready for the (4) of your life! If you are (5) about how much the trip will cost, here's some good news. The park will (6) the cost for each scout who has earned a service badge. We plan to (7) seats on the bus, so tell Mr. Sato who you'd like to sit with.

Science Fiction

Jason's writing group invented two plots for a science fiction skit. Complete them using each list word once.

| squeeze | studying | smallest | screen | writing | attack | wreck | unknown |

The skit might be about alien creatures who come to Earth in a battered (1) of a spaceship plastered with bumper stickers.

They have come in the hopes of (2) the human sense of humor.

In one scene, the very (3) alien, measuring 2 feet, 6 inches, says, "Take me to your ladder!"

He uses it to climb up to the TV (4) so he can watch old Marx Brothers reruns.

The skit could be about time travel. Six students (5) into a small time machine and visit the year 2096.

Their Time-Travel Guide tells them that they will go to a distant place, but the exact location is (6).

In one scene, forces on Planet Circon prepare to (7) Mars with high-impact squirt guns.

When the kids return, they begin (8) a tell-all biography of their amazing adventure.

1. _____
2. _____
3. _____
4. _____
5. _____
6. _____
7. _____
8. _____

STRATEGY WORKSHOP

Divide and Conquer

DISCOVER THE STRATEGY Do long words give you spelling problems? Help is on the way. It's the divide-and-conquer strategy, and it consists of the following three ways to divide long words:

1. Divide them into syllables.	2. Divide them into prefixes, suffixes, and base words.	3. Divide them into base words if they're compounds.

choc / o / late

un / known
violin / ist

sky / scraper
butter / fly

Use the way that works best for you to divide each long word. Then study the word part by part.

TRY IT OUT Now practice the divide-and-conquer strategy yourself. Follow the directions on the next page.

1. Divide into Syllables Use this method with any long word. Remember: A syllable is a word or part of a word that you say as a unit: **(choc/o/late)**.

✝ Write *America, alphabet,* and *elephant.* Listen for the syllables and draw lines between them. Check a dictionary for any words you're not sure of.

2. Divide Prefixes and Suffixes This method will help you see the parts of the word with a prefix or suffix. You will also see if adding a suffix changes the spelling of the base word.

✝ Write *unhappy, beautiful,* and *rewrite.* Draw lines between each base word and any prefixes or suffixes.

Look back at the words you wrote. Underline the base word in which the spelling changed when the suffix was added.

3. Divide Compounds This method will show you that two words have been put together with no letters lost.

✝ Write *everybody, afternoon,* and *something.* Draw a line between the two base words in each compound.

✝ **LOOK AHEAD** Look ahead at the next five lessons. Write two list words that are long and look hard to spell. Divide each word to make it easier to study.

1. _____

2. _____

3. _____

4. _____

5. _____

6. _____

7. _____

8. _____

9. _____

1. _____   2. _____

Words with sh, ch, tch, wh

1. _____

2. _____

3. _____

4. _____

5. _____

6. _____

7. _____

8. _____

9. _____

10. _____

11. _____

12. _____

13. _____

14. _____

15. _____

16. _____

17. _____

18. _____

19. _____

20. _____

■ **FOCUS** Look at each word and read the meaning phrase. Find the **sh, ch, tch,** and **wh** in each word.

watch ♻	**watch** an archery contest
anywhere	can't find it **anywhere**
punish	**punish** a naughty child
church	the ringing of the **church** bell
wheat	a piece of **wheat** bread
kitchen	ate in the **kitchen**
shown	**shown** how to do something
awhile	had to wait **awhile**
pitcher	a **pitcher** on a baseball team
flashlight	shine a **flashlight** in the dark
somewhere	**somewhere** in the city
short	a **short** visit
catcher	threw the ball to the **catcher**
whatever	**whatever** you do
chapter	reading **chapter** two
whenever	**whenever** possible
shelter	take **shelter** under a tree
chocolate ♻	ate **chocolate** pudding
trash	took out the **trash**
March	born in **March**

■ **DISCOVER** Sometimes consonant combinations have only one sound: **sh**ort, Mar**ch**, wa**tch**, **wh**eat. Which two combinations sound the same? Be sure to use the right combination when you write words with these letters.

■ **WRITE**
- six words with **sh**
- four words with **tch**
- four words with **ch**
- six words with **wh**

CHALLENGE!

champion
touchdown
squash
crutches
wherever

BURIED WORDS Each word below is hidden in a list word. Write the list word.

1. eat
2. pitch
3. what
4. pun
5. arch

6. or
7. rash
8. own
9. chap
10. catch

MAKING ASSOCIATIONS Write the list word that you would associate with each word or phrase below.

11. protection ____
12. a short time ____
13. worship ____
14. clock ____
15. dark candy ____
16. cook's place ____

1. _____
2. _____
3. _____
4. _____
5. _____
6. _____
7. _____
8. _____
9. _____
10. _____
11. _____
12. _____
13. _____
14. _____
15. _____
16. _____

STRATEGIC SPELLING

The Divide and Conquer Strategy

Study long words piece by piece. Write *flashlight, somewhere, anywhere, whenever, chocolate,* and *pitcher.* Draw lines to break each word into smaller parts. Study the parts.

17. _____
18. _____
19. _____

20. _____
21. _____
22. _____

Did You Know?
The word **chocolate** was borrowed from Mexican Spanish. It came from *chocolatl,* a word in Nahuatl, the language of the Aztecs and Toltecs.

☰	Make a capital.
/	Make a small letter.
∧	Add something.
ℓ	Take out something.
⊙	Add a period.
⌗	New paragraph

PROOFREAD A SIGN A spelling error on a large outdoor sign really stands out. Find the mistake in the photograph below, and spell it correctly.

PROOFREADING TIP
Watch out! Don't be caught making a big mistake. Keep a dictionary handy when you write signs.

WACH AND
JEWELRY REPAIR

$1   UP TO

_____

CREATE A SIGN Think of one of your favorite stores. Create a sign for an item that is sold there. Try to use words from your spelling list. Check your sign for careless errors.

Word List

watch	somewhere
anywhere	short
punish	catcher
church	whatever
wheat	chapter
kitchen	whenever
shown	shelter
awhile	chocolate
pitcher	trash
flashlight	March

Personal Words

1. _____

2. _____

WORD HISTORIES A **word history**, or **etymology**, tells us the origin and history of a word. Most dictionaries display word histories at the end of an entry.

The word histories for the names of our months can be traced back to the ancient Romans. Julius Caesar was a famous Roman emperor. A month was named *Julius* in his honor. *Julius* eventually became *July*.

Following are etymologies for other months in our calendar. Write the name of the month that completes each history.

1. In Roman times the Latin phrase *Martius mensis* meant month of Mars. In Old French this became *marche*, and in English it became ___.
2. In honor of the ruler Augustus, the Romans named a month *Augustus*. In English it became ___.
3. The Latin word *Januarius* is from *Janus,* a two-faced god said to look back at the old year and ahead to the new. This became the month of ___.

1. _____
2. _____
3. _____

ENRICHMENT Pick one.

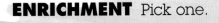

Back to the Present
Look up the word histories for *punish* and *kitchen*. Write a sentence describing your discoveries.

Where Is It From?
Work with a partner to look up these words in a dictionary: *denim, nicotine, jumbo, hamburger,* and *bloomers.* Which words came from the name of a city? Which came from the name of a person?

CHALLENGE!
Research the terms Old English and Middle English. When were they spoken? Find examples of English words spoken today that came from Old and Middle English.

Words with Double Consonants

1. _____

2. _____

3. _____

4. _____

5. _____

6. _____

7. _____

8. _____

9. _____

10. _____

11. _____

12. _____

13. _____

14. _____

15. _____

16. _____

17. _____

18. _____

19. _____

20. _____

■ **FOCUS** Look at each word and read the meaning phrase. Notice the double consonant letters in each word.

different ♻	many **different** animals
offer	**offer** to help
suffer	**suffer** from illness
slippers	wear **slippers** around the house
supper	have **supper** at 5:00
grasshopper	a **grasshopper** on a leaf
tomorrow	finish up **tomorrow**
worry	**worry** about someone's safety
current	study **current** events
borrow	**borrow** someone's pencil
written	a **written** party invitation
matter	does not **matter**
bottle	a **bottle** of juice
lettuce	a **lettuce** salad
ridden	has **ridden** a horse
paddle	**paddle** a canoe
shudder	**shudder** in the cold
odd	an **odd** cat with no hair
bubble	blow a big **bubble**
hobby	painting as a **hobby**

■ **DISCOVER** The double letters in **offer** and **supper** have only one sound, but to spell the words correctly you must use two letters. What letters are doubled in **bottle, worry, shudder,** and **grasshopper?**

■ **WRITE** First write the words in the list you think are easy to spell. Then write the words you think are difficult. Underline the double consonants in each word.

CHALLENGE!

allowance
antennas
impossible
Mississippi
recess

ANTONYM ARGUMENT   Write the list word that is the opposite of the underlined word in each sentence.

1. Mo and Al are as <u>alike</u> as they can be.
2. At <u>breakfast</u> yesterday they didn't even eat.
3. "Why can't I <u>lend</u> your knit hat?" asked Mo.
4. "Because losing hats is a <u>job</u> with you," said Al.
5. "But I like its <u>ancient</u> style," responded Mo.
6. Mo agreed to a <u>spoken</u> contract before wearing the hat.
7. These <u>ordinary</u> fellows enjoy disagreeing.

WORDS IN CONTEXT   Write the list word that completes each sentence.

8. Both of my parents ___ from allergies.
9. Rabbits eat greens such as ___ and spinach.
10. I forgot to do it today, but I will be sure to do it ___.
11. I am learning how to ___ a canoe.
12. After her bath, she put on a robe and ___.
13. What is the ___ with that howling dog?
14. I bought this gum so I could blow a ___.
15. Do you buy apple juice in a can or a ___?
16. I had never ___ on a Ferris wheel before.
17. The ___ jumped from the leaf to the ground.

1. _____
2. _____
3. _____
4. _____
5. _____
6. _____
7. _____
8. _____
9. _____
10. _____
11. _____
12. _____
13. _____
14. _____
15. _____
16. _____
17. _____

STRATEGIC SPELLING

Building New Words

Write *worry*, *offer*, and *shudder*. Add **-ed** to complete the chart. Remember: Change the **y** to **i** before adding **-ed**.

Base word	Add-ed
18. _____	_____
19. _____	_____
20. _____	_____

RECYCLED WORDS

To spell **different** correctly be sure to pronounce every syllable: **dif fer ent.**

≡	Make a capital.
/	Make a small letter.
∧	Add something.
ℯ	Take out something.
⊙	Add a period.
⌗	New paragraph

PROOFREADING TIP

Lucas is careless with the same word twice. He repeats it in one place, and leaves it out in another. These mistakes are easy to catch if you proofread.

PROOFREAD A MESSAGE

Lucas read about someone finding an important message in a bottle. He wrote a message of his own. Find four spelling errors and two careless errors and correct them.

Dare to be diffrent!

If you padel your own canoe today, you you may captain the ship tommorow.

If your buble bursts, can blow another one.

WRITE A MESSAGE

Pretend you are writing a message for a bottle. Tell someone what you think is important in life. Use list words and personal words.

Word List

different	written
offer	matter
suffer	bottle
slippers	lettuce
supper	ridden
grasshopper	paddle
tomorrow	shudder
worry	odd
current	bubble
borrow	hobby

Personal Words

1. _____

2. _____

EXPLORING LANGUAGE: ACROSTICS An acrostic is a way of connecting letters to spell different words, often about a particular subject. To make an acrostic, write a noun across or down the page. Then connect words that describe that noun. Try it with *grasshopper.* Use the words shown and add your own, or make up a new one.

l

grasshopper r

g r e g

r e e n y

ENRICHMENT Pick one.

All About YOU
Print your first name, leaving space between each letter. Then make an acrostic like the one above, adding words that you think describe you best.

Across Your Home Town
Work with a partner. Use large pieces of paper to write the name of your town in colorful letters. Add the words that tell about it. Decorate your acrostic.

CHALLENGE!

Write the names of two characters from a book or story that your class has read. Add words that tell about each character to make acrostics. Compare your acrostics to those made by classmates. Discuss their differences and similarities.

Short e and Long e

1. _____

2. _____

3. _____

4. _____

5. _____

6. _____

7. _____

8. _____

9. _____

10. _____

11. _____

12. _____

13. _____

14. _____

15. _____

16. _____

17. _____

18. _____

19. _____

20. _____

■ **FOCUS** Say each word and phrase. Notice how the **long e** and **short e** sounds are spelled in these words.

credit	buy new furniture on **credit**
speak	**speak** to a neighbor
alley	trash cans in the **alley**
fence	a white picket **fence**
least	the **least** expensive shirt
hockey	play ice **hockey**
went	**went** to see a play
contest	a juggling **contest**
beat	**beat** eggs until fluffy
honey	put **honey** on toast
reason	a good **reason** for that
valley	a river in the **valley**
money	**money** to buy food
engine	a car **engine**
them	gave it to **them**
steal	**steal** someone's property
monkey	a **monkey** in the jungle
treat	**treat** a friend to lunch
season	the fall **season**
donkey	a braying **donkey**

■ **DISCOVER** The **long e** sound is spelled **ea** in **speak**. How is it spelled in **honey?** What letter spells the **short e** sound?

■ **WRITE** Sort the words by writing
- seven words with **long e** spelled **ea**
- seven words with **long e** spelled **ey**
- six words with **short e** spelled **e**

CHALLENGE!

bleachers
squeaked
escaped
celery
jersey

WORDS IN CONTEXT   Write the list word that completes each sentence.

1. I can't hear you. Please ___ up.
2. Bees were in the hive making ___.
3. The necklace cost a great deal of ___.
4. Around the yard was a picket ___.
5. She had the most homework and I had the ___.
6. The king gave ___ all silver swords.
7. The child sat upon a long-eared ___.
8. The peasants farmed the fertile ___.
9. The cook ___ the eggs for the omelet.
10. She hid the gold so no one would ___ it.
11. The knight ___ riding off.

DEFINITIONS   Answer each question with a list word.

12. Which list word is a sport?
13. What can you use to buy things if you have no cash?
14. What animal chatters and often lives in trees?
15. Which word means to think and understand?
16. Which names a narrow driveway behind a building?
17. What piece of machinery gives a car power?
18. Which word describes what winter is?
19. Which names something special that gives pleasure?

1. _____
2. _____
3. _____
4. _____
5. _____
6. _____
7. _____
8. _____
9. _____
10. _____
11. _____
12. _____
13. _____
14. _____
15. _____
16. _____
17. _____
18. _____
19. _____

STRATEGIC SPELLING

Seeing Meaning Connections

| contestant |
| uncontested |

Write the list word related in spelling and meaning to the boxed words.

20. _____

Complete the sentences using the words in the box.

Mai was a (21) on a new TV quiz show. All of her answers were correct, so her victory was (22) by her opponent.

21. _____   22. _____

Take a Hint
Do you have trouble remembering how to spell **beat** and **beet** ?
This riddle may help:
What do you do when you can't **beat the heat?** Sweat!

49

≡	Make a capital.
/	Make a small letter.
∧	Add something.
℮	Take out something.
⊙	Add a period.
¶	New paragraph

PROOFREAD A LETTER Find the four misspelled words in this letter to an advice columnist. Write them correctly and add the two missing punctuation marks.

PROOFREADING TIP
Don't forget what you know about the parts of a letter. What punctuation is needed at the end of the greeting and closing?

May 8, 1997

Dear Ms. Understanding

Michelle and I have practiced all seson for the dance contist. We whent to the finals last year, but Michelle dropped out at the last second. We didn't speek for weeks! How can I help her?

Yours truly

Riana

Word List

credit	reason
speak	valley
alley	money
fence	engine
least	them
hockey	steal
went	monkey
contest	treat
beat	season
honey	donkey

Personal Words

1. _____

2. _____

ANSWER A LETTER Pretend you are Ms. Understanding. Answer Riana's letter. Use spelling words.

_____
_____
_____
_____
_____
_____
_____
_____

MULTICULTURAL CONNECTION: PROVERBS A **proverb** is a short, wise saying. People everywhere use proverbs to pass along common beliefs. Proverbs may mention crops or animals that are important to the area.

The Chinese proverb **Talk does not cook rice** is much like the English proverb **Actions speak louder than words**.

Read each proverb below. Choose a proverb from above that has a similar meaning and write it.

The water buffalo plays an important part in proverbs from Thailand, such as:
1. You don't force a buffalo to eat grass.

The Senegalese say:
2. To catch a monkey requires patience.

The Iranians say:
3. One finger cannot lift a pebble.

From Bulgaria comes:
4. Gentle words open iron gates.

> You can lead a horse to water, but you can't make it drink.
>
> You catch more flies with honey than you do with vinegar.
>
> In unity there is strength.
>
> Good things come to those who wait.

1. _____

_____

2. _____

_____

3. _____

4. _____

_____

ENRICHMENT Pick one.

Animal Proverbs
Think of a familiar proverb about an animal. Write it down. Or make up your own animal proverb and write that.

Proverbial Partners
Get together with a friend. Each of you find two proverbs and copy them. Then write a proverb of your own. Guess which proverbs are traditional and which were just written.

CHALLENGE!
Like proverbs, **maxims** and **epigrams** are short, thought-provoking sayings. Check your library for collections of some of these, and write down your favorites. Share them with your classmates.

Short Vowels a, i, o, u

1. _____

2. _____

3. _____

4. _____

5. _____

6. _____

7. _____

8. _____

9. _____

10. _____

11. _____

12. _____

13. _____

14. _____

15. _____

16. _____

17. _____

18. _____

19. _____

20. _____

■ **FOCUS** Say each word and phrase. Notice how the **short a, i, o,** and **u** sounds are spelled in these words.

cousin ♻	my oldest **cousin**
cash	took **cash** to the bank
into ♻	went **into** the castle
closet	coats hung in a **closet**
with ♻	going **with** a friend
couple	just a **couple** of days
block	run around the **block**
January	the month of **January**
river	canoe down a **river**
young	too **young** to see the movie
chop	**chop** some wood
finger	a **finger** pointed at me
blanket	warm under the **blanket**
forgot	**forgot** to return a book
band	joined the school **band**
trouble	problems that **trouble** me
window	looking out the **window**
backpack	a **backpack** full of books
tough	a **tough,** overcooked roast
pond	a fishing **pond**

■ **DISCOVER** Short vowel sounds can be spelled with one letter: **short a** in **blanket, short i** in **into, short o** in **closet.** Short vowel sounds can be spelled with two letters: **short u** in **cousin.** What letters spell the **short u** sound in **trouble?**

■ **WRITE** ▪ five words with **short a** spelled **a**
  ▪ five words with **short o** spelled **o**
  ▪ five words with **short u** spelled **ou**
  ▪ five words with **short i** spelled **i**

CHALLENGE!

southern
ignored
Pilgrims
package
o'clock

DEFINITIONS   Write the list word that fits each definition. Use the Spelling Dictionary if you need to.

1. the first month of the year
2. one of the five slender parts on a hand
3. to the inside of
4. water that flows into a lake or ocean
5. a small room for storing clothes or supplies
6. a group of musicians performing together
7. didn't remember
8. money in the form of coins and bills

VOWEL TRADE   Change the vowel in each word to make a list word with the **short o** sound.

9. black   10. chap   11. pend

BASE WORDS   Write the list words that are the base words for the words below.

12. coupled   15. cousins   18. untroubled
13. toughness   16. youngster   19. windowless
14. blanketed   17. backpacking

STRATEGIC SPELLING

Seeing Meaning Connections

withstand
withdraw
withhold

20. Write the list word that is related to the words in the box.

_____

Then write the words from the box that fit the definitions.

21. to draw back or draw away   _____

22. to refuse to give   _____

23. to stand against or resist   _____

Did You Know?
The word **couple** comes from the Old French word *cople*. *Cople* came from the Latin word *copula*, meaning bond. A married couple is thought to be bonded together.

1. _____
2. _____
3. _____
4. _____
5. _____
6. _____
7. _____
8. _____
9. _____
10. _____
11. _____
12. _____
13. _____
14. _____
15. _____
16. _____
17. _____
18. _____
19. _____

≡	Make a capital.
/	Make a small letter.
∧	Add something.
ℰ	Take out something.
⊙	Add a period.
¶	New paragraph

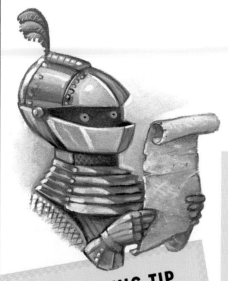

PROOFREAD A MESSAGE Jane took a message for her cousin, Hiro, from his teacher, Mrs. Cortez. Find four spelling errors and one handwriting error.

You Have a Message!!!

To: _Hiro_   **Date:** _Janurary 5_

Time: _4_   A.M. (P.M.)   **From:** _Ms. Cortez_

Phone #: _555-1219_   **Taken by:** _Jane_

Message

She has the bagpack you left at school. She will drop it off here tomarrow. It's no troble.

PROOFREADING TIP
Did Jane write "7279" or "1219"? When you take a phone message, be sure to write the phone number carefully.

WRITE A MESSAGE Read the following telephone message. Write down only the important information.

"Hello, is Jane there? No? Well this is Hiro, her cousin. I'm calling from a pay phone. Tell her I won't be there until 5:00. I'm at school, looking for my backpack."

You Have a Message!!!

To: _____   **Date:** _____

Time: _4:15_   A.M. (P.M.)   **From:** _____

Phone #: _____   **Taken by:** _____

Message

_____

_____

Word List

cousin	chop
cash	finger
into	blanket
closet	forgot
with	band
couple	trouble
block	window
January	backpack
river	tough
young	pond

Personal Words

1. _____

2. _____

ɑ	hat	ī	ice	u̇	put	ə stands for	
ā	age	o	not	ü	rule	ɑ	in about
ä	far, calm	ō	open	ch	child	e	in taken
âr	care	ȯ	saw	ng	long	i	in pencil
e	let	ô	order	sh	she	o	in lemon
ē	equal	oi	oil	th	thin	u	in circus
ėr	term	ou	out	ᴛH	then		
i	it	u	cup	zh	measure		

DICTIONARY: PRONUNCIATION Dictionaries include a **pronunciation key** on every other page in the book. It helps you pronounce the symbols in the dictionary. It might look like this: →

Each word in the dictionary is followed by its **pronunciation** in parentheses. The entry *window* might look like this: →

Using the pronunciation key, you see the **i** is pronounced like the **i** in *it* and the **ow** is pronounced like the **o** in *open.*

win‧dow (win′ dō), an opening in an outer wall or roof of a building, or in a vehicle, that lets in air or light. It is usually a wooden or metal frame that surrounds panes of glass or plastic. *n.*

The dot between **win** and **dow** tells you that *window* has two syllables. The **accent mark** (′) tells you to say the first syllable in *window* with more force than the second.

Read each pronunciation below. Write the word that the pronunciation symbols stand for. In each two-syllable word, underline the syllable you would say with more force.

1. (tuf)
2. (kloz′it)
3. (wiᴛH or with)
4. (snak)
5. (kuz′n)
6. (bot′l)

1. _____

2. _____

3. _____

4. _____

5. _____

6. _____

ENRICHMENT Pick one.

Be a Pronunciation Decoder

Translate this message:

mī kuz′n and i dōv in′tü ᴛHə riv′ər wiᴛH nō trub′əl.

Write it. Don't forget to capitalize.

Accent on Friendship

Form a group of four. Using pronunciation symbols, write everyone's name. For example, Jack Johnson would be jak jon′sen. For help, use the pronunciation key in the dictionary.

CHALLENGE!

Look at the pronunciation key at the top of this page. Think of other words that could also be used as examples for **ɑ, i, o, u,** and **ou.** For example, **ɑ:** *map, land, fast.* Write them.

Long Vowels a, i, o

■ **FOCUS** Say each word. Notice how the **long a, i,** and **o** sounds are spelled. Then read the meaning phrase.

smoke	**smoke** from a campfire
cable	a television **cable** into the house
whole ♻	ate the **whole** apple
invite	**invite** the queen to dinner
April	**April** showers
behind	getting **behind** in one's work
remote	a **remote** cabin in the woods
lion	the roar of a **lion**
vacation ♻	a **vacation** by the sea
pint	a **pint** of cream
broke	**broke** a glass
station	waiting at the train **station**
stole	**stole** into their hideaway
arrive	will **arrive** at noon
danger	staying out of **danger**
drove	**drove** to the countryside
hide	run away and **hide**
bacon	cook **bacon** for breakfast
wild	a **wild**, bucking horse
decide	**decide** to get a pet

1.
2.
3.
4.
5.
6.
7.
8.
9.
10.
11.
12.
13.
14.
15.
16.
17.
18.
19.
20.

■ **DISCOVER** Long vowel sounds are often spelled with one letter, as in **bacon** and **wild**. They can also be spelled **vowel-consonant-e**, as in **smoke** and **hide**. What letters spell the long vowel sound in **danger** and **whole?**

■ **WRITE** Sort the list words by writing
- six words with **long a**
- eight words with **long i**
- six words with **long o**

CHALLENGE!

behavior
operation
private
apologize
Rhode Island

56

COMPARE Write a list word that has the same first letter, last letter, and number of syllables as each word below.

1. lotion
2. beacon
3. stallion
4. Abdul
5. ramble
6. veteran
7. drier
8. divide
9. pant
10. wood
11. beyond
12. inside

VOWEL TRADE Change the vowel in each word to make a list word with the **long o** sound.

13. whale   14. brake   15. drive   16. stale

STRATEGIC SPELLING

Using the Rhyming Helper Strategy

A rhyming helper rhymes with a word and is spelled the same at the end. Write *hide, cable, arrive,* and *smoke.* Write a rhyming helper alongside each word. Underline the matching letters. Be sure your helper is spelled right.

List Word	Rhyming Helper
17.	
18.	
19.	
20.	

1. _____
2. _____
3. _____
4. _____
5. _____
6. _____
7. _____
8. _____
9. _____
10. _____
11. _____
12. _____
13. _____
14. _____
15. _____
16. _____

RECYCLED WORDS

Can't remember when to use **whole** or **hole?** Remember this: A complete **whole** has a wide w, while **hole** has just an empty middle.

≡	Make a capital.
/	Make a small letter.
∧	Add something.
ℯ	Take out something.
⊙	Add a period.
¶	New paragraph

PROOFREAD A SUMMARY

Shanieka's class enjoyed a documentary film about Africa. Shanieka wrote a summary of what she saw. Correct four misspellings and one run-on sentence.

PROOFREADING TIP

Shanieka forgot this simple rule: To avoid a run-on sentence, use a comma and and.

Africa has deserts, jungles, and large cities. It is a place where willd animals roam and buildings touch the sky. A line roars loudly smock floats from a house. It would be a wonderful place to vacashun.

WRITE A SUMMARY

Think of an interesting film you saw lately. Write a summary of the film. Try to use some of your list words and personal words.

Word List

smoke	broke
cable	station
whole	stole
invite	arrive
April	danger
behind	drove
remote	hide
lion	bacon
vacation	wild
pint	decide

Personal Words

1. _____

2. _____

_____

_____

_____

_____

_____

_____

_____

_____

EXPLORING LANGUAGE: IDIOMS An **idiom** is a word picture that means something more than the words in it would suggest. One idiom has an interesting history.

Long ago in France, the people of Paris did not want Henry IV as their king. Henry decided to make war on them to "teach them a lesson." A wise counselor said to Henry, "If you destroy Paris, you will be king of a dead city. Would you chop off your nose to teach your face a lesson?" Henry spared Paris, became a popular king, and helped coin the idiom **cut off one's nose to spite one's face.**

Use the phrases in the box to help you write the meaning of each idiom below.

1. bring home the bacon _____

2. blow one's own horn _____

3. lose one's head _____

4. lead by the nose _____

praise oneself; boast
earn a living
have control over
get excited

ENRICHMENT Pick one.

Anatomy of an Idiom
Look in the Spelling Dictionary to find an idiom based on each of these words: *leg, eye, hand, mouth, ear.* Write each idiom and its meaning.

Idioms Delight
Get together with a friend to collect idioms. Ask family and friends for contributions, or check a dictionary. Share your idioms by using them in sentences.

CHALLENGE!
Track down the histories of each of the idioms above. A good place to start is with the book *Put Your Foot in Your Mouth* by James A. Cox.

Review

Look back at the word lists in Lessons 7–11 and think about how you are doing in spelling.

1. The most interesting word that I have learned to spell is_____.

2. I learned to spell a hard word by
   ☐ dividing the word into smaller parts and studying the parts.
   ☐ thinking of another word that sounds like it and is spelled in a similar way.
   ☐ underlining the part of the word that is a problem for me and studying it.

3. When I learn a new spelling word, I spell it correctly
   when I write stories.   Yes   No   Sometimes

4. I think I am a good speller for my age.   Yes   No   Don't Know

5. I try to use words I am learning to spell in my writing. Yes   No   Sometimes

6. A word that is always hard for me to spell is _____.

WIN A TRIP

Use the list words to complete the sentences.

contest   invite   anywhere   vacation   remote

PASSPORT

FREE TICKET

We _____ you to win a free_____

to a _____ island in the Pacific. To enter the

_____ just write the answer (in 50 words

or less) to, "Where would you go if you could go

_____ in the world?" Good luck!

Suitcase Travel Company

Nat's Story

couple   them   whatever   smoke
young   decide   odd

Nat is telling the story of *Aladdin* to his classmates, but he has forgotten a few of the details. Use the list words to complete his story.

ALADDIN AND THE MAGIC LAMP

Aladdin is a (1) man who finds a magic lamp. He rubs the lamp and an (2) fellow, called a genie, floats out in a puff of (3). The genie gives Aladdin (4) he asks for. Aladdin falls in love with the Emperor's daughter and must (5) how to win her. The genie helps (6), and the happy (7) are finally married.

1. _____
2. _____
3. _____
4. _____
5. _____
6. _____
7. _____

While in Los Angeles, Aponi sent her friend Ray this postcard. Use the list words to complete her message.

church   April   window
river   speak   season
station

1. _____
2. _____
3. _____
4. _____
5. _____
6. _____
7. _____

POSTCARD FROM L.A.

Dear Ray,   April 3, 1995

We arrived in Los Angeles on the first of (1). Our train pulled into the (2) at midnight. It's supposed to be the rainy (3), but each day is sunny. It's fun to (4) Spanish with my friend Carlota. Today we visited Watts Towers. They look like steeples on a (5). I can see them from my bedroom (6). Tomorrow we will find a (7) and do some fishing. Have fun.

Aponi

61

Household Chores

Complete the list of weekly chores using each list word once.

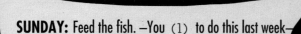

List words:
forgot   with   bottle
alley   offer   trash
fence   slippers

SUNDAY: Feed the fish. —You (1)_____ to do this last week—

MONDAY: Clean the hamster's water (2)_____.

TUESDAY: Mend torn bedroom (3)_____.

WEDNESDAY: Help Mom—Remember to (4)_____ to wash dishes.

THURSDAY: Clean the tub (5)_____ scouring powder.

FRIDAY: Take old newspapers and other (6)_____ out to the (7)_____.

SATURDAY: Paint the picket (8)_____.

1. _____

2. _____

3. _____

4. _____

5. _____

6. _____

7. _____

8. _____

The Big Game

pitcher   stole   watch
catcher   beat   drove
into   tough   trouble

Kelly couldn't wait to write in her journal after the championship baseball game. Complete the sentences. Use each list word once.

We played the big game against Evanston yesterday and we_____ them by one run!!! Dad said it was an incredibly exciting game to_____ .
It sure was a_____game to play! We had a lot of_____getting on base the first five innings, but then Chris got to first and_____two bases.
I_____home the winning run! Our_____struck out five of their batters, and our_____tagged two runners sliding_____home. The final score was 2-1.

A Family Meal

The local high school is offering a family cooking class. Complete the description using each of the list words once.

— Cooking Together 101 —

If you want to (1) your family to a great time, this course is for you. Come into the (2) and learn how to prepare an entire (3). You will learn how to make a delicious omelet, using eggs, (4) milk, and crisp (5). Children will enjoy making Caesar salad, using fresh garden (6). They will also learn how to (7) and arrange vegetables for a dip. Dessert will be a (8) cake you prepare without flour! Only five families per class.

supper	kitchen	chocolate	treat
lettuce	chop	bacon	whole

5. _____

2. _____

6. _____

3. _____

7. _____

1. _____

4. _____

8. _____

Camping Out

tomorrow
somewhere
shelter
blanket
flashlight
backpack

Use the list words to complete the conversation.

Place: Middle of the woods
Time: Twilight

1. _____
2. _____
3. _____
4. _____
5. _____
6. _____

Lewis: I'm glad we set up camp here. The trees will give us (1).

Clark: Can you help me get my arm out of this heavy (2)?

Lewis: Gosh, it's cold. I hope you packed an extra (3).

Clark: It may be in here, but I can't see anything, it's so dark. I need the (4).

Lewis: It's here (5), but I can't find it. It's too dark.

Clark: Let's just roll out our sleeping bags. We'll find everything (6), when it's light.

STRATEGY WORKSHOP

Meaning Helpers

DISCOVER THE STRATEGY Even a short word like *every* can be hard to spell—until you discover where it comes from.

You don't hear the second **e** when you say *every*, but you do hear it when you say *ever*. *Ever* is a meaning helper for *every* because a sound clue in *ever* helps you spell *every*.

TRY IT OUT Now try the meaning-helper strategy yourself. Follow the directions on the next page.

Work with a partner to figure out what sound clue in the top word helps you spell the bottom word. The first two pairs are done for you.

major
majority

The **long a** in **major** reminds me that **majority** is spelled with an **a** too. The sound of **a** is different in the two words, but the spelling of that sound is the same.

act
action

The sound of **t** in **act** reminds me that **action** is spelled with a **t** too.

1. press
   pressure

_____

_____

2. fast
   fasten

_____

_____

_____

Write a meaning helper of your own for each word below. Mark the letter or letters that give the sound clue.

3. national

4. election

5. confession

_____   _____   _____

LOOK AHEAD Look ahead at the next five lessons. Write two list words and the helpers that you could use with this strategy. Underline the letters that give the sound clues.

1. _____

2. _____

_____   _____

Related Words

1. _____
2. _____
3. _____
4. _____
5. _____
6. _____
7. _____
8. _____
9. _____
10. _____
11. _____
12. _____
13. _____
14. _____
15. _____
16. _____
17. _____
18. _____
19. _____
20. _____

■ **FOCUS** Look at each word and read the meaning phrase. Notice how each pair of words is alike.

crumb	ate every **crumb** of the cake
crumble	**crumble** to the ground
sign	a stop **sign**
signal	**signal** a left turn
soft	a **soft,** dreamy song
soften	**soften** my dry skin
mean	didn't **mean** to hurt you
meant	**meant** what I said
heal	medicine to **heal** a burn
health	grateful for good **health**
meter	about 39 inches in a **meter**
metric	a **metric** measurement
deal	**deal** the number cards
dealt	**dealt** six math fact cards
able	**able** to do a back flip
ability	the **ability** to juggle
relate	**relate** well to one's sister
relative	a distant **relative**
compose	**compose** a symphony
composition	a new piano **composition**

■ **DISCOVER** The words **crumb** and **crumble** are similar in spelling and meaning, but the **b** is silent in **crumb** and spoken in **crumble.** Related words often have parts that are pronounced differently. What letter is silent in **sign** but spoken in **signal?**

■ **WRITE** Write the related word pairs. For each pair, first write the word that is easier for you to spell. The easier word should help you spell the related word.

CHALLENGE!

direct	invade
direction	invasion
personal	
personality	

CONTRASTS   Write list words to complete the sentences.

1. A small bit of water is a drop.
   A small bit of bread is a ___.
2. Lack of rest and a virus may cause sickness.
   Rest and medicine may bring about ___.
3. If you fail at something, you are unable to do it.
   If you finally succeed, you are ___ to do it.
4. A person who helps you is kind.
   A person who harms you is ___.
5. You use your voice in spoken language.
   You use your hands in ___ language.
6. Apples should be sweet and hard.
   Raisins should be sweet and ___.

SYNONYMS   Write the list word that means the same as the underlined word or words. Use the Spelling Dictionary.

7. I wrote a short essay about my dog.
8. Please shuffle and pass out the division facts cards.
9. The arrangement of beats in a polka is very quick.
10. Mozart was able to put together twenty-two operas.
11. She was able to tell the exact details of the event.
12. Is that what you intended to say?
13. The cut will become well in a few days.
14. Dogs have the power to hear high-pitched sounds.
15. A red light is a sign giving notice to stop.
16. The old wall was beginning to decay.
17. Asia uses the measurement-that-counts-by-tens system.

1. _____
2. _____
3. _____
4. _____
5. _____
6. _____
7. _____
8. _____
9. _____
10. _____
11. _____
12. _____
13. _____
14. _____
15. _____
16. _____
17. _____

STRATEGIC SPELLING

Using the Meaning Helper Strategy

Take a Hint
Watch out for the **mean ant** in **meant.**

18.–20. Meaning helpers can help you spell words. Write the list words related to *soft, relate,* and *deal.* Mark the letters that match the underlined letters in the helpers.

18. _____
19. _____
20. _____

☰	Make a capital.
/	Make a small letter.
∧	Add something.
℮	Take out something.
⊙	Add a period.
⁋	New paragraph

PROOFREAD A PERSUASIVE PARAGRAPH   Min and her friends are trying to convince their principal to allow music during lunch. They are writing their reasons on index cards to be delivered on a cafeteria tray. Correct the five spelling errors Min has made.

PROOFREADING TIP
Min wrote *brother* when she meant to write something else. Always proofread your writing for words that are spelled correctly but have the wrong meaning.

It is meen not to let us listen to music at lunch. Good music is good for our helth. It helps us relax and be abel to face the next class. We will only play sof music. It won't brother anyone.

Min Yi

WRITE A PERSUASIVE PARAGRAPH   Think of something you would like to persuade someone to do or to allow you to do. Write about it. Try to use list words and a personal word.

Word List

crumb	meter
crumble	metric
sign	deal
signal	dealt
soft	able
soften	ability
mean	relate
meant	relative
heal	compose
health	composition

Personal Words

1. _____

2. _____

_____

_____

_____

_____

_____

_____

_____

_____

EXPLORING LANGUAGE: TRIPLETS Here's a challenging vocabulary game called **Triplets.** It's a game in which you supply the one word that is often associated with three others. For example, what list word would you associate with the three words below?

post   language   up

The answer is **sign,** as in **signpost, sign language,** and **sign up.** Here are more for you to try. Remember, the missing word always goes in front. Use the boxed words for help.

soft	night	whole	music	dry

1. drink   boiled   soap
2. cleaner   run   dock
3. gown   crawler   mare
4. video   hall   box
5. milk   note   wheat

1. _____
2. _____
3. _____
4. _____
5. _____

ENRICHMENT Pick one.

Triplets Times Two
Make up your own triplet. Write a short paragraph using all the triplets you've created. Use the Spelling Dictionary if you need help.

Triplet Trade-off
Pick a partner. One of you work with list A and the other with list B. Choose two words from your list and write triplets. Give your partner the words in the triplet. He or she guesses the word that fits in front of them all.

List A	List B
watch	bag
book	table
glass	egg
land	home

CHALLENGE!
Try to write a **Quadruplet,** four words that can be associated with one word. If you accomplish that, try a **Quintuplet** (five words).

Consonant Sounds /j/, /ks/, /kw/

■ **FOCUS** Say each word and phrase. Notice how each word looks and sounds.

bridge	a **bridge** across a river
queen	the **queen** of a Pacific island
except ♻	everyone **except** me
change	**change** my wet clothes
relax	**relax** and listen to music
quart	a **quart** of milk
edge	the **edge** of a cliff
extra	**extra** credit for doing more work
village	a charming country **village**
liquid	medicine in **liquid** form
expect	**expect** a package in the mail
quick	a **quick** dance step
explain	**explain** how to do something
Texas	a ranch in **Texas**
charge	**charge** a purchase
equal	all **equal** under the law
excellent	an **excellent** orchestra
quilt	a **quilt** made of colorful scraps
excited	**excited** about a trip
fudge	delicious chocolate **fudge**

1. _____
2. _____
3. _____
4. _____
5. _____
6. _____
7. _____
8. _____
9. _____
10. _____
11. _____
12. _____
13. _____
14. _____
15. _____
16. _____
17. _____
18. _____
19. _____
20. _____

■ **DISCOVER** The sound /j/ is spelled **ge** in **change** and **dge** in **bridge**. How is it spelled in **edge**? The sound /ks/ is spelled **x** in **extra** and **xc** in **except**. How is it spelled in **Texas**? The sound /kw/ is spelled **qu**, as in **queen**.

■ **WRITE**
- six words with /j/ spelled **ge** or **dge**
- three words with /ks/ spelled **xc**
- five words with /ks/ spelled **x**
- six words with /kw/ spelled **qu**

CHALLENGE!

pledge
explosion
question
advantage
excess

TONGUE TWISTERS   Write the list word that would best complete each tongue twister.

1. Fran fasts Fridays, frequently forgetting flavorful ____.
2. The ____ quickly quashed the quarrelsome quibbler.
3. Tula took trips to ____ a total of ten times.
4. Beside the bay ____, Binita built a bungalow.
5. Running relentlessly, Russ will rarely ____ or rest.
6. Chang's chum can ____ cheese into cheesecake.
7. This Vermont ____ is veiled in the vast verdant valley.
8. Lassie lapped at the ____ in the ladle.
9. Ed is edgy at the ____ of the edifice.

WORD SEARCH   Find the ten list words in the puzzle below. They may be printed down or across. Write them.

```
c e x c e l l e n t e e
h x e q u a r t e a x x
a p e x t r a q u i c k
r e x p l a i n q u e e
g c e x c i t e d e p p
e t q u i l q u i l t x
```

STRATEGIC SPELLING

Seeing Meaning Connections

20. Write a list word that is related in spelling and meaning to the words in the box.

_____

equator
equally
equation

Finish the sentences with words from the box.

21. Divide this _____ among you.

22. (2 x 2) + 3 = 7 is a math _____.

23. The _____ circles the earth.

1. _____
2. _____
3. _____
4. _____
5. _____
6. _____
7. _____
8. _____
9. _____
10. _____
11. _____
12. _____
13. _____
14. _____
15. _____
16. _____
17. _____
18. _____
19. _____

RECYCLED WORDS

Because they sound alike, *except* and *accept* are often confused. Make an **ex**tra effort to remember the **ex** in **ex**cept.

☰	Make a capital.
/	Make a small letter.
∧	Add something.
ℯ	Take out something.
⊙	Add a period.
¶	New paragraph

PROOFREAD A RECIPE Read the following recipe. Correct four misspellings and one place where *good* is used incorrectly.

PROOFREADING TIP
Good food, good kids, good home are good ways to use the word *good*. *Good* describes a person, place, or thing. Use *well* to describe how you do something: cook *well*.

Here's a recipe for very good fuge.

In a pan over low heat mix together good:

2 tablespoons butter

2 cups marshmallows

2 cups exellent chocolate

2 cups sugar

Pour liqid into pan. Allow to cool. Cut into bars. For a good snack, freeze exdra pieces.

WRITE A RECIPE Think of something you enjoy eating. Find out how to make it and write the recipe. You might want to make the dish and share it with your classmates.

_____
_____
_____
_____
_____
_____

Word List

bridge	expect
queen	quick
except	explain
change	Texas
relax	charge
quart	equal
edge	excellent
extra	quilt
village	excited
liquid	fudge

Personal Words

1. _____

2. _____

DICTIONARY: FINDING THE RIGHT MEANING

If someone said, "I can't eat without my bridge," would you understand the person? *Bridge* has many meanings. If you looked it up in a dictionary, you might find these definitions. ➡

bridge (brij), **1** something built over a river, road, or railroad, so that people can get across. **2** to build a bridge over: *The engineers bridged the river.* **3** the false tooth or teeth in a mounting fastened to natural teeth. **4** a thin, arched piece over which the strings of a violin and other stringed instruments are stretched. 1, 3-4 *n.,* 2 *v.,* **bridged, bridg•ing.**

The second definition is followed by a **sentence.** This sentence helps you to see how the word is used.

At the end of the entry, each definition is identified by its **part of speech** (whether noun, verb, adjective, etc.) These are called part-of-speech labels.

Look at the entry for *bridge* again. Write the number of the definition that answers each question below.

1. Which definition of *bridge* fits the meaning, "I can't eat

   without my bridge"? _____

2. Which definition of *bridge* is a part of a stringed

   instrument? _____

3. Which definition is a verb?

   _____

ENRICHMENT Pick one.

Build a Bridge
Look at the definitions for *bridge* again. Write a short paragraph that uses one noun meaning and one verb meaning of the word.

Bridging the Gap
Find the three definitions that are not followed by a sentence. With a partner, write a sentence using each word as it is defined.

CHALLENGE!
With a classmate, take turns choosing other spelling words that have more than four definitions in a dictionary. Make up a sentence using the word you chose, and have your partner tell you the definition number and the part of speech.

73

Adding -s and -es

1. _____

2. _____

3. _____

4. _____

5. _____

6. _____

7. _____

8. _____

9. _____

10. _____

11. _____

12. _____

13. _____

14. _____

15. _____

16. _____

17. _____

18. _____

19. _____

20. _____

■ **FOCUS** Read the words in each column. Notice whether **-s** or **-es** is added to make each list word.

friend	*friends* ♻
tiger	*tigers*
flower	*flowers*
holiday	*holidays*
delay	*delays*
monkey	*monkeys*
ash	*ashes*
eyelash	*eyelashes*
beach	*beaches*
bunch	*bunches*
circus	*circuses*
glass	*glasses*
class	*classes*
tax	*taxes*
suffix	*suffixes*
hobby	*hobbies*
enemy	*enemies*
memory	*memories*
mystery	*mysteries*
supply	*supplies*

■ **DISCOVER** In words that end in a vowel and **y**, as well as many other base words, add **-s: holidays, friends.**
- In words ending with **sh, ch, s, ss,** or **x,** add **-es: ashes.**
- In words ending with a consonant and **y,** change the **y** to **i** and add **-es: hobbies.**

■ **WRITE** Sort the words by writing
- five words in which the **y** is changed to **i**
- nine words in which just **-es** is added
- six words in which **-s** is added

CHALLENGE!

couches
accidents
skis
injuries
libraries

74

MAKING COMPARISONS Complete each comparison using a list word.

1. The children chattered like ____ in a tree.
2. Her sweet perfume smelled like fresh ____.
3. The long threads were as thin and dark as ____.
4. Their faces were as dry and gray as ____.
5. The play had more problems than one of my math ____.
6. The two round puddles shined like a pair of ____.
7. The floor was as sandy as ten ____.
8. Deep-sea photography is like having two ____ in one.
9. They ate the roast like ferocious, snarling ____.

WORD ASSOCIATIONS Write the list word that you would associate with the words or phrases below. Use the Spelling Dictionary for help.

10. stops along the way
11. grapes in groups
12. July 4, Thanksgiving
13. groups at war
14. clowns and acrobats
15. money citizens pay

16. sleeping bags, canteens
17. good pals
18. puzzling secrets
19. -ment, -ly, -ous
20. things remembered

STRATEGIC SPELLING
Building New Words

Write the plural form of each word. Remember what you learned.

21. scratch _____

22. guess _____

23. play _____

1. _____
2. _____
3. _____
4. _____
5. _____
6. _____
7. _____
8. _____
9. _____
10. _____
11. _____
12. _____
13. _____
14. _____
15. _____
16. _____
17. _____
18. _____
19. _____
20. _____

Take a Hint
Here's another way to remember when to add **-es:**
Say the plural form aloud. If the ending you hear adds a syllable, the ending you add is **-es:**
watch•es   tax•es

≡	Make a capital.
/	Make a small letter.
∧	Add something.
ℯ	Take out something.
⊙	Add a period.
¶	New paragraph

PROOFREAD A DESCRIPTION

Byron wrote this description of reggae, his favorite music. Read what he wrote, and then correct three misspellings and one pronoun error.

PROOFREADING TIP

My friends and I means the same thing as we. Byron should use one or the other, never both.

> In Jamaica, my homeland, my freinds and I we listen to reggae music. Reggae has a strong beat, like rock music. It is not as hard as rock, though, because it was born on island beachs. It is like the blues, but brighter. It has the sound of sunshine and floweres.

Word List

friends	circuses
tigers	glasses
flowers	classes
holidays	taxes
delays	suffixes
monkeys	hobbies
ashes	enemies
eyelashes	memories
beaches	mysteries
bunches	supplies

Personal Words

1. _____

2. _____

WRITE A DESCRIPTION Write a description of your favorite music. Use list words and personal words.

_____
_____
_____
_____
_____
_____
_____
_____

MULTICULTURAL CONNECTION: ENVIRONMENT

People of all nations delight in flowers. They use flowers to express feelings and to symbolize love. The flowers pictured below are national flowers. Read about them. Then write a name from the box to match each description. Look up the flowers you don't know in the Spelling Dictionary.

> lotus
>
> almond blossom
>
> cattleya orchid
>
> edelweiss

1. _____
2. _____
3. _____
4. _____

1. a small flower that grows in Austria, made famous in a song

2. a bright, showy flower that grows in the tropics of Costa Rica

3. a kind of water lily found in India

4. the flower of the almond tree, often seen in Israel

ENRICHMENT Pick one.

Names in Bloom
The cattleya orchid was named for William Cattley. Look up three of the following flowers in the Spelling Dictionary to discover for whom they were named: *begonia*, *zinnia*, *dahlia*, *fuchsia*, and *peony*. Write about your findings.

Flower Symbols
Suppose you could have a flower as your symbol. Write a paragraph telling why you would choose this flower. Sign the back of the paper. Trade papers with classmates and try to guess who chose which flower.

CHALLENGE!

Pick one of the countries below and use an encyclopedia to gather information about the flowers that grow there. Is one of these a national flower? Write a short report.

Japan   Scotland
Malaysia   Turkey
Mexico   Chad

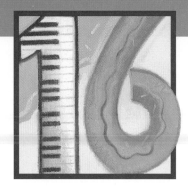

Using Just Enough Letters

■ **FOCUS** Say each word to yourself. Notice how it looks and sounds, as well as how many letters it has.

hamster	a furry little **hamster**
a lot ♻	like to dance **a lot**
ugly	an **ugly** duckling
washed	**washed** the dinner dishes
hotel	a **hotel** in the city
always ♻	**always** buckle seat belts
father	a **father** with six children
missed	**missed** my bus
until ♻	wait **until** later
coming	**coming** to your house
eleven	**eleven** different flavors
didn't ♻	**didn't** want to go
upon	sat **upon** a bench
crazy ♻	performed a **crazy** stunt
lazy	felt **lazy** all day
wasn't	**wasn't** ready to begin
almost	**almost** finished her homework
want ♻	**want** a glass of milk
feelings	hurt someone's **feelings**
during	quiet **during** the concert

1. _____
2. _____
3. _____
4. _____
5. _____
6. _____
7. _____
8. _____
9. _____
10. _____
11. _____
12. _____
13. _____
14. _____
15. _____
16. _____
17. _____
18. _____
19. _____
20. _____

■ **DISCOVER** Sometimes you may mistakenly add an extra letter or two to certain words. Pronouncing a word correctly and trying to picture its spelling in your mind can help you avoid mistakes.

■ **WRITE**
- the only two-word form
- one word that has three syllables
- three words that have one syllable
- fifteen words that have two syllables

CHALLENGE!

delivery
drowned
magnet
mustard
replied

78

CLASSIFYING   Write the list word that fits in each group.

1. sister, mother, ____
2. ten, ____, twelve
3. inn, resort, ____
4. wish, desire, ____
5. in the course of, at the time, ____

6. foolish, nutty, ____
7. emotions, thoughts, ____
8. careless, not working, ____
9. guinea pig, gerbil, ____

WORDS IN CONTEXT   Write the missing list words to complete the paragraph below.

Once (10) a time, there was a little boy who thought of himself as an (11) duckling, although his grandmother always told him, "You're truly a handsome fellow." She (12) kidding, but the boy (13) believe her. He would frown at himself in a mirror (14) his face would begin to hurt. Other children would ask him to play quite (15), but he would (16) find an excuse to smile and say, "Not today, thanks." One day a little girl invited him to a party. He (17) didn't go, but his grandmother convinced him that the girl would feel hurt if he stayed home. When he finally arrived at the party, his friend rushed to him, saying, "I was worried you weren't (18)! We would have (19) your friendly face!"

STRATEGIC SPELLING
Using the Meaning Helper Strategy

| wishy-washy |
| washable |
| washcloth |

20. Write a list word that is related to the words in the box. _____

Now write words from the box that fit the clues.

21. Use it when you take a bath. _____

22. If asked an opinion, don't be this. _____

23. Your play clothes should definitely be this. _____

RECYCLED WORDS

The two-word form **a lot** is misspelled a lot! Remember, **a lot** is NEVER one word. It is NEVER more than four letters.

1. _____
2. _____
3. _____
4. _____
5. _____
6. _____
7. _____
8. _____
9. _____
10. _____
11. _____
12. _____
13. _____
14. _____
15. _____
16. _____
17. _____
18. _____
19. _____

≡	Make a capital.
/	Make a small letter.
∧	Add something.
ℓ	Take out something.
⊙	Add a period.
¶	New paragraph

PROOFREAD A WARNING One morning the sign below appeared beside the cage of Scratch the Hamster. Correct four misspellings and one place where the punctuation is wrong.

PROOFREADING TIP
Remember that *it's* has an apostrophe because it's short for *it is*. Say *it is* aloud when you write *it's* or *its*. If *it is* doesn't fit, take out the apostrophe.

WARNING

This hamster is on strick untill it's cage is

cleaned. Hamsters have feellings too.

Please, allways be aware of its needs!

WRITE A WARNING Think of a warning sign you would like to write. Try to use your list words and your personal words.

Word List

hamster	eleven
a lot	didn't
ugly	upon
washed	crazy
hotel	lazy
always	wasn't
father	almost
missed	want
until	feelings
coming	during

Personal Words

1. _____

2. _____

EXPLORING LANGUAGE: WORD PLAY Janna believes that the word *ugly* looks just like what it means. "It's an ugly word," she says. "Just look at that open, gaping *u*, and the hanging *g* and *y*. It just says 'ugly' to me!" Janna drew the word *ugly* to illustrate her point.

Lee had other ideas. "That's a neat drawing, Janna," he said, "but I don't see it that way. I think there's some beauty to be found in the word *ugly*." Lee drew the word his way.

Now it's your turn. Find a way to make a word look like what it means. You might want to take Lee's approach and do the opposite.

ENRICHMENT Pick one.

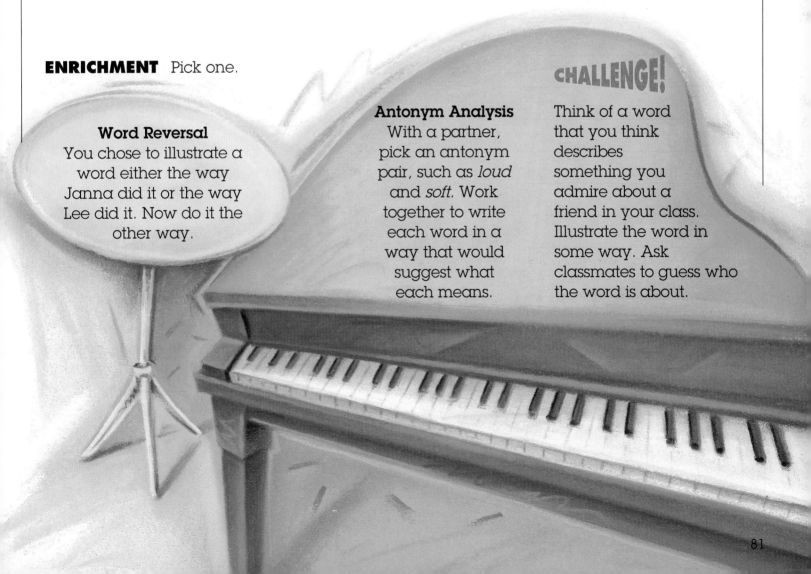

Word Reversal
You chose to illustrate a word either the way Janna did it or the way Lee did it. Now do it the other way.

Antonym Analysis
With a partner, pick an antonym pair, such as *loud* and *soft*. Work together to write each word in a way that would suggest what each means.

CHALLENGE!
Think of a word that you think describes something you admire about a friend in your class. Illustrate the word in some way. Ask classmates to guess who the word is about.

Contractions

1. _____

2. _____

3. _____

4. _____

5. _____

6. _____

7. _____

8. _____

9. _____

10. _____

11. _____

12. _____

13. _____

14. _____

15. _____

16. _____

17. _____

18. _____

19. _____

20. _____

■ **FOCUS** A **contraction** is a shortened form of two words. Say each pair of words and then say its contraction.

I + am	=	*I'm* ♻
I + would	=	*I'd*
you + would	=	*you'd*
they + would	=	*they'd*
he + would	=	*he'd*
I + will	=	*I'll*
he + will	=	*he'll*
she + will	=	*she'll*
we + will	=	*we'll*
they + will	=	*they'll*
it + is	=	*it's* ♻
that + is	=	*that's* ♻
what + is	=	*what's*
let + us	=	*let's* ♻
would + not	=	*wouldn't*
should + not	=	*shouldn't*
does + not	=	*doesn't*
we + have	=	*we've*
would + have	=	*would've*
could + have	=	*could've*

■ **DISCOVER** An apostrophe (') replaces the letters that are left out when a contraction is formed. What letters are left out when **she will** is shortened to **she'll** and **I am** to **I'm?**

■ **WRITE**
- five words ending in **-'ll**
- four words ending in **-'d**
- four words ending either in **-'ve** or **-'m**
- seven words ending either in **-'t** or **-'s**

CHALLENGE!

we'd
it'll
mustn't
might've
who'll

HOMOPHONES   Write the contraction that sounds just like each word below.

1. heed
2. weave
3. aisle
4. eyed
5. heel
6. lets

CREATING CONTRACTIONS   Write the contractions for the words below.

7. they will
8. we will
9. what is
10. they would
11. that is
12. could have
13. would have
14. she will

DON'T QUOTE ME   Write list words to help the famous people below complete sentences they might have said.

15. Nathan Hale: "____ sorry I have but one life to give."
16. Rosa Parks: "Would I give up my seat on the bus? I ____!"
17. Mohandas Gandhi: "One should resist oppression, but one ____ use violence to do so."
18. Pablo Picasso: "Painting isn't beautiful, ____ magical."
19. Confucius: "Do to others what ____ want done to you."
20. Amelia Earhart: "Peace comes with courage. It ____ come easily."

STRATEGIC SPELLING
Building New Words

1. _____
2. _____
3. _____
4. _____
5. _____
6. _____
7. _____
8. _____
9. _____
10. _____
11. _____
12. _____
13. _____
14. _____
15. _____
16. _____
17. _____
18. _____
19. _____
20. _____

Add the contraction for *will* to the base words. Remember what you learned.

Base word	Contraction with 'll
21. you	_____
22. who	_____

Did You Know?
I is a capital because in old handwritten manuscripts a small *i* would often be lost or attached to a neighboring word. A capital *I* helped separate it.

≡	Make a capital.
/	Make a small letter.
∧	Add something.
ℓ	Take out something.
⊙	Add a period.
¶	New paragraph

PROOFREAD A SIGN The photograph below contains a misspelled word. Since a question is being asked, the punctuation is also incorrect. Write the word correctly as well as the punctuation mark.

PROOFREADING TIP
It's easy to make a mistake in a word with an apostrophe when making a sign. Be sure you carefully proofread your sign before others see it.

WOULD'T AN AUTOMATIC
GARAGE DOOR OPENER
BE GREAT!
CALL US 555-9757

WRITE A SIGN Isn't there a question you'd like to ask in a big way? Use a few list words to create your message.

Word List

I'm	it's
I'd	that's
you'd	what's
they'd	let's
he'd	wouldn't
I'll	shouldn't
he'll	doesn't
she'll	we've
we'll	would've
they'll	could've

Personal Words

1. _____

2. _____

EXPLORING LANGUAGE: PYRAMID SENTENCES

Pyramid sentences start with one word, the subject, and get longer and longer. Each word that is added must begin with the same letter. Arranged one atop the other, the sentences look like a pyramid. Here's an example:

Subject word: she'll

She'll sing.

She'll sing songs.

She'll sing six songs.

Shelly says she'll sing six silly songs.

Now you try writing your own pyramid sentences. Begin with one of these words: *They'll, I'm, It's, He'd,* or *We'll.*

_____

_____

_____

_____

ENRICHMENT Pick one.

Pyramids, Part II
Create another pyramid, this time choosing your own word. Decorate your pyramid.

Upside-down Pyramid
Get together with one or two classmates and write a long sentence whose words begin with the same letter. Make a reverse pyramid by taking words out and writing shorter sentences, until all that remains is the subject word.

CHALLENGE!
Use what you know about pyramid sentences to write sentences in the shape of a diamond. Remember to begin all words with the same letter. Compare your results with others in your class.

Review

HOW AM I DOING?

Look back at the word lists in Lessons 13–17 and think about how you are doing in spelling.

1. The word I am proudest about learning to spell is _____ .

2. I learned to spell a hard word by
   ☐ thinking of a sound clue from a related word.
   ☐ underlining the part of the word that is a problem for me and studying it.
   ☐ dividing the word into smaller parts and studying the parts.

3. When I learn a new spelling word, I spell it
   correctly in my writing.   Yes   No   Sometimes

4. When I just can't figure out how to spell
   a word, I check the dictionary.   Always   Sometimes   Never

5. A word that has always been hard for me to spell is _____ .

   In order to spell it correctly, I think about

   _____

   _____

   _____ .

R for Good Health

excellent

lazy

we'll

heal

charge

health

Take (1) of your own life. Eat sensibly! Exercise!

To maintain good (2), always get plenty of rest.

Don't be (3)! Get out and do things!

Exercise is an (4) way to reduce stress.

If a sore doesn't (5), see your doctor.

If we follow these simple rules, (6) all stay healthy.

The students in health class put together the following rules. Supply the missing words and think about how the rules apply to you.

1. _____
2. _____
3. _____
4. _____
5. _____
6. _____

Daily Record — mon., may 7

5:30	(1) _____ up and dressed.
5:40	Breakfast: two (2) _____ of orange juice. 7-grain cereal, and ½ (3) _____ of 2% milk
6:30	30 sit-ups
7:00	My (4) _____ comes in and says, "Son, (5) _____ talk."
7:05	I tell him I'm not (6) _____ to take the time.
7:30	I run 5 miles, worrying about hurting Dad's (7) _____.
8:30	Home to change clothes for school.
9:00	Take a shortcut that (8) _____ go anywhere.
10:00	I'm so late for school, I've missed two (9) _____! Tomorrow will be better.

N'Jabi decided to keep a record of his daily routine. Complete the entry for Monday, May 7.

quart   glasses   father
able   feelings   classes
I'm   doesn't   let's

1. _____
2. _____
3. _____
4. _____
5. _____
6. _____
7. _____
8. _____
9. _____

GOOD SPORTS

Use the words below to complete each person's statement.

1. _____
2. _____
3. _____
4. _____

signal

missed

beaches

always

I MADE TEN BASKETS AND ONLY (1) _____ ONCE.

I RIDE THE WAVES RIGHT ONTO THE SANDY (2) _____.

GIVE ME THE (3) _____, AND I'LL TACKLE ANYTHING IN SIGHT.

I (4) _____ TRY TO SERVE AND VOLLEY.

87

Off the Shelf

The items below are missing words.
Complete each item with a list word.

1. _____
2. _____
3. _____
4. _____

5. _____
6. _____

WHEAT CRUNCHIES
Breakfast of Eaters

with (5) helpings of honey clusters

SLICK SHOES
"If you want to be (1), wear Slick. They'll (2) the way you run... for the better!"

the ROACHES SING the BEETLES

" I liked it (3)."
– Paula McCartney

"You'll (4) to hear more!"
– Ringlet Starr

MY FLIGHTY LIFE
by Carl Canary

"You (6) miss this one!"

Interview

Karli loves music and wondered what it would be like to discuss it with a famous composer. She wrote this imaginary interview with J. S. Bach.

KARLI: Mr. Bach, can you _____ why you became a composer?

J. S.: Yes. I _____ want to do anything in my life

but _____ music.

KARLI: Did you have musical _____ at a young age?

J. S.: I believe so. I wrote my first _____ as a young man.

KARLI: What was it about music that _____ you?

J. S.: Everything! The notes, the _____ , the harmonies!

KARLI: You write music that is loud and triumphant

or _____ and romantic. Which do you prefer?

J. S.: I think _____ all a challenge. Music is my life.

didn't
meter
ability
compose
excited
it's
explain
soft
composition

Visiting the Lone Star State

holidays
eleven
friends
memories
relative
village
Texas

Rafael gave a talk to his class about a place that is very important to him. Use the list words to complete his sentences.

- EL PASO
- PECOS
- SOCORRO

I love the state of _____ .

I have wonderful _____ of El Paso. I spend all my school _____ there.

My good _____ Juana and Paul live in Pecos.

I have _____ cousins who live in the small _____ of Socorro.

I am the only _____ who doesn't live in this state.

School Fund-Raiser

Martin Luther King, Jr. School is having its annual fund-raiser. Use the list words to finish the posters.

fudge	quilt	washed
crumb	edge	relax
flowers	bunches	liquid

1. _____
2. _____
3. _____
4. _____
5. _____
6. _____
7. _____
8. _____
9. _____

Raffle Tickets
TAKE A CHANCE ON THIS BEAUTIFUL HANDMADE (1).
NOTICE THE SCALLOP ALONG EACH (2).

Fresh garden (5)
Daisies, Roses, Snapdragons, and more!! Buy two (6) in a big bouquet, get one free! Hurry while the supply lasts!!

Quench Your Thirst
25¢ each
Sodas, apple juice, and other (9) refreshments. Straw-free.

Homemade Chocolate (3) for sale here. You'll gobble up (4)! every fifty cents apiece

Car Wash $2.50
We'll have it (7) in 5 minutes. You just sit back and (8).

Strategy Workshop

Memory Tricks

DISCOVER THE STRATEGY Some words seem so tricky to spell that we need to outsmart them with tricks of our own. Follow these steps.

1. Mark the letters that give you a problem.	2. Find words you know with those same letters.	3. Use your problem word and the word you know in a phrase or sentence.

Your memory trick might be more than one word. It might rhyme. Just be sure you can spell the helping word and that the problem letters match. Here are more memory tricks.

wheat—Heat the wheat.

liquid—quick liquid
young—You are young.
bubbles— big beautiful bubbles

TRY IT OUT Now practice the memory-tricks strategy yourself. Follow the directions on the next page.

† Complete each memory
trick using a word from the box to the right.

1. Ride _____ the lion.

2. A couple is _____.

3. Flick the kitchen _____.

4. Give _____ lettuce.

switch
on
Bruce
plenty

†† With a partner, write your own memory tricks for each pair
of words below. It's all right if they sound silly. The point is
to find ways to remember how to spell tricky words.
Underline the matching letters.

5. hotel—Elvis _____

6. blanket—thank _____

7. window—down _____

† Make a memory trick for one of the words in the box to the
right. Follow steps 2 and 3 on page 90. Mark the matching
letters.

8. _____

_____

cable
closet
season
tomorrow

† **LOOK AHEAD** Look ahead at the next five lessons. Find
one list word that looks hard to spell and write a memory
trick for it. Share your trick with the class.

_____

_____

Getting Letters in Correct Order

1. _____

2. _____

3. _____

4. _____

5. _____

6. _____

7. _____

8. _____

9. _____

10. _____

11. _____

12. _____

13. _____

14. _____

15. _____

16. _____

17. _____

18. _____

19. _____

20. _____

■ **FOCUS** Read each word and phrase. Notice the order of the underlined letters.

believe	♻	**believe** someone's story
friend	♻	help a **friend**
piece		a **piece** of cake
field		a **field** full of corn
weird		**weird** shadows on the wall
height		a **height** of six feet six inches
weight		a **weight** of two hundred pounds
neighbor		my next-door **neighbor**
said	♻	couldn't hear what she **said**
again	♻	doing it over **again**
heard	♻	**heard** the good news
heart		a kind **heart**
rattle		a **rattle** for the baby
pickle		a sour **pickle**
brought	♻	**brought** a friend along
asked		**asked** for my help
toes		wiggling their **toes**
build		**build** a new tree house
only		**only** on Tuesdays
hospital	♻	in the **hospital** with a broken leg

■ **DISCOVER** Many people misspell words by getting letters in the wrong order. What letters might give you a problem in the words **friend, weight,** and **pickle?**

■ **WRITE** Think about which of the list words you use most in your writing. Then write them in order, from the ones you use most to the ones you use least. Underline any letter combinations that are hard for you to keep in order.

CHALLENGE!

tongue
unusual
interview
sword
poetry

EQUATIONS   Write each list word using the math clues.

1. a + gain =
2. on + lye -e =
3. we + bird -b =
4. ask + led -l =
5. rat + tile -i =
6. fried -d + nd =

7. is -i + aid =
8. pick + led -d =
9. outfield -out =
10. built -t + d =
11. be + lie -e + eve=
12. neigh + born -n =

HOMOPHONES   Write the list word that sounds like each word below.

13. herd
14. peace

15. wait
16. tows

17. hart

Strategic Spelling

Using the Memory Tricks Strategy

Use memory tricks to help you spell. Write a list word to complete each trick. Underline the matching letters.

18. e<u>ight</u> feet in _____

19. <u>p</u>at<u>i</u>en<u>t</u>s in traction in a _____

20. I _____ <u>g</u>rapes, <u>h</u>oney, and <u>t</u>ea to the

party.

1. _____

2. _____

3. _____

4. _____

5. _____

6. _____

7. _____

8. _____

9. _____

10. _____

11. _____

12. _____

13. _____

14. _____

15. _____

16. _____

17. _____

Take a Hint
Is it **peace** or **piece?**
Just remember:
Slice a **pie**ce of **pie.**

☰	Make a capital.
/	Make a small letter.
∧	Add something.
℮	Take out something.
⊙	Add a period.
⨍	New paragraph

PROOFREAD A DESCRIPTION

While blindfolded, Bria felt an object and then wrote a description of it. First correct three misspellings and two careless errors in her description below. Then write the name of the object. Hint: It's a list word.

PROOFREADING TIP

Bria tried so hard to get the description right that small words were left out. Such mistakes are easy to catch if you proofread.

It is a long peice of plastic with a round part on top.

Its weight is about two ounces.

Its hight about five inches.

It makes wierd sound when you shake it.

What is it? _____

WRITE A DESCRIPTION

Play this guessing game with your classmates. While blindfolded, each player feels a different object and writes a description of that object. After everyone has written descriptions, read them aloud one by one and guess the names of the objects.

_____
_____
_____
_____
_____
_____
_____
_____

Word List

believe	heard
friend	heart
piece	rattle
field	pickle
weird	brought
height	asked
weight	toes
neighbor	build
said	only
again	hospital

Personal Words

1. _____

2. _____

AFFIXES Affixes are added to words to change their meanings. An affix added to the beginning of a word is called a **prefix.** An affix added to the end of a word is called a **suffix.** Look at the table below.

AFFIXES

PREFIXES			SUFFIXES		
Meaning		**Example**	**Meaning**		**Example**
un	not	(unhappy =not happy)	**-less**	without	(hopeless=without hope)
re	again	(replay=play again)	**-ly**	in a ___ way	(slowly=in a slow way)
mis	badly	(misbehave=behave badly)	**-ness**	being __	(happiness=being happy)

Use the list words below and the affixes in the chart to make new words that will finish the sentences. One sentence will need a word with two affixes.

build   friend   heard   weight

1. The cat's noisy meowing was _____ by its owner.

2. The astronauts floated around in a _____ state.

3. The beavers were able to _____ their home.

4. I backed away from the growling, _____ dog.

ENRICHMENT Pick one.

Antonym Affixes
Choose two list words. Try to write the opposite of each by adding one or more affixes to the list word.

Affixing Suffixes
Choose a list word to which you can add a suffix. Write a sentence leaving a blank for the new word. Trade papers with a friend, fill in the blank, and read your completed sentences.

CHALLENGE!
Pick one list word. Write as many new words as you can by combining this word with various affixes.

Vowels with r

1. _____
2. _____
3. _____
4. _____
5. _____
6. _____
7. _____
8. _____
9. _____
10. _____
11. _____
12. _____
13. _____
14. _____
15. _____
16. _____
17. _____
18. _____
19. _____
20. _____

■ **FOCUS** Say each word and phrase. Find the letters that make the vowel sounds you hear in **pour** and **nerve**.

pour	**pour** a glass of milk
morning ♻	woke up early in the **morning**
course	take a **course** in woodworking
Florida	eat an orange from **Florida**
storm	trees bending in a **storm**
fourth	entering **fourth** grade
forest	a deep, green **forest**
fourteen	**fourteen** apartments in a building
form	filled out an application **form**
court	met on the tennis **court**
nerve	have the **nerve** to sing a solo
dirty	**dirty** after a week of camping
first ♻	be the **first** in line
serve	**serve** a salad with dinner
girlfriend	trust the advice of a **girlfriend**
certain	be **certain** a problem is solved
thirsty	**thirsty** after a hard game of soccer
perfect	**perfect** weather for a picnic
skirt	wore a **skirt** and blouse
herself	finished the job **herself**

■ **DISCOVER** The vowel sound you hear in **pour** is spelled **our**, but how is it spelled in **form**? The vowel sound you hear in **nerve** is spelled **er**, but how is it spelled in **skirt**?

■ **WRITE**
- five words with **er**
- five words with **ir**
- five words with **or**
- five words with **our**

CHALLENGE!

whirl
commercial
determine
unfortunately
resources

MAKING CONNECTIONS Write the list word that answers each question.

1. What follows second and third?
2. In what kind of place could you see many trees?
3. What type of clothing is often worn with a blouse?
4. What do you call that special female pal?
5. What does a waiter do with the meal you order?
6. When you play basketball, what do you play it on?
7. What comes next: myself, yourself, himself,____?
8. If something is absolutely wonderful, what is it?

POETRY Write the list words that complete the poem.

Early one (9) in their Michigan dorm,
The students could hear the raging (10).
They hadn't the (11) to go out the door,
Because rain continued to pour and (12).
Then the temperature dropped to a cold (13).
Snow mounds began to (14) all over the green.
Said one, "I'm (15) now of nature's force.
Mother Nature always takes her own (16)."
Well, they did the same—on the (17) bus they could reach.
They arrived in sunny (18) and headed for the beach.

1. _____
2. _____
3. _____
4. _____
5. _____
6. _____
7. _____
8. _____
9. _____
10. _____
11. _____
12. _____
13. _____
14. _____
15. _____
16. _____
17. _____
18. _____

Strategic Spelling

Building New Words

Write *dirty* and *thirsty*. Write the forms of these words that complete the chart. **Remember:** In words that end in **y**, you change the **y** to **i** before adding **-er** or **-est**.

> **Take a Hint**
> If you think it may r**ain**,
> But you're not quite cert**ain**,
> Spare yourself some p**ain**.
> Open up the cur**tain**.

	Spelling Word	Add -er	Add -est
19.	_____	_____	_____
20.	_____	_____	_____

≡	Make a capital.
/	Make a small letter.
∧	Add something.
ℒ	Take out something.
⊙	Add a period.
⁋	New paragraph

PROOFREAD AN ADVERTISEMENT

The ad below was written for a small travel magazine. Correct four misspelled words and two incorrect verbs.

PROOFREADING TIP
The writer used the verbs swam and saw incorrectly. It's swim, swam, (have) swum. Check a dictionary for how to handle see.

Have you ever swam in the ocean?

Have you ever eaten fresh lobster?

Have you ever saw grate blue herons flying?

No? Then you must visit **Flordia!**

It is the perfect vacation for anyone thursty for sun and fun!

Call us today. **Travel Masters**

WRITE AN ADVERTISEMENT

Write an advertisement for a place you think others might like to visit. Use a few list words and personal words.

Word List

pour	nerve
morning	dirty
course	first
Florida	serve
storm	girlfriend
fourth	certain
forest	thirsty
fourteen	perfect
form	skirt
court	herself

Personal Words

1. _____

2. _____

EXPLORING LANGUAGE: ONOMATOPOEIA   This

big word is pronounced on′ ə mat′ ə pē′ ə. It's what we call words like *buzz, hum,* and *splash.* When you use **onomatopoeia,** the words sound just like the sounds they describe. Read the poem below aloud. Emphasize the words that are examples of onomatopoeia.

> *Whack! The tennis ball is served.*
> *It whizzes 'cross the net.*
> *Bing! It bounces on the court.*
> *Wham! It's hard to get.*
> *Then...thud!*
> *Oh ...*
> *No!*
> *It's collapsed into the net.*

Now use onomatopoeia to write words you might use to describe the sounds of:

1. walking on leaves in wet tennis shoes _____

2. bees building a honeycomb _____

3. dropping pebbles in a puddle _____

4. eating soup and salad _____

ENRICHMENT   Pick one.

Onomatopoeia Animals
Use onomatopoeia to write about the sounds and actions of two of the following animals: pigeon, cat, snail, sheep, and fly. Draw or find pictures of the animals too. Label your creations.

Sounds Where You Live
Think about the sounds you hear on the way to school. Write them down. Work with a partner to write a poem or story using these sounds as words.

CHALLENGE!
Write a paragraph using each of these onomatopoeic words:
boom   clatter
crash   snore

Vowel Sounds in *put* and *out*

1. _____
2. _____
3. _____
4. _____
5. _____
6. _____
7. _____
8. _____
9. _____
10. _____
11. _____
12. _____
13. _____
14. _____
15. _____
16. _____
17. _____
18. _____
19. _____
20. _____

■ **FOCUS** Say each word and phrase. Find the letters that make the vowel sounds you hear in **put** and **out**.

took ♻	**took** an afternoon nap
cushion	a soft sofa **cushion**
football	throw a **football**
July	vacation in **July**
brook	a little bubbling **brook**
butcher	meat from the **butcher**
stood	**stood** at the door
pudding	ate chocolate **pudding**
bush	birds sitting in a **bush**
wood	**wood** for the fireplace
shower	took a hot **shower**
mountain	high atop the **mountain**
power	a senator with great **power**
proud	**proud** of your success
house ♻	build a brick **house**
however	**however** you prefer
cloud	a billowy white **cloud**
crowd	a large **crowd** of moviegoers
loud	heard a **loud** bang
outside ♻	went to play **outside**

■ **DISCOVER** The vowel sound you hear in **put** is spelled **oo** in **took**. How is it spelled in **bush**? The vowel sound you hear in **out** is spelled **ow** in **crowd**. How is it spelled in **cloud**?

■ **WRITE**
- six words with **ou**
- four words with **ow**
- five words with **u**
- five words with **oo**

CHALLENGE!

barefoot
coward
announced
thousand
jury

SYLLABLE SCRAMBLE Each group of letters is one syllable of a two-syllable word. Match one from each column to make list words.

1. moun	ball
2. butch	ly
3. foot	er
4. cush	ding
5. Ju	tain
6. pud	ion

RHYME TIME Write the list words that rhyme with the underlined words and make sense in the sentences. Circle the list word that ends differently than its rhyming word.

The tiny <u>mouse</u> crept through the (7).
With one swift <u>push</u> I fell into the (8).
Lee <u>Loud</u> looked up at a fluffy white (9)
The actors <u>bowed</u> before the cheering (10).
"Milk a <u>cow</u>? <u>Never</u>!" "You may have to, (11)."
I (12) a <u>book</u> and read beside the (13).
Tired Ms. <u>Good</u> (14) beside the cut (15).
<u>Gower</u> lacked the (16) to turn off the dripping (17).
Mr. <u>Doud</u> shouted out (18) because he was so (19).

Strategic Spelling

Seeing Meaning Connections

Write the words from the box that fit the definitions.

20. a person who is driven away from home and friends _____

21. not inside; outdoors _____

22. a way of looking at things; point of

   view _____

Words with *out*
outlook
outside
outcast

1. _____
2. _____
3. _____
4. _____
5. _____
6. _____
7. _____
8. _____
9. _____
10. _____
11. _____
12. _____
13. _____
14. _____
15. _____
16. _____
17. _____
18. _____
19. _____

Take a Hint
If you have trouble with
wood and **would,** remember
the two round knotholes in
wood.

101

≡	Make a capital.
/	Make a small letter.
∧	Add something.
ℯ	Take out something.
⊙	Add a period.
¶	New paragraph

PROOFREAD A LIST Lamont has written a list of the things he must do Saturday morning. Correct four misspelled words and two words that should be capitalized.

PROOFREADING TIP

Lamont has developed a "lazy-lower-case" habit. He forgets to capitalize people's names and the days of the week. Don't let this happen to you.

saturday chores

1. Take a shouwer.

2. Help auntie clean the hous.

3. Make puding for the party.

4. Practice foot ball.

WRITE A LIST Write a list of the things you plan to do this weekend. Use some of your list words and a few personal words.

Word List

took	shower
cushion	mountain
football	power
July	proud
brook	house
butcher	however
stood	cloud
pudding	crowd
bush	loud
wood	outside

Personal Words

1. _____

2. _____

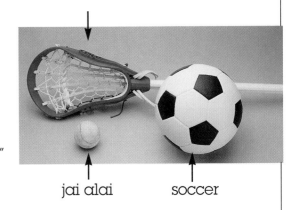

lacrosse

jai alai   soccer

MULTICULTURAL CONNECTION: SPORTS All over the world, sports are played in which players try to get a ball from one place to another. Read about three sports. Use the picture and the labels at right to help you name each sport. The Spelling Dictionary will help also.

1. North American Indians invented this game. It is played with a small rubber ball and sticks, or "crosses." It is called ___.

2. South Americans play a very fast game using a small, hard ball called a "pelota." Curved baskets are worn on the hands. The game is pronounced hī′ lī′. It is called ___.

3. This is the most popular game in the world. It is played without using the hands. Most Africans and Europeans call it "football," but you may know it as ___.

1. _____

2. _____

3. _____

ENRICHMENT Pick one.

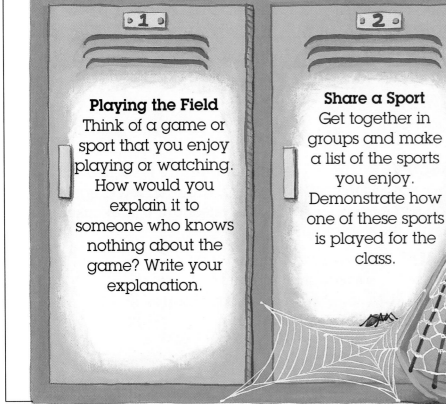

•1•

Playing the Field
Think of a game or sport that you enjoy playing or watching. How would you explain it to someone who knows nothing about the game? Write your explanation.

•2•

Share a Sport
Get together in groups and make a list of the sports you enjoy. Demonstrate how one of these sports is played for the class.

•3•

CHALLENGE!

Find out about a game that is very popular in another country. Write the rules and objectives of the game. Teach the game to friends and classmates.

Vowel Sounds in *few* and *moon*

1. _____

2. _____

3. _____

4. _____

5. _____

6. _____

7. _____

8. _____

9. _____

10. _____

11. _____

12. _____

13. _____

14. _____

15. _____

16. _____

17. _____

18. _____

19. _____

20. _____

■ **FOCUS** Say each word and phrase. Find the letters that make the vowel sounds you hear in **few** and **moon.**

bruise	a purple **bruise** on her leg
cool	**cool** weather for July
juice	drank a glass of **juice**
school	ride the bus to **school**
fruit	ate three pieces of **fruit**
mood	in a bad **mood**
suit	a blue business **suit**
shoot	**shoot** a few baskets
cruise	a Caribbean **cruise**
shampoo	**shampoo** my hair
pupil	a **pupil** in the third grade
few	waited a **few** minutes
fuel	**fuel** a car with gasoline
excuse	no **excuse** for rudeness
nephew	a **nephew** in college
huge	a **huge** office building
curfew	in before 9:00 **curfew**
confuse	**confuse** her with her sister
usual	took the **usual** route home
menu	order food from a **menu**

■ **DISCOVER** The vowel sound in **bruise** is spelled **ui.** How is it spelled in **cool**? The vowel sound in **few** is spelled **ew.** The same sound is spelled **u-consonant-e** in **excuse.** How is it spelled in **pupil**?

■ **WRITE**   ▪ five words with **oo**
　　　　　　▪ five words with **ui**
　　　　　　▪ six words with **u-consonant-e** or **ew**
　　　　　　▪ four words with **u**

CHALLENGE!

reunion
universe
commute
fireproof
pursuit

ANALOGIES Write the list word that completes each phrase.

1. hot and warm, cold and ____.
2. most and many, least and ____.
3. aunt and uncle, niece and ____.
4. small and tiny, large and ____.
5. carrot and banana, vegetable and ____.
6. apple and sauce, orange and ____.
7. teeth and toothpaste, hair and ____.
8. train and schedule, restaurant and ____.
9. doctor and patient, teacher and ____.

TONGUE TWISTERS Write the list word that would best complete each tongue twister.

10. Being bucked by a bronco brought about Brian's ____.
11. The sensational singer sported a silky silver ____.
12. Should Shelly snap the shutter and ____ the shy sheep?
13. Curt's camp counselor calls "Come in!" at ____.
14. Maybe Maya managed to maintain a merry ____.
15. Chemistry quiz questions ____ and confound Cornelius.
16. Chris chartered a craft to ____ the Caribbean.
17. The extravagant explorers had an ____ for the expensive expedition.

Strategic Spelling

Seeing Meaning Connections

Write the list word that completes each sentence. The underlined word is a clue. Circle the letters in each list word that are the same as in the underlined word.

18. The schoolwork at our ____ is very challenging.
19. I am usually on time if I take the ____ route.
20. We had to stop and refuel when we ran out of ____.

1. _____
2. _____
3. _____
4. _____
5. _____
6. _____
7. _____
8. _____
9. _____
10. _____
11. _____
12. _____
13. _____
14. _____
15. _____
16. _____
17. _____
18. _____
19. _____
20. _____

> **Did You Know?**
> The word *curfew* comes from the French words *covrir,* to cover, and *feu,* fire. When the curfew bell rang, people covered, or put out, their fires each night.

105

≡	Make a capital.
/	Make a small letter.
∧	Add something.
ℯ	Take out something.
⊙	Add a period.
¶	New paragraph

PROOFREAD DIRECTIONS The owner of Cozy's Café left these directions for her after-school assistant. Correct four misspelled words and add three missing end marks.

PROOFREADING TIP

Cozy forgot to use an exclamation mark in her final sentence. What other mark did she forget (twice)?

> P. J.,
>
> How was shcool Please squeeze oranges and cut up apples. Type up a new menu to include frut salad and fresh orange joos. Are you in the mude to make one of your special soups They are terrific
>
> Cozy

WRITE DIRECTIONS Isn't there something you'd like to ask someone to do in writing? Use spelling words and personal words to write your directions.

Word List

bruise	pupil
cool	few
juice	fuel
school	excuse
fruit	nephew
mood	huge
suit	curfew
shoot	confuse
cruise	usual
shampoo	menu

Personal Words

1. _____
2. _____

EXPLORING LANGUAGE: COLLECTIVE NOUNS

You know the phrase, "a herd of elephants," but did you know a group of geese is called a "gaggle"? Words like *herd* and *gaggle* are called **collective nouns.** Sometimes they reflect a quality possessed by the subject. This is why we speak of a *pride* of lions—because they seem proud to us.

Read each sentence below. Find the collective noun at the right that you think would best describe each group. Your Spelling Dictionary will help you.

1. Just one is called a goldfish.
Two are goldfish or goldfishes.
As a group, they are called a _____.

2. One alone is a bee.
More than one are bees.
As a group, they are called a _____.

swarm
school
skulk

3. One is called a fox.
Two or more are called foxes.
As a group, they are called a _____.

ENRICHMENT   Pick one.

Collective Coinage
Create your own collective phrase. Choose a word from your spelling list and combine it with something it could describe. An example might be: a cruise of spaceships.

Collective Creations
Draw a picture of a collective phrase based on one of these words: *pod, nonsense, wisp, humor,* and *group.* Write the word under your picture. Ask a classmate to title the picture using a collective phrase (example: a *humor* of comedians).

CHALLENGE!
Find out the meaning of the collective nouns listed below. Use each in a sentence. Share them with your classmates.
bevy   colony   covey   gang   pod

Homophones

1. _____

2. _____

3. _____

4. _____

5. _____

6. _____

7. _____

8. _____

9. _____

10. _____

11. _____

12. _____

13. _____

14. _____

15. _____

16. _____

17. _____

18. _____

19. _____

20. _____

■ **FOCUS** Read each word and phrase. Pay attention to the spellings of the words that sound exactly alike.

beat	**beat** a drum
beet	ate a pickled **beet**
break	**break** a glass
brake	**brake** at a stop sign
wood	chopped a pile of **wood**
would ♻	asked if I **would** help
clothes	bought some new **clothes**
close	told me to **close** the door
piece	ate a **piece** of cheese
peace	hoped for world **peace**
your	borrowed **your** book
you're ♻	asked when **you're** going
thrown	has **thrown** her old toys away
throne	a queen on her **throne**
to	went **to** work
too ♻	**too** tired to stay up
two	**two** sisters and a brother
there ♻	have never been **there** before
their ♻	finished **their** work
they're ♻	if **they're** not too busy

■ **DISCOVER** A homophone is a word that sounds exactly like another word but has a different meaning and spelling: **beat** and **beet**. Studying the meaning phrases above will help you remember the spelling of each homophone group.

■ **WRITE** First write the homophone groups that may be difficult for you to keep straight. Then write the rest of the homophones.

CHALLENGE!

guessed	aisle
guest	isle
waste	
waist	

HOMOPHONE PHOTOS Write the list word that labels each photograph. Below that word, write another list word that sounds just like it.

1. _____

2. _____

3. _____

4. _____

5. _____

6. _____

HOMOPHONE QUOTES Complete the statements of the people below by writing list words that sound alike.

King: "I was so unpopular, I was (7) from my (8)."
Teacher: "If they stay (9), I know (10) going to miss (11) bus."
Twins: "The (12) of us would like (13) ride the bus (14)."
Driver: "If I (15) suddenly, the dishes in the back will (16)."
Dentist: "Tino, (17) going to have to brush (18) teeth more."

Using the Memory Tricks Strategy

Use memory tricks to help you spell. Write a list word to complete each trick. Underline the matching letters.

19. a _____ of <u>pie</u>

20. _____ for <u>pe</u>ople <u>a</u>ll over

7. _____

8. _____

9. _____

10. _____

11. _____

12. _____

13. _____

14. _____

15. _____

16. _____

17. _____

18. _____

≡	Make a capital.
/	Make a small letter.
∧	Add something.
ℯ	Take out something.
⊙	Add a period.
¶	New paragraph

PROOFREAD AN OUTLINE Sara is giving a speech tomorrow. Read her outline. Correct four misspelled words and two errors in capitalization.

PROOFREADING TIP
Sara knows that the first word in each main topic and subtopic of her outline must be capitalized. Proofreading would have helped her do just that.

How to Build a Birdhouse
I. Gather your materials
    A. Seven squares of wod (sides, bottom, roof)
    B. Hammer and nails
II. assemble you're materials
    A. Cut hole in one peace
    B. Nail four sides together (opening in front)
    C. nail bottom to sides
    D. Nail the last to pieces on top for roof
III. Paint your birdhouse

WRITE AN OUTLINE Write an outline of a speech you would like to give. Use list words.

Word List

beat	your
beet	you're
break	thrown
brake	throne
wood	to
would	too
clothes	two
close	there
piece	their
peace	they're

Personal Words

1. _____

2. _____

DICTIONARY: HOMOGRAPHS
If you looked up *brake* in a dictionary, here is what you would find:

There is more than one entry for *brake. Brake* is a **homograph.** Homographs are spelled exactly alike, but they have different word histories and different meanings. The raised number alerts you to this.

brake¹ (brāk), **1** anything used to slow or stop the motion of a wheel or vehicle by pressing or scraping or by rubbing against. **2** slow or stop by using a brake: *The driver braked the speeding car and it slid to a stop. 1 n., 2 v.,* **braked, brak•ing.**
brake² (brāk), a thick growth of bushes; thicket. *n.*

Study the entries above. Write *brake¹* or *brake²* to answer each question below.

1. Which entry can be more than one part of speech?
2. Which entry has an example sentence?
3. Which entry would you find in a forest?

1. _____

2. _____

3. _____

ENRICHMENT Pick one.

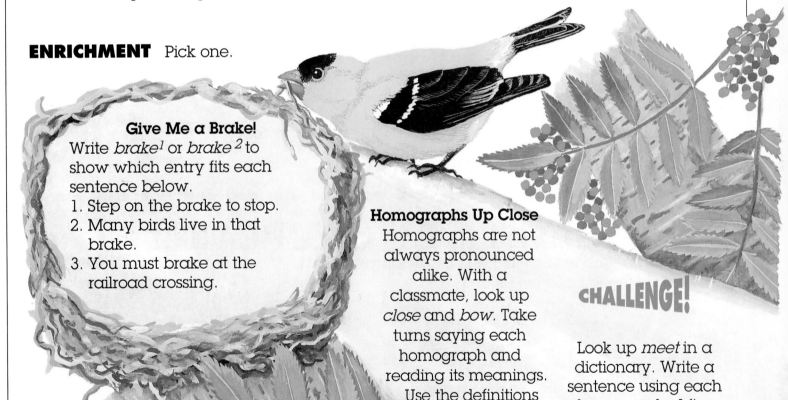

Give Me a Brake!
Write *brake¹* or *brake²* to show which entry fits each sentence below.
1. Step on the brake to stop.
2. Many birds live in that brake.
3. You must brake at the railroad crossing.

Homographs Up Close
Homographs are not always pronounced alike. With a classmate, look up *close* and *bow*. Take turns saying each homograph and reading its meanings. Use the definitions in sentences.

CHALLENGE!
Look up *meet* in a dictionary. Write a sentence using each homograph. After each sentence write the part-of-speech label that shows how *meet* was used in each sentence.

111

Review

Look back at the word lists in Lessons 19–23 and think about how you are doing in spelling.

1. I'm learning to spell many new words correctly.   Yes   No   Maybe

2. I learned to spell a hard word by
   ☐ using memory tricks to link problem words with words I already knew.
   ☐ saying the word aloud and picturing it in my mind.
   ☐ dividing the word into smaller parts and studying the parts.

3. When I misspell a word I usually know it doesn't
   look correct.   Yes   No   Sometimes

4. When I try to spell a word I can usually picture
   the word in my head.   Yes   No   Sometimes

5. The most interesting word that I have learned to spell is _____ .

   In order to spell it correctly, I think about _____

   _____ .

CLARINETISTS' COMPLAINT

Band members are filing an official complaint with their leader. Write the words they left out.

usual
suit
clothes
believe
crowd

Dear Mr. Seiferth,

   We, the Woodwind Section, (1) it is unfair that we must wear (2) pants to play in school concerts. The (3) comes to hear us play, not to admire our (4). Please consider letting us wear our (5) school clothes at future concerts.

            Thank you,

            The Woodwinds

1. _____

2. _____

3. _____

4. _____

5. _____

Labels

Tess received a small label maker and went around her house labeling items. Match the name of each item to the number next to it.

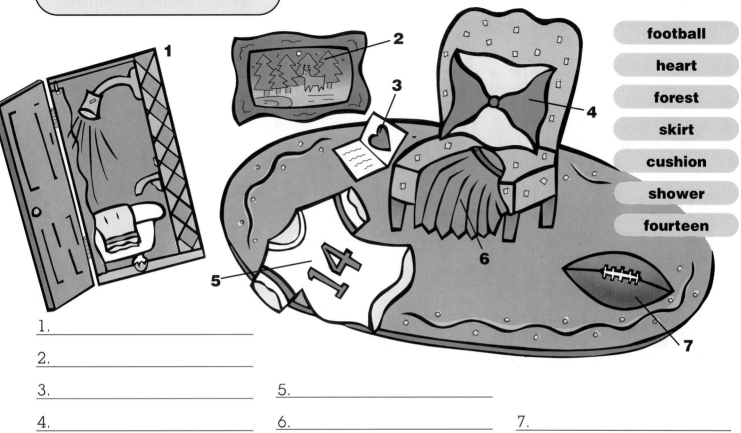

football
heart
forest
skirt
cushion
shower
fourteen

1. _____
2. _____
3. _____   5. _____
4. _____   6. _____   7. _____

Descriptions

Guess what each person is describing below. Write your answers.

cloud
hospital
wood
storm
nephew

It may look fluffy and white, but a (2) is simply water vapor. I predict there will be a major (3) moving in from the east.

There's nothing like the smell of freshly cut pine (4).

She's my dad's sister, and I'm her (1).

I spend long hours operating in the (5).

1. _____
2. _____
3. _____
4. _____
5. _____

113

Wally

– a cartoon by Sam
Help Sam finish his comic strip about a big baby named Wally.

dirty	rattle	shampoo	friend	nerve	huge	toes

1. _____
2. _____
3. _____
4. _____
5. _____
6. _____
7. _____

Wally is bigger than most babies. Actually, he is (1).

He can wiggle his gigantic (2). He makes music by shaking his (3).

Wally loves mud puddles!

I'm all (4)!

But he hates (5)!

You have some (6) messing with my hair!!!

He is a (7) to all animals.

Pen Pals

Read Marissa's card to her pen pal in Moscow, Russia. Supply the missing words.

fourth	school	height	your	too
they're	July	weight	again	

May 2, 1997

Dear Svetlana,

I enjoyed reading _____ letter. Here are some facts about me: My birthday is _____ 22. My _____ is 4 feet 2 inches. My _____ is 62 pounds. I am in the _____ grade. I go to _____ on a bus. I like to wear sweat shirts because _____ so comfortable. Please write once _____. I want to hear more about you _____!

Sincerely,
Marissa

Chicago

114

PETITE POEMS

1. _____
2. _____
3. _____
4. _____
5. _____
6. _____
7. _____
8. _____

Read each short poem below and supply the missing rhyming word.

piece
fuel
neighbor
heard
morning
mountain
there
menu

Here's a handy driving rule:
Don't go on the highway
when you're low on (1).

When you've lost something,
you look everywhere.
The last place you look, it's sure
to be (2).

Did I hear the squawks of the
early bird? For an hour and a half
it was all I (3)!

Do yourself a great big favor.
Get to know your next-door (4).

It's easy to order a fine meal when you,
Take a good look at the restaurant's (5).

If this arguing doesn't cease,
The cake will vanish; no one gets a (6).

The storm came up without a warning,
And rocked the city early one (7).

Here's one thing you can always count on:
A hill is never as large as a (8)!

$hopping List

Denzel left this list for Jacqui. Write the missing items.

few   butcher   fruit   Florida   juice
two   pickle   perfect   pudding

• fresh orange juice from_____

• a large dill_____

• oranges, apples, bananas, and other_____

• one gallon of sweet apple_____—not cider

• six red roses—must be_____!

• one stick of butter and_____loaves of bread

• just a_____sprigs of parsley

• ready-made thick chocolate_____

• Have the_____cut up a three-pound chicken.

MOSCOW

115

Pronouncing for Spelling

DISCOVER THE STRATEGY 1   To avoid making the mistake Josh made in the cartoon below, use this strategy:

1. Pronounce the word carefully and correctly. Listen to the sound of each letter.
2. Pronounce the word again as you write it.

TRY IT OUT   Now practice this strategy yourself.

✝ Pronounce each word in dark type slowly and correctly. Pay special attention to the sounds of the underlined letters. Pronounce each word again as you write it.

1. Say **su<u>r</u>prise** (NOT su-prise) _____

2. Say **pic<u>t</u>ure** (NOT pi-ture) _____

3. Say **stren<u>gth</u>** (NOT strenth) _____

4. Say **diff<u>e</u>rent** (NOT diff-rent) _____

5. Say **chas<u>ing</u>** (NOT chas-in) _____

DISCOVER THE STRATEGY 2 Pronouncing the word correctly won't work for a word like *thumb*. How can you remember to include the silent **b?** Use the "secret pronunciation" strategy below.

1. Pronounce any silent letters to yourself. Don't worry if the word sounds funny. Say the **b** in *thumb* and the **k** in *knit*. Say "thum-**b**" and "**k**-nit."

2. Exaggerate or change a sound in the word. You might pronounce *million* by exaggerating the smaller word *lion* inside it. Say "mil-**li-on**" to yourself.

TRY IT OUT Now practice this strategy.

With a partner, make up secret pronunciations for the words below. Pay special attention to the underlined letters. Write each word correctly. Say its secret pronunciation to yourself.

1. lam<u>b</u>
2. <u>k</u>nit
3. <u>w</u>rist
4. g<u>u</u>ess
5. ever<u>y</u>one
6. tal<u>k</u>
7. on<u>c</u>e
8. <u>h</u>our
9. <u>c</u>lothes
10. movi<u>e</u>

LOOK AHEAD Look ahead at the next five lessons. Write four list words you could use these strategies with. Mark the part of each word that you'll pay special attention to when you pronounce it.

1. _____
2. _____
3. _____
4. _____

1. _____
2. _____
3. _____
4. _____
5. _____
6. _____
7. _____
8. _____
9. _____
10. _____

Including All the Letters

1. _____

2. _____

3. _____

4. _____

5. _____

6. _____

7. _____

8. _____

9. _____

10. _____

11. _____

12. _____

13. _____

14. _____

15. _____

16. _____

17. _____

18. _____

19. _____

20. _____

CHALLENGE!

broccoli
kindergarten
cabinet
serious
temperature

118

■ **FOCUS**   Say each word to yourself. Notice how it looks and sounds, as well as how many letters it has.

camera	took a picture with her **camera**
finally ♻	**finally** heard from my pen pal
really ♻	see things as they **really** are
known	**known** as a fine student
everybody ♻	saw **everybody** at the party
everyone ♻	asked **everyone** their opinion
they ♻	if **they** want to
remember	**remember** an important event
February	a valentine in **February**
December	cold weather in **December**
surprised	**surprised** to see you
might ♻	**might** go to a movie
often	**often** read comic books
island	an **island** in the Pacific Ocean
caught ♻	**caught** the ball
evening	an **evening** of entertainment
swimming ♻	**swimming** in the lake
several	**several** close friends
beginning	**beginning** to learn sign language
interesting	an **interesting** science experiment

■ **DISCOVER**   To spell words on this list, pronounce them correctly or exaggerate the sounds of certain letters. In **often,** you'd exaggerate the **t.** What letter would you exaggerate in **known?**

■ **WRITE**
- four words with one syllable
- five words with two syllables
- eight words with three syllables
- three words with four syllables

PUZZLE IT OUT What do you shoot people with that makes them smile? When you write the list words that match the clues, the answer to this riddle will appear in the box.

1. the twelfth month
2. truly; actually
3. call back to mind
4. early part of night
5. astonished; shocked
6. grabbed; took and held
7. The answer to the riddle is a ____.

1. _ _ _ _ _ _ _ _
2. _ _ _ _ _ _ _
3. _ _ _ _ _ _ _ _
4. _ _ _ _ _
5. _ _ _ _ _ _ _ _
6. _ _ _ _ _ _

SYLLABLE ALERT Write the list word that starts and ends with the same letter and has the same number of syllables as each word below.

8. ballooning
9. keen
10. eventfully
11. tray
12. sweeping

13. exercise
14. inward
15. open
16. moat

7. _____
8. _____
9. _____
10. _____
11. _____
12. _____
13. _____
14. _____
15. _____
16. _____

STRATEGIC SPELLING

Pronouncing for Spelling

We sometimes misspell words because we say them wrong. Write *February, finally, interesting,* and *several.* Now say each word carefully. Be sure to pronounce the underlined syllable.

17. _____
18. _____
19. _____
20. _____

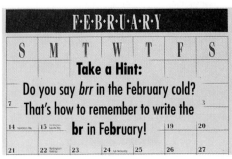

F·E·B·R·U·A·R·Y

S	M	T	W	T	F	S

Take a Hint:
Do you say *brr* in the February cold? That's how to remember to write the **br** in February!

≡	Make a capital.
/	Make a small letter.
∧	Add something.
ℓ	Take out something.
⊙	Add a period.
¶	New paragraph

PROOFREAD A MATH PROBLEM

Ms. Yasutaki's class is keeping a math journal. Read the journal entry below and correct four misspelled words and add the missing quotation marks.

PROOFREADING TIP

A speaker's exact words are called a **quotation.** Quotations begin with a capital letter and have quotation marks at the beginning (") and end (") of the speaker's words.

I multiplied 22 X 15 in 3 seconds! Everyone was suprised by my speed. They asked, How do you do it? I finely told them this secret: "You know 22 X 10 is 220. Half of 220 is 110. So just add them up to get 330.

Math is intresting if you now the shortcuts!

WRITE A MATH PROBLEM

You probably have a math shortcut or interesting problem you'd like to share. Use list words as well as personal words.

Word List

camera	surprised
finally	might
really	often
known	island
everybody	caught
everyone	evening
they	swimming
remember	several
February	beginning
December	interesting

Personal Words

1. _____

2. _____

DICTIONARY: WORDS THAT AREN'T ENTRIES

You won't find **inflected forms,** words like *surprised* and *dirtiest,* as entry words in most dictionaries. If a dictionary included words like these as entries, it would be too large and heavy to use! To find inflected forms, look for the base words. You will find *dirtiest* at the end of *dirty* and *surprised* at the end of *surprise.*

Write the entry word you would look for in order to find the definition of each word below.

1. smuggled _____

2. funnier _____

3. speeches _____

4. largest _____

dirt‧y (dèr′tē), 1 soiled by dirt; not clean: *I got dirty emptying the garbage.* 2 not fair or decent: *Fooling me was a dirty trick. adj.,* **dirt‧i‧er, dirt‧i‧est.**

sur‧prise (sər prīz′) 1 a feeling caused by something that happens suddenly. 2 to cause to feel surprise; astonish: *The news surprised us.* 3 something unexpected: *I have a surprise for you.* 1 *n.,* 2,3 *v.* **sur‧prised, sur‧pris‧ing.**

ENRICHMENT   Pick one.

What Would You Look Under?
Read the sentence below. Look up any words you don't know in the Spelling Dictionary. Write the base word for any word you look up. "Luxuriating in the steaming intensity of the hottest bath water imaginable, I felt blissfully enervated."

The Ending Game
Get together with a group of classmates. Write the following on six separate cards: **s, es, ed, ing, er, est.** On a piece of paper write three nouns, three verbs, and three adjectives. Take turns matching endings to the words and writing the words. To check your spelling, look in a dictionary.

CHALLENGE!
Read the nonsense words below. What do you think is the base word for each? Write that word—the word you would look under if you had a dictionary of nonsense words.
kerfluming   fladitudiness gadifibiest

Compound Words

1. _____

2. _____

3. _____

4. _____

5. _____

6. _____

7. _____

8. _____

9. _____

10. _____

11. _____

12. _____

13. _____

14. _____

15. _____

16. _____

17. _____

18. _____

19. _____

20. _____

CHALLENGE!

courtroom
heartbroken
ourselves
teammate
skateboard

■ **FOCUS** Say each compound word and look at the words that formed it. Then read the meaning phrase.

basketball ♻	a tall **basketball** player
something ♻	have **something** on your mind
sometimes ♻	**sometimes** read action stories
baseball	play **baseball** after school
anyway	did what I shouldn't **anyway**
chalkboard	wrote the answer on the **chalkboard**
earrings	beautiful golden **earrings**
nighttime	raccoons hunting in the **nighttime**
myself ♻	gave **myself** a haircut
motorcycle	rode a red **motorcycle**
upstairs	in an **upstairs** closet
downstairs	went **downstairs** to watch TV
newspaper	read a **newspaper** article
softball	play **softball** all summer
weekend	spent the **weekend** at Grandma's
classroom	a **classroom** full of students
classmate	asked my **classmate** for a pencil
doorbell	rang the **doorbell** twice
driveway	cars pulling into a **driveway**
highway	lots of traffic on the **highway**

■ **DISCOVER** A compound is made of two or more words. Notice that the list words are two-word compounds. Keep all the letters when spelling compounds. If **base** and **ball** make the compound **baseball,** how would you spell a compound word made of **soft** and **ball?**

■ **WRITE** Write the words in alphabetical order.

CLASSIFICATIONS   Add the list words that belong in each group. The words already listed are clues.

Sports	School	Time
football	*homeroom*	*weeknight*
1. _____	4. _____	6. _____
2. _____	5. _____	7. _____
3. _____	*schoolmate*	*sometime*

JOINING WORDS   Find two words in each sentence that can be joined to make a list word. Write the word.

8. Because I was so worried, I was not my old self.
9. Were there any sights along the way?
10. The dog ran to the door when the bell rang.
11. The good news is that I got an A on my paper.
12. Here are some crackers for that thing in the cage.
13. I got up and walked to the stairs near the porch.
14. When the sirens blast, my ear always rings.
15. There are some of us who enjoy good times.
16. The chalk was ordered by a member of the board.
17. He fell and went rolling down the stairs.
18. The washer's motor failed, so the cycle didn't finish.

8. _____
9. _____
10. _____
11. _____
12. _____
13. _____
14. _____
15. _____
16. _____
17. _____
18. _____

STRATEGIC SPELLING

Seeing Meaning Connections

Write the word from the box that answers each question.

Words with *way*
driveway
runway
highway

19. Where does an airplane take off? _____

20. Where do cars go whizzing along? _____

21. Where might a car be parked? _____

Did You Know?
Today basketball players throw a ball through a net to score points. When the game was invented in 1891, they used a real basket. This is how the game got its name.

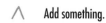

	Make a capital.
/	Make a small letter.
∧	Add something.
℮	Take out something.
⊙	Add a period.
¶	New paragraph

PROOFREAD AN ESSAY Nan wrote this essay about an important event in her life. Correct four misspelled words and one incorrectly used adjective.

PROOFREADING TIP

Nan forgot this rule about using the adjectives more and most: Don't use more or most with words that end in -er or -est.

My Proud Moment

I play basket ball in the Adapted Athletics Program. At first it was hard dribbling from my wheelchair, but I soon got more better at it. Once, I faked out my classmat, Pete. I drove my self around him and swished the ball trough the net. I felt like Supergirl!

WRITE AN ESSAY Write about one of your proud moments. Use your spelling words and a personal word.

Word List

basketball	upstairs
something	downstairs
sometimes	newspaper
baseball	softball
anyway	weekend
chalkboard	classroom
earrings	classmate
nighttime	doorbell
myself	driveway
motorcycle	highway

Personal Words

1. _____

2. _____

MULTICULTURAL CONNECTION: ARTS Throughout history, people have worn jewelry. Read about the hand-crafted jewelry pictured at right. Complete each description below with the name of one of the items pictured.

1. The ancient Egyptians used blue and red gemstones in jewelry such as this beautiful _____

2. The Greeks valued fine metalwork and often used lacelike *filigree*, as seen in this _____

3. Carved jade and metal were popular in China. This white jade _____ is an example.

4. The Inca of South America worked in gold and silver. This _____ shows their craftsmanship.

ENRICHMENT Pick one.

necklace

earring

pendant

brooch

Be a Craftsman
Before beginning work on a piece of jewelry, artisans often draw the design on paper first. Think of a piece of jewelry you would like to make and draw the design.

Write a Description
Without naming it, write a description of one of the jewelry pieces above. Trade descriptions with a friend and identify which piece he or she has written about.

CHALLENGE!
Make a necklace or bracelet using string and materials that can be strung. You might use painted macaroni, shells, or small strips of rolled paper. Use your imagination and work with everyday items.

Suffixes -ful, -ly, -ion

■ **FOCUS** Read the words in each column. Notice what happens to the base word when a suffix is added.

peace + ful =	*peaceful*	
thought + ful =	*thoughtful*	
power + ful =	*powerful*	
cheer + ful =	*cheerful*	
pain + ful =	*painful*	
beauty + ful =	*beautiful*	
safe + ly =	*safely*	
slow + ly =	*slowly*	
week + ly =	*weekly*	
sudden + ly =	*suddenly*	
late + ly =	*lately*	
day + ly =	*daily*	
truthful + ly =	*truthfully*	
careful + ly =	*carefully*	
hopeful + ly =	*hopefully*	
invent + ion =	*invention*	
correct + ion =	*correction*	
act + ion =	*action*	
pollute + ion =	*pollution*	
locate + ion =	*location*	

■ **DISCOVER** When **-ful, -ly,** and **-ion** are added to most base words, the base stays the same: **peaceful, safely, action.** If the base word ends in **y**, the **y** is changed to **i** before adding **-ful** or **-ly: beautiful, daily.** If the base word ends in **e,** the **e** is dropped before adding **-ion: location.**

■ **WRITE** In alphabetical order, write
- nine words with the suffix **-ly**
- six words with the suffix **-ful**
- five words with the suffix **-ion**

1.
2.
3.
4.
5.
6.
7.
8.
9.
10.
11.
12.
13.
14.
15.
16.
17.
18.
19.
20.

CHALLENGE!
grateful
suspenseful
completely
exactly
separation

SUFFIX ADDITION   Write the list word that has each meaning and ending shown below.

1. gladness and joy + ful
2. seven days + ly
3. feeling hope + ly
4. not early + ly
5. quiet and still + ful
6. without warning + ly

7. good looks + ful
8. not fast + ly
9. feeling hurt + ful
10. free from harm + ly
11. strength and might + ful
12. twenty-four hours + ly

WORD FORMS   Add **-ion, -ly,** or **-ful** to the base words below to make list words. Write the list words. Circle the word in which the spelling changed when the suffix was added.

13. act _____

14. thought _____

15. pollute _____

16. invent _____

17. truthful _____

18. careful _____

1. _____
2. _____
3. _____
4. _____
5. _____
6. _____
7. _____
8. _____
9. _____
10. _____
11. _____
12. _____

STRATEGIC SPELLING

Using the Meaning Helper Strategy

Use meaning helpers to help spell hard words. Write the list word that goes with each meaning helper. Mark the letter that matches the underlined sound clue.

19. correct_

20. loca_te

_____   _____

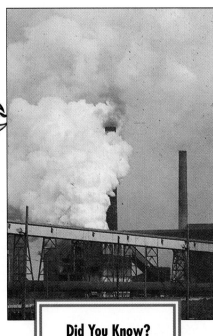

Did You Know?
The word *pollution* comes from a Latin word meaning "soiled," "dirty."

≡	Make a capital.
/	Make a small letter.
∧	Add something.
℮	Take out something.
⊙	Add a period.
⁋	New paragraph

PROOFREAD CAPTIONS Hassan and his friend Bill have written captions for the photos they took on their camping trip. Correct four misspellings and one sentence that contains more than one negative word.

PROOFREADING TIP

No and *not* are **negative words.** Contractions formed with the adverb *not* are also negative words. Use ONLY ONE negative word per sentence.

> *Here we are in beatiful Mesa Verde.*

> *We carfully climb the ladder to the house.*

> *Our campsite is in a peacefull locashun.*

> *This deer didn't have no fear of humans.*

WRITE A CAPTION Think about a photo that shows you and a friend doing something. Draw a picture of it. Then write a caption for the picture. Use a spelling word and a personal word.

Word List

peaceful	lately
thoughtful	daily
powerful	truthfully
cheerful	carefully
painful	hopefully
beautiful	invention
safely	correction
slowly	action
weekly	pollution
suddenly	location

Personal Words

1. _____

2. _____

EXPLORING LANGUAGE: CODES There are many different kinds of codes that can be used to disguise what we write. Can you read the message below?

When you understand how the **tick-tack-toe code** works, the message is easy to read.

A	B	C
D	E	F
G	H	I

J	K	L
M	N	O
P	Q	R

S	T	U
V	W	X
Y	Z	

All the letters of the alphabet are on three tick-tack-toe grids. To spell a word in code, look at where the letter is on the grid, then draw the lines that appear around it. If there are dots, draw those too. So, B = ⊔ M = ⸛ F = ⊏
Now read the words above and write them.

_____   _____   _____

ENRICHMENT Pick one.

Write a Coded Message
Use the tick-tack-toe code to write a message to a friend.

Create a Code
Get together with a classmate and come up with a code of your own. It may be based on letters, symbols, numbers—whatever works. Write to each other using this code.

CHALLENGE!
When do you think it might be important to use a code? Write about it.

Suffixes -less,-ment,-ness

1. _____

2. _____

3. _____

4. _____

5. _____

6. _____

7. _____

8. _____

9. _____

10. _____

11. _____

12. _____

13. _____

14. _____

15. _____

16. _____

17. _____

18. _____

19. _____

20. _____

■ **FOCUS** Read the words in each column. Notice how the word is spelled when a suffix is added.

pave + ment =	*pavement*	
state + ment =	*statement*	
move + ment =	*movement*	
pay + ment =	*payment*	
treat + ment =	*treatment*	
punish + ment =	*punishment*	
great + ness =	*greatness*	
fair + ness =	*fairness*	
good + ness =	*goodness*	
soft + ness =	*softness*	
dark + ness =	*darkness*	
bright + ness =	*brightness*	
busy + ness =	*business*	
breath + less =	*breathless*	
care + less =	*careless*	
spot + less =	*spotless*	
help + less =	*helpless*	
use + less =	*useless*	
hope + less =	*hopeless*	
worth + less =	*worthless*	

■ **DISCOVER** When **-less, -ment,** and **-ness** are added to most base words, the base word stays the same: **spotless, treatment, softness.** If the base ends in a consonant and **y,** the **y** changes to **i** before adding **i: business.**

■ **WRITE** In alphabetical order, write
■ seven words ending in **-ness**
■ six words ending in **-ment**
■ seven words ending in **-less**

CHALLENGE!

assignment
announcement
appointment
homelessness
consciousness

ADDING ENDINGS Complete each sentence by adding **-less**, **-ment**, or **-ness** to the word in parentheses.

1. (busy)   She was out of town on ___.
2. (pay)   He just made his last car ___.
3. (help)   The trapped fox was ___.
4. (use)   This old map is ___.
5. (move)   I watched the dancer's graceful ___.
6. (great)   The child was destined for ___.
7. (state)   The lawyer began her closing ___.
8. (hope)   Our unfortunate situation looked ___.
9. (good)   He helped us out of the ___ of his heart.
10. (worth) Throw away that ___ old inner tube.
11. (breath) I ran so fast I was soon ___.
12. (pave)   We rode our bikes on the concrete ___.
13. (fair)   In all ___, I don't want to take sides.
14. (soft)   The child loved the ___ of the blanket.

MATCH UP Match each word with one of the suffixes below to form a list word. Write each word.

ness	less	ment

15. care   18. spot
16. treat   19. dark
17. bright   20. punish

1. _____
2. _____
3. _____
4. _____
5. _____
6. _____
7. _____
8. _____
9. _____
10. _____
11. _____
12. _____
13. _____
14. _____
15. _____
16. _____
17. _____
18. _____
19. _____
20. _____

STRATEGIC SPELLING

Building New Words

Add the suffix to each base word to make a new word.

Base word	Suffix	New word
21. home	-less	_____
22. enjoy	-ment	_____
23. cold	-ness	_____

Take a Hint
It's easy to leave out the **i** in **business** because you don't say it. Just remember this phrase: Take the **bus in** when you have **busin**ess in town.

131

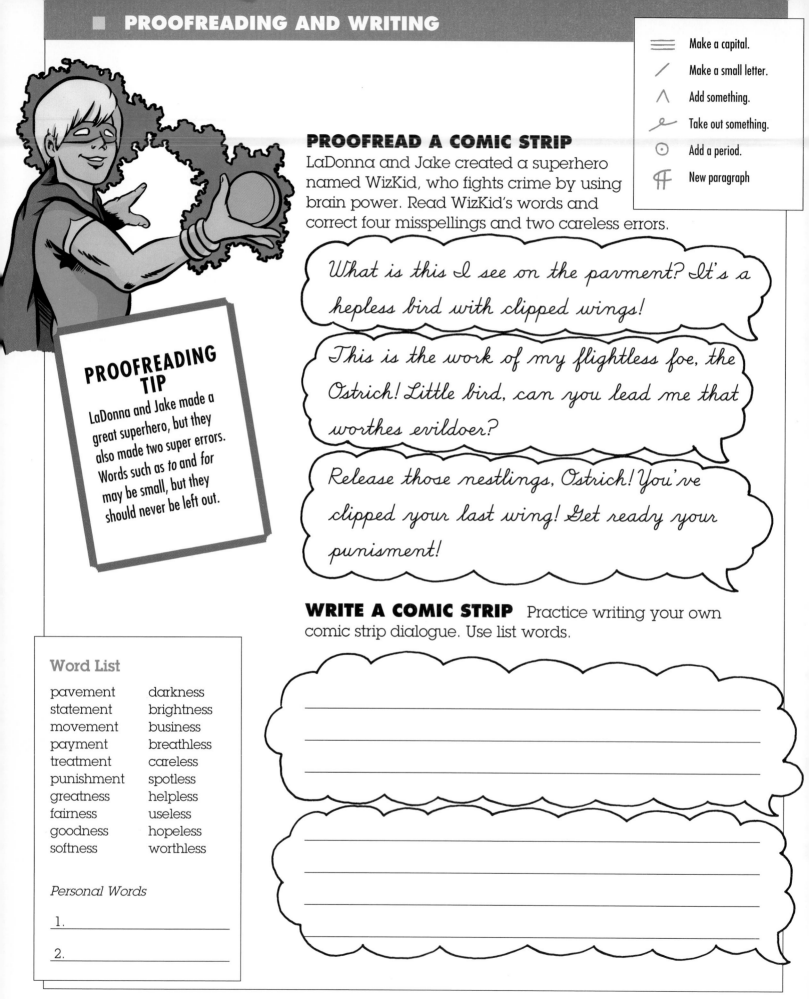

≡	Make a capital.
/	Make a small letter.
∧	Add something.
ℰ	Take out something.
⊙	Add a period.
⨏	New paragraph

PROOFREAD A COMIC STRIP

LaDonna and Jake created a superhero named WizKid, who fights crime by using brain power. Read WizKid's words and correct four misspellings and two careless errors.

> What is this I see on the pavment? It's a hepless bird with clipped wings!

> This is the work of my flightless foe, the Ostrich! Little bird, can you lead me that worthes evildoer?

> Release those nestlings, Ostrich! You've clipped your last wing! Get ready your punisment!

PROOFREADING TIP

LaDonna and Jake made a great superhero, but they also made two super errors. Words such as *to* and *for* may be small, but they should never be left out.

WRITE A COMIC STRIP   Practice writing your own comic strip dialogue. Use list words.

Word List

pavement	darkness
statement	brightness
movement	business
payment	breathless
treatment	careless
punishment	spotless
greatness	helpless
fairness	useless
goodness	hopeless
softness	worthless

Personal Words

1. _____

2. _____

EXPLORING LANGUAGE: HAIKU   Long ago in Japan a contest was held in which competitors added lines to existing poems. Those who created the best lines won. The name **haiku,** pronounced hī′kü, comes from this contest. Read the two haiku below.

The falling flower
I saw drift back to the branch
was a butterfly.

Poor crying cricket,
perhaps your little husband
was caught by our cat.

A haiku is usually three lines long. The first line has five syllables, the second line has seven syllables, and the third line has five syllables. Often, a haiku describes a scene in nature.

Write your own haiku. Start with the line below. Use a dictionary if you need help counting syllables.

Raindrops on a leaf,

_____

_____

ENRICHMENT   Pick one.

Draw a Haiku
Read the two haiku above once again. Draw a picture of one of them.

Haiku Partners
With a classmate, decide on a subject you would describe in a haiku. Write the first line together.

CHALLENGE!
Use the poems above as your models and write a haiku about a force in nature, such as fire or wind.

Prefixes dis-, in-, mis-, re-

1. _____

2. _____

3. _____

4. _____

5. _____

6. _____

7. _____

8. _____

9. _____

10. _____

11. _____

12. _____

13. _____

14. _____

15. _____

16. _____

17. _____

18. _____

19. _____

20. _____

■ **FOCUS** Read the words in each column. Notice the base word does not change when a prefix is added.

dis + appear	=	*disappear*
dis + trust	=	*distrust*
dis + honest	=	*dishonest*
dis + agree	=	*disagree*
dis + like	=	*dislike*
in + visible	=	*invisible*
in + correct	=	*incorrect*
in + complete	=	*incomplete*
in + active	=	*inactive*
in + dependent	=	*independent*
mis + place	=	*misplace*
mis + spell	=	*misspell*
mis + treat	=	*mistreat*
mis + led	=	*misled*
mis + behave	=	*misbehave*
re + act	=	*react*
re + place	=	*replace*
re + call	=	*recall*
re + build	=	*rebuild*
re + use	=	*reuse*

■ **DISCOVER** Prefixes added to base words create new meanings. Don't drop letters when adding prefixes.
- **dis-** means "opposite of"
- **in-** means "not"
- **mis-** means "bad or wrong"
- **re-** means "again"

■ **WRITE**
- five words with **dis-** in alphabetical order
- five words with **re-** in alphabetical order
- five words with **in-** in alphabetical order
- five words with **mis-** in alphabetical order

CHALLENGE!

disobedience
inconvenient
incredible
misfortune
recycling

SUPER ANTONYMS Complete each statement with a list word that means the opposite of the underlined word.

1. Superguy said, "I <u>like</u> good guys, but I ___ criminals."
2. Spygirl stated, "I <u>trust</u> that you won't ___ me."
3. X-ray Man boasted,"What is <u>visible</u> to me is ___ to you."
4. Wiseguy said, "Treat others <u>well</u> and they won't ___ you."
5. Plastic Woman asked, "Do you <u>agree</u> or ___ with me?"
6. Supergirl warned, "The <u>honest</u> are rewarded, but the ___ are never happy."

PREFIX ADDITION Write the list word that has each beginning and meaning indicated below.

7. re + do something
8. dis + come into sight
9. in + without mistakes
10. mis + put down
11. re + put into service
12. in + finished
13. mis + went in front of
14. in + ready to do things
15. re + put down
16. mis + act politely
17. in + needing help
18. re + speak or shout
19. mis + write words
20. re + put pieces together

STRATEGIC SPELLING

Building New Words

Add the prefix **dis-** or **re-** to each word to make a new word. Remember what you learned.

21. able   _____
22. design   _____
23. charge   _____
24. band   _____

Take a Hint
Miss Pell will never misspell the word misspell!

1. _____
2. _____
3. _____
4. _____
5. _____
6. _____
7. _____
8. _____
9. _____
10. _____
11. _____
12. _____
13. _____
14. _____
15. _____
16. _____
17. _____
18. _____
19. _____
20. _____

≡	Make a capital.
/	Make a small letter.
∧	Add something.
℮	Take out something.
⊙	Add a period.
¶	New paragraph

PROOFREAD A LETTER Editors at a textbook publisher received the letter below. Correct four misspellings and four handwriting errors.

PROOFREADING TIP

People appreciate hearing your opinion, but they have to be able to read what you write. Make it easy for them—always cross your t's and loop your l's.

April 8, 1995

Dear Editors,

Your spelling book is fun and some times challenging, but we all have sertain lessons we dislik. We enjoy finding words other writers mispell.

Sincerely,

Lill School Fourth Graders

WRITE A LETTER Let the editors of one of your textbooks know what you think of their product. Use list words.

Word List

disappear	misplace
distrust	misspell
dishonest	mistreat
disagree	misled
dislike	misbehave
invisible	react
incorrect	replace
incomplete	recall
inactive	rebuild
independent	reuse

Personal Words

1. _____

2. _____

EXPLORING LANGUAGE: SYNONYMS Words that have the same meanings are called **synonyms.** The words in dark type in the sentences below are synonyms.

When I rub my powerful ring, my assistant will **disappear.**

When I rub my powerful ring, my assistant will **vanish.**

Write the list word that is a synonym for each underlined word or words below.

1. I'm sorry that the number I gave you was <u>wrong</u>.
2. Doctors often <u>differ</u> about the way to treat patients.
3. You've made a good start, but your work is <u>unfinished</u>.
4. I cannot <u>remember</u> the words to that song.

1. _____
2. _____
3. _____
4. _____

ENRICHMENT Pick one.

Using Synonyms
Use the Spelling Dictionary to find the synonyms for these words: *courageous, gallant, fearless,* and *plucky.* What do they all have in common?

The Synonym Twins
With a classmate, write a play starring the Synonym Twins. Every sentence one twin speaks has a word that the other twin substitutes with a synonym. For example: Twin # 1: This comic book I'm reading is **humorous.** Twin # 2: It's not as **amusing** as watching you read it!

CHALLENGE!

Write a comic strip about an action hero. Pack each scene full of synonyms. Have your classmates list the synonyms they find in your writing.

Review

Look back at the word lists in Lessons 25–29 and think about how you are doing in spelling.

1. The hardest word that I have learned to spell is _____.

2. I learned to spell a hard word by
   ☐ being sure I pronounced the word correctly before writing it.
   ☐ pronouncing silent letters secretly to remember them when writing.
   ☐ thinking of a sound clue from a related word.
   ☐ saying it as I wrote it.

3. I try to use words I am learning to spell
   in my writing.   Yes   No   Sometimes

4. I think spelling words correctly
   in my writing is   Very important   Somewhat important   Unimportant

5. My reasons for the above opinion are _____

_____

_____.

Adopt-a-Pet

These animals are looking for good homes. Read their stories, and supply the words that are missing.

1. _____

2. _____

3. _____

4. _____

5. _____

6. _____

brightness
newspaper
independent
daily
dislike
rebuild

Rico
Rico is a quiet cat. He's a bit of a loner, and very (1). The (2) of his wide, green eyes will delight you. Rico likes kids but would (3) living with another cat.

Mim
When Mim first arrived, she distrusted everyone. Help her (4) her trust by giving her a loving home. Mim must have (5) exercise. She loves to fetch the (6)!

138

Tricks of the Trade

Read the chapter subtitles from the book *Magic to Annoy Those Around You.* Write the words that have been left out.

reuse   downstairs   everybody

invisible   December   caught   disappear

1. _____

2. _____

3. _____

4. _____

5. _____

6. _____

7. _____

1. Writing on your Grandpa's best shirt with ____ ink

2. New ways to ____ old paper towels

3. Ten foolproof ways to grab cookies without getting ____

4. Making your little sister ____ without a trace

5. Throwing your voice all the way ____ when you are upstairs

6. Convincing ____ at home that you're asleep when you're not

7. Creating ____ snowstorms in July with the spurting whipped-cream trick

classmate
powerful
baseball
island
several
camera
swimming

Necessities of Life

Use list words to complete the list below.

I would want these things along if I were stranded on a desert _____:

- my _____ cap—for cool dips in the sea
- my _____ Alex—for good company
- a _____ — to capture the sights

- a _____ to toss around with Alex
- _____ books—about wilderness camping
- a _____ speedboat—for escape— HA HA!

Jack and the Beanstalk and the Three Little Pigs had their sides of the story told, but what do the giant and the wolf have to say? You supply the missing words.

Story Book Secrets

Daily Report ★ ★ ★ ★ ★ ★ ★ **Read all about it!**

Giant Tells All

Bigtown, Austria—The giant of the beanstalk legend has (1) agreed to share his story. He feels that the (2) the press has given him lacks (3). "I strongly (4) with what's been written about me," he said. "Jack stole my (5) harp and golden eggs! He brought disorder to my once quiet, (6) household. He gets to be the hero, and I'm the (7) one! Well, I'm here to defend (8)!"

1. _____
2. _____
3. _____
4. _____
5. _____
6. _____
7. _____
8. _____

From the Trial of B. B. Wolf

Bailiff: Do you swear that the (1) you are about to give is the whole truth, and nothing but the truth?

Wolf: I do.

Bailiff: Be seated.

Defense Lawyer: Tell us, Mr. Wolf, do you (2) the night of August 6?

Wolf: Yes, I think about it (3). It is the night I huffed and puffed and blew. . . .

Defense Lawyer: To be sure, but how were you feeling that particular (4)?

Wolf: I had a terrible cold. My sinuses were blocked and very (5). Whenever I sneezed, a house fell to the (6)!

Defense Lawyer: So it wasn't your intention to destroy the homes of these squealing piglets?

Wolf: Certainly not! I am a peaceful wolf who minds his own business.

1. _____
2. _____
3. _____
4. _____
5. _____
6. _____

The Leszczynsky family is celebrating the birthday of their dog, Spot. Supply the words that are missing from the card they wrote.

1. _____
2. _____
3. _____
4. _____
5. _____

BIRTHDAY GREETINGS

to One Fine Canine

You know (1) said that we were thoughtless,
For naming you Spot, although you are (2)!

Will you be (3) to find steak in your bowl,
And to have us take you for a (4) stroll?

Just (5), dear old Spot,
We all love you quite a lot!

Hugs and kisses,
Your family

Benjamin Banneker— American Genius

By Yael Rubin

Learning about Benjamin Banneker was very (1). He became famous for the (2) of his mathematical abilities.

He was (3) taught to read and write by his grandmother. He was further educated in the (4) of a Quaker school. George Ellicott, who owned a large flour mill (5), also encouraged Benjamin's (6) pursuit of knowledge.

Write the words that are missing from Yael's report on a famous American.

business
carefully
interesting
thoughtful
classroom
greatness

1. _____
2. _____
3. _____
4. _____
5. _____
6. _____

invention   **hopeless**   **suddenly**
incomplete   **something**

7. _____
8. _____
9. _____
10. _____
11. _____

page 2

At the age of 24, Benjamin built a clock that struck the hour. This clock is thought to be the first such (7) made in the United States.

Later, Benjamin was appointed by George Washington to help plan Washington, D.C. The chief architect (8) left the project, so the work was (9). The architect had taken the plans with him, and re-creating them seemed (10). Benjamin came to the rescue, drawing all the plans from memory. The building of the capital city is (11) people can thank Benjamin Banneker for.

141

STRATEGY WORKSHOP

Choosing the Best Strategy

DISCOVER THE STRATEGY You've learned that it is important to use the Steps for Spelling when studying spelling words. Don't forget to also use the strategies you've learned when a spelling word gives you a problem. Read about the strategies in the chart below.

Steps for Spelling Use the step-by-step strategy for studying most spelling words. 1. Look. 2. Spell. 3. Think. 4. Picture. 5. Look. 6. Cover and write.	**Divide and Conquer** Divide long words into shorter pieces. choc/o/late un/known	**Memory Tricks** Link the tricky word with a helper you can spell. <u>You</u> are <u>you</u>ng. <u>qui</u>ck l<u>i</u>qu<u>i</u>d
Problem Parts Identify the problem part and study it extra hard. <u>w</u>rong lau<u>g</u>hed	**Pronouncing for Spelling** Pronounce the word correctly, say a silent letter, or exaggerate a sound. Say "thum**b**." Say "mil-**li-on**."	**Meaning Helpers** Find a related word that gives you a sound clue. ever—ev<u>e</u>ry ac<u>t</u>—ac<u>t</u>ion

TRY IT OUT Now it's time to practice choosing the best strategies. Read the exercises below and on the next page. Write the name of each strategy. Use the chart.

✦ 1. Which tricky strategy helps you remember the two **r**'s in *arrives*?

_____

♦ 2. Which strategy helps you conquer a long word like *caterpillar?*

_____

♦ 3. Which strategy helps you remember to pronounce the **o** in *favorite?*

_____

♦ 4. Name the meaningful strategy that is helpful when trying to remember that *operation* is spelled with a **t.**

_____

♦ 5. Which strategy would you use if a certain part of the word were giving you a spelling problem?

_____

♦♦ Compare your results with others in your class. It's fine to have different choices as long as you can explain them.

♦ **LOOK AHEAD** Look ahead at the next five lessons. Find three words that look hard to spell. Write the word and strategy you would use to help spell each word.

1. _____   _____

2. _____   _____

3. _____   _____

Vowels with No Sound Clues

■ **FOCUS** Say each word. Notice that each underlined vowel has the same sound. Then read each phrase.

an<u>i</u>mals	saw the **animals** in the zoo
buff<u>a</u>lo	**buffalo** roaming the plains
especi<u>a</u>lly	like sports, **especially** soccer
fav<u>o</u>rite	my **favorite** teacher
gi<u>a</u>nt	saw a **giant** panda
Aug<u>u</u>st	go swimming in **August**
supp<u>o</u>se	**suppose** it would be alright
usu<u>a</u>lly	**usually** asleep by now
ir<u>o</u>n	need to **iron** a shirt
Can<u>a</u>da	a vacation in **Canada**
c<u>a</u>noe	**canoe** down a stream
ma<u>ch</u>ine	fix the sewing **machine**
mom<u>e</u>nt	stopped for a **moment**
rel<u>a</u>tives	**relatives** in Bombay
stom<u>a</u>ch	a growling **stomach**
cem<u>e</u>nt	pour **cement** for a sidewalk
yest<u>e</u>rday	finished it **yesterday**
prob<u>a</u>bly	**probably** on her way
s<u>u</u>pport	offer a friend **support**
welc<u>o</u>me	**welcome** visitors

_1. _____

_2. _____

_3. _____

_4. _____

_5. _____

_6. _____

_7. _____

_8. _____

_9. _____

_10. _____

_11. _____

_12. _____

_13. _____

_14. _____

_15. _____

_16. _____

_17. _____

_18. _____

_19. _____

_20. _____

■ **DISCOVER** Sometimes the vowel sounds you hear in a word give you no clue as to its spelling. When that happens, use a strategy. To help spell **stomach,** you might use this memory trick: the **stomach** is an eating **machine.** Can you think of a meaning helper for **especially?**

■ **WRITE** Sort the words by first writing those that you know how to spell. Then write the ones you think are difficult. Tell which strategy you used for hard words.

CHALLENGE!

dictionary
multiplication
salmon
recognize
separate

DRAWING CONCLUSIONS   Write a list word that fits the clues below.

1. A bricklayer uses this material to keep things in place.
2. If you want to paddle down a river, do it in this.
3. These people may be your aunts, uncles, and cousins.
4. When friends come to visit, greet them with a big one.
5. This is what you call the one you like more than others.
6. Use this to straighten out a wrinkled shirt.
7. A fairy tale might include one of these large fellows.
8. This is the month before September.
9. To sew a dress quickly, learn to operate one of these.
10. Sit-ups firm up the muscles in this part of your body.
11. This country is the United States neighbor to the north.

SYNONYMS   Write the list word that means the same as each word below. Use the Spelling Dictionary for help.

12. particularly; chiefly
13. assume; believe
14. help; comfort
15. instant; short time
16. normally; customarily

1. _____
2. _____
3. _____
4. _____
5. _____
6. _____
7. _____
8. _____
9. _____
10. _____
11. _____
12. _____
13. _____
14. _____
15. _____
16. _____

STRATEGIC SPELLING

Choosing the Best Strategy

Write *yesterday, probably, buffalo,* and *animals.* Which strategy could help you spell all four words? Name the strategy and tell why you chose it. Compare choices with a partner. For a list of strategies, see page 142.

17. _____
18. _____
19. _____
20. _____

Name of strategy: _____

Why I chose it: _____

_____

RECYCLED WORDS

To be an e**special**ly good speller include the word *special* inside *especially* whenever you write it.

☰	Make a capital.
/	Make a small letter.
∧	Add something.
ℓ	Take out something.
⊙	Add a period.
¶	New paragraph

PROOFREAD A LETTER Anya wrote this letter home after her first day at camp. Correct five misspelled words, one of which is an incorrectly formed plural.

PROOFREADING TIP

Remember, to make words that end in a consonant and **y** plural, you must change the **y** to **i** and add **-es.**

July 8, 1997

Dear Mom and Aunt Carol,

I arrived yesterdey. Flies are everywhere. My canoe tipped over. The food is relly bad. I supose one day I'll have fond memorys of camp, but so far it's not my favrite place.

Love,

Tenderfoot

Word List

animals	canoe
buffalo	machine
especially	moment
favorite	relatives
giant	stomach
August	cement
suppose	yesterday
usually	probably
iron	support
Canada	welcome

Personal Words

1. _____

2. _____

WRITE A LETTER Pretend you are at camp. Write a letter home telling all about your first day. Use list words.

_____
_____
_____
_____
_____
_____
_____
_____

DICTIONARY: FINDING A WORD WHEN YOU CAN'T SPELL IT

Many sounds in the English language can be spelled lots of different ways. Take the sound /s/, for example. It can be spelled **s**upport, **c**ement, **sc**ent, li**st**en, walt**z,** and about six other ways. So if you wanted to look up *sword* and only knew it began with the sound /s/, what would you do?

You'd check the Spellings of English Sounds chart in your dictionary (and in this book on page 245). It shows you all the ways any given sound in English can be spelled.

Look at each pronunciation below. Write the word you would look under in the dictionary to find its spelling. If you are unsure, check the Spellings of English Sounds chart. Check the Spelling Dictionary for the correct spelling.

1. (hwēt)
2. (brij)
3. fō′tō

ENRICHMENT Pick one.

1. _____
2. _____
3. _____

Spelling the Sounds of English

Look at the pronunciations below. The Spellings of English Sounds chart on page 245 will help you figure out the words they represent. Find the words in the Spelling Dictionary, and use each one in a sentence.

hwėrl   pēt′sə
skwosh   gest

A Sound Idea

Get together with a classmate and write as many words as you can think of that have the sound /sh/. Look up some of the words in a dictionary. Are the words spelled the way you thought they would be? Use the Spellings of English Sounds chart if you need help.

CHALLENGE!

Ask a classmate to read you three of the challenge words from an upcoming lesson. Use the Spellings of English Sounds chart to help you locate the words in a dictionary. Write a brief definition of each word.

Vowels in Final Syllables

■ **FOCUS** Say each word and take special notice of the sound of the last two letters. Then read the meaning phrase.

people	♻	many **people** at the beach
gallon		a **gallon** of milk
color		the **color** green
broken		a **broken** flower pot
October		a cool **October** evening
angle		a right **angle** of 90%
number		wore the **number** ten
barrel		rainwater in a **barrel**
motor		the **motor** in a car
model		a role **model** to a young cousin
sudden		caught in a **sudden** rainstorm
another	♻	**another** day of fun
button		**button** a child's jacket
other		no **other** news
simple		give **simple** directions
doctor		saw the **doctor** for an injury
oven		a roast in the **oven**
title		the **title** of a book
angel		an **angel** with silvery wings
common		a **common** summer vegetable

1. _____
2. _____
3. _____
4. _____
5. _____
6. _____
7. _____
8. _____
9. _____
10. _____
11. _____
12. _____
13. _____
14. _____
15. _____
16. _____
17. _____
18. _____
19. _____
20. _____

■ **DISCOVER** **People** and **model** sound alike at the end but are spelled differently. What do you notice about the last two letters in **doctor** and **number?** What do you notice about the last two letters in **button** and **broken?**

■ **WRITE**
- seven words that end with **or** and **er**
- seven words that end with **el** and **le**
- six words that end with **en** and **on**

Underline the last two letters in each word.

CHALLENGE!

receiver
counselor
citizen
cinnamon
article

CONTEXT CLUES   Write the list word that ends like the underlined word and completes the sentence.

1. An ___ with wings was carved into each door panel.
2. Tex was my ___ when I learned how to yodel.
3. The little squirrel jumped into the wooden ___.
4. To cure a pimple, try this ___ solution.
5. No one ___ than Mother will be waiting.
6. The inventor built a new automobile ___.
7. My cotton shirt is missing a ___.
8. I would not bother to look for ___ pen.
9. Drinking tea with lemon is ___ in many countries.
10. A ___ rainstorm will sadden picnickers.
11. The poor little chicken had a ___ wing.

ABBREVIATIONS   Write the list word that corresponds to each abbreviation below. Use the Spelling Dictionary if you need help.

12. Dr.
13. Oct.
14. gal.
15. no.

CATEGORIZING   Write the list word that names the category to which you would assign each group below.

16. men, women, children
17. turquoise, mauve, orange
18. your highness, her majesty
19. gas, electric

STRATEGIC SPELLING

Seeing Meaning Connections

| rectangle |
| triangle |

20. Write a list word that is related to the words in the box.

Write the words from the box that fit the definitions.

21. a three-sided shape _____

22. a four-sided shape _____

1. _____
2. _____
3. _____
4. _____
5. _____
6. _____
7. _____
8. _____
9. _____
10. _____
11. _____
12. _____
13. _____
14. _____
15. _____
16. _____
17. _____
18. _____
19. _____
20. _____

Did You Know?
The word *angel* comes from a Greek word meaning "messenger."

149

☰	Make a capital.
/	Make a small letter.
∧	Add something.
ℓ	Take out something.
⊙	Add a period.
¶	New paragraph

PROOFREAD A CARD Indira received this card from a friend at school. Correct five misspelled words and two careless errors.

PROOFREADING TIP
You may leave out words when you're writing a card you're in a hurry to mail. Take a minute to proofread. Your reader will thank you.

GET WELL SOON!

I sorry about your brokin leg. Does it hurt? Is your docter nice? All the peopel at shcool miss you a lot. Hurry back. I want sighn your cast.

Michael

WRITE A CARD Pretend you are Indira. Write a response to your friend's card. Use a few list words and some personal words.

Word List

people	sudden
gallon	another
color	button
broken	other
October	simple
angle	doctor
number	oven
barrel	title
motor	angel
model	common

Personal Words

1. _____

2. _____

EXPLORING LANGUAGE: WORD WEBS Suppose
you wanted to write a report about spiders. The first thing
you'd want to do is ask yourself what you've learned about
them. "What do they look like? What do they do? What
makes them special?" Your next step would be to create a
word web like the one below.

eight-legged   small

spider

builds webs   insect

Now suppose you were a spider, spinning a word web
about people. Write the words you would use in your web.

people

ENRICHMENT Pick one.

Webs You Know
Make word webs to show
the meanings of the words
doctor and *motor*. Include
words that tell what they
do, where they are found,
and what makes them
special.

Web Mobile
Work with a partner to
make a word web mobile
for a month of the year.
Write the month on a large
piece of colored paper. Next
write words you associate
with that month on smaller
pieces of paper (use
interesting shapes). Attach
the papers to a coat hanger.

CHALLENGE!
Create a word web about
an interesting place you
have visited or what you
like to do during summer
vacation. Write a story that
uses all the words in
your web.

Capitalization and Abbreviation

1. _____

2. _____

3. _____

4. _____

5. _____

6. _____

7. _____

8. _____

9. _____

10. _____

11. _____

12. _____

13. _____

14. _____

15. _____

16. _____

17. _____

18. _____

19. _____

20. _____

■ **FOCUS** Look at each word. Notice that all of them begin with capital letters and some of them end in a period.

Ms.	Hanukkah
Mr.	Christmas ♻
Mrs.	Kwanzaa
Dr.	Chinese New Year
Ave.	Valentine's Day
Rd.	Memorial Day
Sun.	May
Wed.	June
Feb.	September
Dec.	November

■ **DISCOVER** Look at the words in the list again. Remember that titles, holidays, days and months of the year, and words that are part of an address are always capitalized.

- Some titles are abbreviations that end with a period: **Dr.**
- Nouns in addresses are often abbreviated: **Rd., Ave.**
- Most months can be abbreviated: **Feb., Dec.**
- **May** and **June** are months that should never be abbreviated.
- If a name of a holiday has more than one important word, each word is capitalized: **Chinese New Year.**

■ **WRITE** Sort the words by writing

- six list words that name holidays
- two list words that name days
- six list words that name months
- four list words that name people
- two list words that name types of streets

CHALLENGE!

St. Patrick's Day
Fourth of July
English
Blvd.
etc.

ABBREVIATIONS Write the abbreviation on your spelling list that stands for each word below.

1. doctor
2. avenue
3. December
4. Wednesday
5. February
6. mister
7. Sunday
8. road

IDENTIFICATION Write the list word that matches each clue below.

9. This is the ninth month of the year.
10. On this day we remember those who have died.
11. This is the fifth month of the year.
12. This is the eleventh month of the year.
13. This is a title put in front of a married woman's name.
14. This is the sixth month of the year.
15. On this day we may send a card to a sweetheart.
16. This is a title put in front of a woman's name, married or unmarried.

1. _____
2. _____
3. _____
4. _____
5. _____
6. _____
7. _____
8. _____
9. _____
10. _____
11. _____
12. _____
13. _____
14. _____
15. _____
16. _____

STRATEGIC SPELLING

The Divide and Conquer Strategy

Sometimes its helps to study long words piece by piece. Write *Kwanzaa, Hanukkah, Christmas,* and *Chinese New Year.* Draw lines between the syllables. Then study each word syllable by syllable. Use a dictionary if you need help.

17. _____
18. _____
19. _____
20. _____

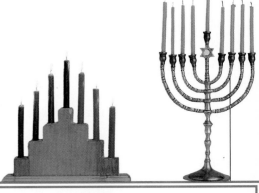

Did You Know?
Both **Hanukkah** and **Kwanzaa** can be spelled in different ways. You may also see **Hanukkah** spelled **Chanukah**. **Kwanzaa** may also be spelled **Kwanza**.

Mark	Meaning
≡	Make a capital.
/	Make a small letter.
∧	Add something.
⸗	Take out something.
⊙	Add a period.
¶	New paragraph

PROOFREAD AN ANNOUNCEMENT

The announcement below was posted on a school bulletin board. Find five misspelled words and four handwriting errors. Write them correctly.

PROOFREADING TIP

Did you stop and try to figure out what an aulhor and an audilorium were? Uncrossed **t**'s can cause confusion. You can catch these errors if you proofread.

Ms Jan Dure to Speak on Novenber 5

Here the aulhor of Hannah's Hannuka, Cal's Cristmas, and Kestra's Kwanzaa speak aboul her wriling.

Time: Wed. 6:00 PM

Place: School Audilorium

WRITE AN ANNOUNCEMENT

Now it's your turn to write an announcement about a visiting author. Use list words and personal words.

____

____

____

____

____

____

____

____

Word List

Ms.	Hanukkah
Mr.	Christmas
Mrs.	Kwanzaa
Dr.	Chinese New Year
Ave.	Valentine's Day
Rd.	Memorial Day
Sun.	May
Wed.	June
Feb.	September
Dec.	November

Personal Words

1. ____________________
2. ____________________

MULTICULTURAL CONNECTION: HOLIDAYS

People everywhere celebrate important occasions. The holidays described below are usually celebrated at the end of the year. Read the descriptions and answer the questions.

Hanukkah celebrates the recapturing of the great temple at Jerusalem over 2,000 years ago. Jewish writings describe how the Jews had barely enough lamp oil for one night in the temple, yet the lamp burned for eight days. Today, the menorah is lit in memory of this. Also called the "Festival of Lights," it is celebrated in November or December.

Christmas celebrates the birth of Jesus, also called Christ. According to the Bible, Jesus was born in a stable and welcomed with gifts from wise men and shepherds. Christians believe Jesus is their savior. Small stable scenes are often seen at Christmas. It comes on December 25.

Kwanzaa is a yearly African American holiday created in 1966. It celebrates black people and their history. There are seven principles of Kwanzaa. The kinara, or candle holder, holds seven candles, one for each principle. Kwanzaa lasts from December 26 through January 1.

1. Which holiday celebrates African traditions?
2. Which holiday celebrates the birth of Jesus?
3. Which holiday is also called the "Festival of Lights"?

ENRICHMENT Pick one.

1. _____
2. _____
3. _____

CHALLENGE!
Read about one of the holidays on your spelling list that you would like to know more about. Take notes and share your findings with the class.

Happy Holidays
What is your favorite holiday? Write a short paragraph about it. Tell when it occurs, how it is celebrated, and why people celebrate it.

Holidays Are for Sharing
Discuss with your classmates the kinds of holidays you share with family and friends. Plan a celebration that incorporates the traditions, meals, songs, and games of these various holidays.

155

Possessives

■ **FOCUS** Look at each possessive and read the phrase. Notice whether the apostrophe comes before or after the **s.**

brother's	my younger **brother's** jacket
brothers'	my two older **brothers'** rock band
boy's	found the **boy's** bicycle
boys'	members of the **boys'** soccer team
girl's	admired the **girl's** self-portrait
girls'	joined the **girls'** basketball league
aunt's	my **aunt's** neighbor
aunts'	our **aunts'** husbands
teacher's	met his **teacher's** mother
teachers'	visited the **teachers'** lounge
lady's	shook the **lady's** hand
ladies'	heard the **ladies'** voices
family's	read my **family's** history
families'	talked about our **families'** holidays
baby's	got the **baby's** bottle
babies'	talked to the **babies'** fathers
grandma's	enjoyed her **grandma's** story
grandpa's	ate his **grandpa's** scrambled eggs
Dad's	took a ride on **Dad's** bicycle
friend's ♻	listened to a **friend's** troubles

1. _____
2. _____
3. _____
4. _____
5. _____
6. _____
7. _____
8. _____
9. _____
10. _____
11. _____
12. _____
13. _____
14. _____
15. _____
16. _____
17. _____
18. _____
19. _____
20. _____

■ **DISCOVER** **Possessives** show who or what has or owns something. To form possessives of
- singular nouns, add an apostrophe and **s: boy's, baby's**
- plural nouns that end in **s,** add only an apostrophe: **boys', babies'**

■ **WRITE** Sort the list words by writing
- twelve singular possessive nouns
- eight plural possessive nouns

CHALLENGE!

someone's
grandparent's
grandparents'
boss's
James's

SINGULAR POSSESSIVES   Complete each sentence by writing the singular possessive of the underlined word.

1. We found the boy cap under the chair.
2. I enjoyed the girl piano playing very much.
3. I visited my aunt office last Tuesday.
4. I accidentally scratched my brother car.
5. I listened to Dad advice.
6. The children loved their grandma lullabies.
7. She always followed her grandpa directions.
8. I stayed the night at my best friend house.

USING CONTEXT CLUES   Write the list word that is a form of the word in parentheses to complete each sentence.

9. I found a (lady) ring at the bottom of the pool.
10. That makes five (lady) rings I've found this week!
11. My (family) way of spending free time is to go hiking.
12. Other (family) free time activities may differ from ours.
13. My math (teacher) classroom is full of large posters.
14. The other (teacher) classrooms have smaller posters.
15. I put the (baby) little jacket on a hook in the closet.

1. _____
2. _____
3. _____
4. _____
5. _____
6. _____
7. _____
8. _____
9. _____
10. _____
11. _____
12. _____
13. _____
14. _____
15. _____

PLURAL POSSESSIVES   Write the possessive of each word.

16. brothers _____   19. babies _____

17. boys _____   20. girls _____

18. aunts _____

Take a Hint
Dad's is capitalized only when it is used as a name. *You read Dad's letter, but you borrow your dad's pen.*

STRATEGIC SPELLING
Building New Words

Write the words that complete the chart.

Singular	Singular Possessive	Plural Possessive
21. father	_____	_____
22. monkey	_____	_____

☰	Make a capital.
/	Make a small letter.
∧	Add something.
✐	Take out something.
⊙	Add a period.
⁋	New paragraph

PROOFREADING TIP

I take, you take, but it takes. Be sure your subject (It) always agrees with your verb (takes).

PROOFREAD AN OPINION Find four misspelled words in this opinion. Write them correctly. Fix two places where the subject and verb don't agree.

Opinion Poll: Should Your TV Watching Be Restricted?

☑ Yes   ☐ No

Comments:

Watching to much TV is bad for you. It take away from the time you'd be doing important stuff. At my frends house, his family watch TV all day! I read, play basball, and help build my grandpas boat instead.

Word List

brother's	lady's
brothers'	ladies'
boy's	family's
boys'	families'
girl's	baby's
girls'	babies'
aunt's	grandma's
aunts'	grandpa's
teacher's	Dad's
teachers'	friend's

Personal Words

1. _____

2. _____

WRITE AN OPINION Do you think that you should restrict the amount of TV you watch? Write the reasons for your opinion. Use list words and personal words.

_____
_____
_____
_____
_____
_____
_____
_____
_____

EXPLORING LANGUAGE: PALINDROMES

Anna, Otto, and Ada have something in common. Their first names are **palindromes.** A palindrome is a word that reads the same backward or forward. To complete the puzzle below, you must write palindromes. You'll find the names of the Palindrome Kids hiding in the puzzle.

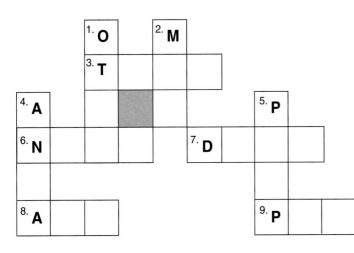

DOWN

1. a boy's name
2. a short word for *mother*
4. a girl's name
5. the sound made by a young bird

ACROSS

3. the sound made by a horn or whistle
6. 12 o'clock in the daytime
7. something done; a good —— should be rewarded
8. a girl's name
9. a young dog

ENRICHMENT   Pick one.

Palindrome Pals

Think of other names that are palindromes. Start with the letter **A** and go right on through to **Z.**

Crossword Palindrome

Work with a partner to make a crossword puzzle of palindromes like the one above. Here are a few words you might want to use: *bib, dad, dud, eve, eye, gag, level, pop, redder, sis, sees, tot, wow.* Write clues for your puzzle and let others try it out.

CHALLENGE!

Try to write a short sentence that is a palindrome. Here is a famous example: Madam, I'm Adam.

Easily Confused Words

■ **FOCUS** Notice how the words are grouped. Pronounce each word carefully. Read the phrases.

were ♲	if I **were** you
we're ♲	told them **we're** not interested
where ♲	don't know **where** it is
quiet	**quiet** in the library
quite	not **quite** three years old
quit	**quit** a job she hated
off ♲	turned **off** the radio
of	a friend **of** mine
our ♲	lost **our** dog
are ♲	**are** going to the museum
then ♲	turned, **then** walked away
than	bigger **than** my sister
lose	didn't want to **lose** the game
loose	shoelaces were coming **loose**
set	began to **set** the table
sit	tried to **sit** on the jagged rocks
when ♲	**when** Grandpa was a child
win	didn't **win** the race
whose	wondered **whose** bicycle it was
who's	asked **who's** going to the game

■ **DISCOVER** Some words are easily confused because they have similar pronunciations or spellings. Studying each word and learning its meaning will help you remember how to spell it.

■ **WRITE** Sort the words by first writing the groups of words that are confusing for you. Then write the rest of the words.

1. _____
2. _____
3. _____
4. _____
5. _____
6. _____
7. _____
8. _____
9. _____
10. _____
11. _____
12. _____
13. _____
14. _____
15. _____
16. _____
17. _____
18. _____
19. _____
20. _____

CHALLENGE!

recent
resent
pedal
petal
diary

160

ANTONYMS   Write the list word that means the opposite of the underlined word to complete each phrase.

1. not <u>tight</u>, but ____
2. not <u>noisy</u>, but ____
3. not <u>on</u>, but ____
4. not <u>begin</u>, but ____
5. not <u>stand</u>, but ____
6. not <u>find</u>, but ___

CONTEXT SENTENCES   Write the list word that completes each sentence.

7. Yes, ___ all going camping tomorrow.
8. I'm not sure just ___ we will return.
9. No, I haven't ___ finished packing.
10. I can't remember ___ the camp is located.
11. No, I don't know ___ tent we'll use.
12. No, I'm not sure ___ going to drive.
13. Yes, ___ trip should be full of surprises.

ALPHA PUZZLES   Decide what letter of the alphabet comes between each pair of letters below. Write the letters to make a list word.

14. **n p** + **e g** =
15. **z b** + **q s** + **d f** =
16. **v x** + **d f** + **q s** + **d f** =
17. **s u** + **g i** + **d f** + **m o** =

1. _____
2. _____
3. _____
4. _____
5. _____
6. _____
7. _____
8. _____
9. _____
10. _____
11. _____
12. _____
13. _____
14. _____
15. _____
16. _____
17. _____

Choosing the Best Strategy

Write *set, win,* and *than.* Name one strategy that would help you spell all three words. Discuss your choice with a partner. For a list of strategies, see page 142.

18. _____

19. _____   Name of Strategy:

20. _____   _____

RECYCLED WORDS

Having trouble with **where** and **were?** Just remember, **where** rhymes with **there** and **we** is part of **were.**

≡	Make a capital.
/	Make a small letter.
∧	Add something.
ℯ	Take out something.
⊙	Add a period.
¶	New paragraph

PROOFREAD A SIGN The sign in the photograph below contains a misspelled word. Can you find it? Write the word correctly.

PROOFREADING TIP

Be sure that words you've written with apostrophes really should have them. Read the words without the apostrophe—who's as who is, for example—to see if it's needed.

CREATE A SIGN Do you have a favorite snack you'd like to tell everyone about? Draw a picture and use a word or two from the word list. Be sure to proofread your writing.

Word List

were	then
we're	than
where	lose
quiet	loose
quite	set
quit	sit
off	when
of	win
our	whose
are	who's

Personal Words

1. _____

2. _____

EXPLORING LANGUAGE: USING EXACT WORDS

Win is a perfectly good word to use when describing a victory. But think how boring sportscasts would be if the scores from baseball games were read using only *win* or *lose*.

> Cozy's Cafe had a 10-9 win against Dee's Diner.

> Harold's Hardware lost 3-5 to Main St. Lumber.

When sportscasters use words that are more exact and descriptive, we get a better (and more interesting) picture.

> Cozy's Cafe slapped Dee's Diner with a 10-9 check that was the upset of the season.

> Main St. Lumber hammered away at Harold's Hardware to gain a 5-3 victory.

Use your own words to complete the sportscast below.

1. The Hawks' superior pitching _____ the

   Pigeons in the first five innings.

2. The Pigeon's _____, but couldn't get a hit.

3. The Pigeons were _____ by the Hawks 6-0.

ENRICHMENT   Pick one.

Be Exact
The sentences below use words that aren't as exact as they should be. Think of better words to replace them. Rewrite the sentences.
Nell petted the cute kitten.
I showed my friend my stuff.
D'Juan looked strange.

Word Trade
Write sentences about something you saw today, something you heard today, and something you felt today. Trade papers with a friend. Suggest ways to one another in which your words could be more exact.

CHALLENGE!

Write a paragraph describing a character in a favorite book or the plot of a favorite movie. Go back over your writing to improve your descriptions.

Review

Look back at the word lists in Lessons 31–35 and think about how you are doing in spelling.

1. The most unusual word that I have learned to spell is _____.

2. I learned to spell a hard word by
   ☐ first deciding which strategy would be most helpful, and then using it.
   ☐ underlining the part of the word that is a problem for me and studying it.
   ☐ picturing the word in my mind to help remember it.

3. When I encounter a hard spelling word I try to apply
   one of the strategies I have learned.   Yes   No   Sometimes

4. I try to use words I am learning to spell in
   my writing.   Yes   No   Sometimes

5. This is what I learned about spelling recently that

   I didn't know before: _____
   _____
   _____

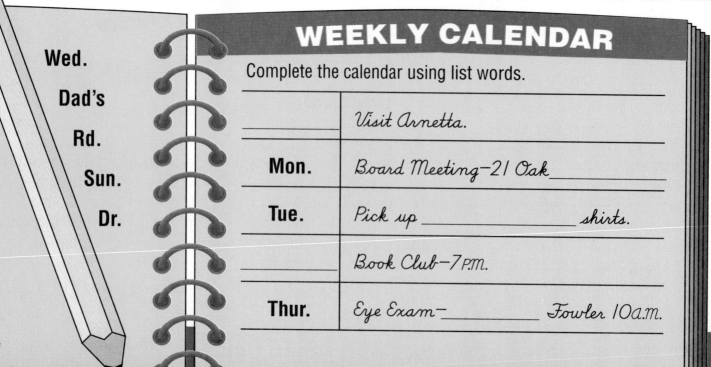

Wed.
Dad's
Rd.
Sun.
Dr.

WEEKLY CALENDAR

Complete the calendar using list words.

_____	*Visit Arnetta.*
Mon.	*Board Meeting—21 Oak_____*
Tue.	*Pick up _____ shirts.*
_____	*Book Club—7 P.M.*
Thur.	*Eye Exam—_____ Fowler 10 a.m.*

Offbeat Greetings

These days, greeting cards say more than just "Happy Birthday" and "Get Well." Supply the missing words in each card below.

Word bank: baby's August probably iron Ave. yesterday loose of

Congratulations!
It's your (1) first tooth! Let's hope it stays in there and doesn't get (2)!

HAPPY BIRTHDAY
(in advance)
I know it's July and you were born in (3), but I like to keep ahead (4) things!

Welcome to the Neighborhood!
You have (5) heard the rumors about Maple (6). Well, most of them are true!

DEAR FRIEND,
I'm sorry I didn't call you (7). I had to (8) my best shirt and that takes time. Maybe tomorrow... after I wash my hair.

1. _____
2. _____
3. _____
4. _____
5. _____
6. _____
7. _____
8. _____

BEING CATERED TO

Jake and Clare make healthy desserts for people giving parties. Supply the list words missing from their advertising brochure.

- Ja'Clare offers your (1) the healthiest and tastiest dessert it's ever had.
- Our treats come direct from our (2) to you!
- Choose from tarts, pies, custards, mousses, and any (3) of your (4) cakes.
- We work seven days a week and (5) always available for consultations.
- You'll find that (6) desserts are (7) the thing for parties, (8) the masterpiece we call Strawberry Rapture.

Word bank: favorite number we're especially stomach oven our quite

1. _____
2. _____
3. _____
4. _____
5. _____
6. _____
7. _____
8. _____

Happy Holidays

Complete the holiday memories using list words.

Hanukkah	Chinese New Year	Valentine's Day
angel	relatives	moment
	giant	

1. What I love best about Christmas is putting the _____ on the tree.

2. I love the glow of the candles in the menorah on _____.

3. My favorite memory of Kwanzaa is seeing all my friends and _____.

4. Memorial Day is a time I like to take a _____ to remember those who have died.

5. I enjoy welcoming in the new year with fireworks and a dragon parade

    during _____.

6. We always buy a _____ pumpkin to carve at Halloween. It's great!

7. I like getting those fancy, heart-shaped greetings on _____.

Canada	button
boys'	animals
machine	model
set	

Moving Out

The Russos are packed and ready to move, but they need help labeling all their belongings. Use each list word once.

Grandma's (1) collection

Mom's five-speed rowing (2)

Leonardo's (3) airplane kits

Dion's miniature tea (4)

(5) skates sizes 5 and 6

Jenelle's stuffed (6)

Angela's map of (7)

1. _____
2. _____
3. _____
4. _____
5. _____
6. _____
7. _____

Where the Buffalo Roam

Read the information below and supply the missing list words.

lose	**buffalo**	**are**	**than**
quit	**were**	**common**	

The American bison, also called the (1), once roamed over most of North America. In the 1700s there (2) thirty to sixty million buffalo in North America. A single herd might be twenty miles wide and more (3) fifty miles long. By the 1800s the slaughter of buffalo by the thousands was a (4) occurrence. It looked as though we might (5) the buffalo forever. By 1900 there were only 20 wild bison left in the United States. Laws were passed to ensure that people would (6) hunting them, and there (7) now parks and preserves that protect the buffalo.

1. _____
2. _____
3. _____
4. _____
5. _____
6. _____
7. _____

Election Time

Lynn Page is running for student council treasurer. Help her finish her campaign slogans.

1. _____
2. _____
3. _____
4. _____
5. _____
6. _____
7. _____
8. _____

If YOU vote for Lynn we're all sure to (1)! Lend your (2) to one who understands money.

Attention: all (3) of voting age. When you vote in (4) be sure it's for (5) Page.

No more (6) promises!! You are all (7) to join LYNN to discuss the issues.

It's time for (8) point of view! Turn to Page!

people
Ms.
support
win
welcome
November
broken
another

Cross-Curricular Lessons

location
latitude
parallels
equator
degrees
hemispheres
longitude
meridians
prime meridian
coordinates

_____

_____

Global Grid

Can you find Ecuador on a map? What about Egypt or Finland? Understanding the words in the list can help you find places in the world. Add your own words to the list. Use your Spelling Dictionary if you need help.

■ GETTING AT MEANING

Locating Places   Look at globes A and B on the next page. Use them to help you complete the sentences.

1. _____

2. _____

3. _____

4. _____

5. _____

6. _____

7. _____

8. _____

9. _____

10. _____

hemispheres   latitude   equator   parallels

Globe
A

The imaginary east-west lines on a map or globe are used to show <u>(1)</u>. They are called <u>(2)</u>. The <u>(3)</u> is at 0° latitude. It divides the Earth into two halves, or <u>(4)</u>—the Northern and Southern Hemispheres.

**degrees   longitude   meridians   location
prime meridian   coordinates**

Globe
B

The imaginary north-south lines that go from pole to pole on a map or globe are used to show <u>(5)</u>. They are called <u>(6)</u>. The <u>(7)</u> is at 0° longitude. It divides the Earth into the Western and Eastern Hemispheres. Both latitude and longitude are measured in <u>(8)</u>. On a globe showing both parallels and meridians, the intersecting lines 20°S, 20°E that go through Africa are called <u>(9)</u>. You can find any <u>(10)</u> on a map or globe when you know its coordinates.

A Parallels
Lines of Latitude

B Meridians
Lines of Longitude

■ SPELL WELL

Double Letters Sometimes double letters can cause spelling problems. Write the words in the list that have double letters. Underline the double letters.

11. _____

12. _____

13. _____

Did You Know?
Suppose you wanted to circle the Earth at the equator. You would have to travel about 24,902 miles to complete your trip.

oak
dune
evergreens
cactus
needleleaf
moisture
forest
broadleaf
desert
sagebrush

_____

_____

Deserts and Forests

What makes a desert? What makes a forest? How are the two alike or different? Use the pictures below to find out. Add your own words to the list. Use the Spelling Dictionary.

■ GETTING AT MEANING

Using Picture Clues   Look at all of the illustrations. Use words from the list to complete each caption.

1. _____

2. _____

3. _____

4. _____

5. _____

| cactus | desert | sagebrush | dune | moisture |

One-seventh of all the Earth's land is dry, sandy <u>(1)</u>. The United States has deserts in the Southwest. Strong, dry winds can blow sand into a mounded <u>(2)</u>.

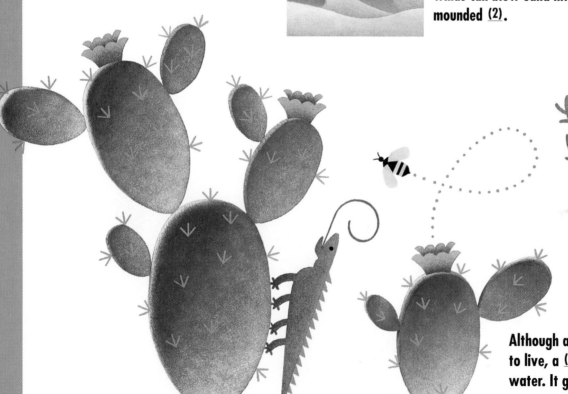

The dry, bushy <u>(3)</u> is found on western plains.

Although all living things require <u>(4)</u> to live, a <u>(5)</u> doesn't need much water. It grows in hot, dry regions.

| evergreens | needleleaf | oak | forest | broadleaf |

6. _____

7. _____

8. _____

9. _____

10. _____

A **(6)** is more than just trees. It includes shrubs, mosses, and flowers. The largest ones in the United States are in the North and East.

Trees with broad, flat leaves are called **(7)** trees. Their leaves change color and fall off. The **(8)** is this kind of tree.

Trees with leaves like thin, sharp needles are called **(9)** trees. These trees are also called **(10)** because they stay green all year.

■ SPELL WELL

Divide and Conquer   Study long words piece by piece. Draw a line between the two base words in each compound below. Write each word.

11. needleleaf _____

12. evergreens _____

CREATE A DIORAMA
Make a three-dimensional desert or forest. First, research your chosen area. What kinds of plants and animals are found there? Next, get a shoe box and pictures, sand, clay, branches, and so on. Create the environment inside the box. Label your diorama.

The Great Lakes

The Great Lakes and the St. Lawrence Seaway are North America's major water highways. Read the list below to learn about them. Add your own words and sentences.

Lake Huron	**Lake Huron** borders Michigan and Canada.
Lake Ontario	**Lake Ontario** borders New York and Canada.
Lake Michigan	**Lake Michigan** borders Wisconsin, Illinois, Indiana, and Michigan.
Lake Erie	**Lake Erie** borders Michigan, Ohio, New York, Pennsylvania, and Canada.
Lake Superior	**Lake Superior** borders Michigan, Wisconsin, Minnesota, and Canada.
St. Lawrence Seaway	**The St. Lawrence Seaway** is a waterway that connects the Great Lakes and the Atlantic Ocean.
Atlantic Ocean	**The Atlantic Ocean** is east of North and South America and west of Europe and Africa.
waterway	A **waterway** is a channel through which boats can navigate.
canal	An artificial waterway for navigation is a **canal.**
lock	An enclosed section of a canal in which the level of water can be changed is called a **lock**.

_____   _____

_____   _____

■ GETTING AT MEANING

Using Written Clues   Complete each sentence using either **lock, canal,** or **waterway.**

1. The St. Lawrence Seaway is a major _____.

2. The ship at right is sailing through a _____.

3. The ship at left enters a _____ and the gates are then closed.

Labeling a Map Label the Great Lakes, the St. Lawrence Seaway, and the Atlantic Ocean using the map below.

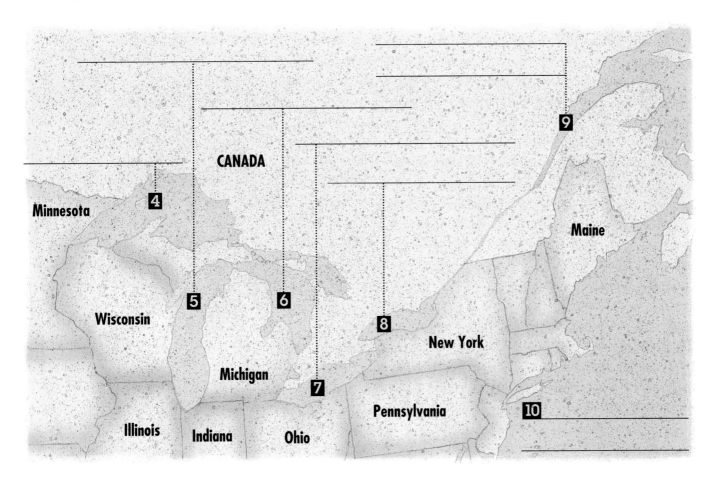

■ SPELL WELL

Divide and Conquer Study the name of each lake syllable by syllable. Then write the names.

11. Lake Su • per • i • or _____

12. Lake On • tar • i • o _____

Lōōk into This

List the names of streams, rivers, lakes, and other bodies of water that influence your environment. Are they natural or made by people? Where do they begin and end? Present your findings in the form of a chart, map, or diagram.

Did You Know?

The first letters of the names of the Great Lakes spell a word that means "places where we live." What is that word? (Once you figure it out, you can use it to help you remember the names of all the Great Lakes!)

Using Natural Resources

Our natural resources are very important to our way of living. Read the sentences below to find out why. Add your own related words and phrases to the list.

energy	We use natural resources to create **energy** to do work.
electricity	**Electricity** is energy that powers lights and machines.
hydroelectric	**Hydroelectric** plants use water power to make electricity.
fuels	**Fuels** are resources that are burned to create energy or heat.
oil	**Oil** is our main fuel for running kinds of transportation.
gasoline	By cleaning and breaking down oil, we get **gasoline.**
natural gas	Another fuel, **natural gas,** is used for heating and cooking.
coal	We burn **coal** to create heat.
steel	**Steel** is a product of iron ore and carbon that is formed into sheets, beams, and other shapes.
products	Steel and gasoline are **products** that are made from natural resources.

_____   _____

_____   _____

■ GETTING AT MEANING

1. _____

2. _____

3. _____

4. _____

5. _____

Using Context Clues   Use the clues in the sentences above to help you choose the right list word for each blank below.

1. In manufacturing and industry, natural resources are made into finished ___.
2. Melting down the natural resource of iron ore and mixing it with carbon produces ___.
3. Factories may burn coal, oil, or other ___ to produce energy.
4. Burning coal turns water into steam that generates electrical ___.
5. The Earth's mineral fuels, including coal, oil, and ___, may be used up in the next few centuries.

Using Visual Clues   Write the list word that best corresponds to each picture below.

6. _____

7. _____

8. _____

9. _____

10. _____

■ SPELL WELL

Seeing Meaning Connections   The word *electric* is related to two list words. Finish each sentence by writing the correct list word.

12. Without _____ I couldn't

watch TV.

13. Hoover Dam is a _____

dam.

DID YOU KNOW?

People in the U.S. use five times more energy per person than any other people in the world.

Constitution
republic
democratic
participate
leaders
elected
represent
local
state
federal

_____

_____

Our Government

What's so special about the United States' government? Plenty! The words in the list will help you find this out. Add more government words to the list. Then do the exercises.

■ GETTING AT MEANING

Context Clues   Use the list words to complete what the people below are saying.

democratic   participate   represent   elected
leaders   republic

1. _____

2. _____

3. _____

4. _____

5. _____

6. _____

America's highest **(1)** are the President and Vice-President.

Government officials are **(2)** by citizens when they vote.

All citizens should take part in, or **(3)** in, elections.

Because the people run our government, we're a **(4)** country.

We also elect senators and representatives to **(5)** us in Congress.

We pledge allegiance to the flag and to the **(6)** for which it stands.

178

State the Facts
Use the list words to answer the questions.

state federal local constitution

7
What written plan gives Americans their power?

8
Do governors and lieutenant governors work on the state or local level?

9
Do the President and Vice-President work on the federal, state, or local level?

10
Do mayors and city council members work on the federal, state, or local level?

7. _____

8. _____

9. _____

10. _____

■ SPELL WELL

Divide and Conquer Some long words are easier to study if you sound them out in syllables. Study each word below, saying it syllable by syllable. Then write the words.

11. Con • sti • tu • tion _____

12. par • tic • i • pate _____

CLASSMATE CONSTITUTION

What kind of government would work best in your classroom? Work in small groups to author a "Classroom Constitution" that establishes the kind of government you want. Think about the number of leaders, their powers, limitations, and responsibilities, as well as the role of the rights and responsibilities of classroom citizens. Use the Constitution of the United States as your guide.

Did You Know?

The Constitution of the United States is one of the oldest written constitutions. Many other countries have patterned their constitutions after it.

pueblo
adobe
corn
ceremony
pottery
Navajo
hogans
silver
weaving
reservation

_____

_____

Southwest American Indians

Many Southwest American Indians keep the traditions their ancestors kept hundreds of years ago. The list words reflect their past as well as their present life. Add your own words. Use the Spelling Dictionary as you do the exercises.

■ GETTING AT MEANING

Using Picture Clues Look at the illustrations. Complete the sentences using words from the list.

1. _____

2. _____

3. _____

4. _____

5. _____

adobe   ceremony   pottery   pueblo   reservation

These American Indians of New Mexico and Arizona get their name from the apartmentlike villages in which they live. Each village is called a (1). The pueblos are made of stone or sun-dried (2) bricks. In one religious (3), the Pueblo pray for harmony and order in the universe. The Pueblo make beautiful clay (4), which they sell to tourists who visit the (5).

silver   hogans   weaving   Navajo   corn

The (6) are also American Indians of the Southwest. Many of them are farmers, growing (7) and raising sheep. Others are gifted at (8) wool into beautiful blankets, while others are engineers, teachers, and technicians. The Navajo are also famous for the artistic turquoise and (9) jewelry they make. A single ring can cost over $20,000. Many Navajo live in (10), shelters made of log frames covered with earth.

■ SPELL WELL

Seeing Meaning Connections   Write the list word that completes each sentence. The underlined word is a clue.

11. That beautiful clay <u>pot</u> is just one of a large (11) collection.
12. A parcel of land <u>reserved</u> exclusively for American Indians is a (12).

Design Your Own Pottery
Each Pueblo village creates pottery using its own special design. Draw a pot and decorate it with your own one-of-a-kind design.

Inuit
seal
whale
walrus
polar bear
caribou
blubber
fur
tundra
kayak

_____

_____

Arctic Life

The Arctic is quite a place! How do people and animals live and travel there? The list words will help you answer these questions. Add your own Arctic words to the list.

■ GETTING AT MEANING

Using Photographs   Use list words to complete the caption for each photograph.

blubber   **Inuit**   **kayak**   **polar bear**   **whale**

Many of the people who live in the Arctic, such as the (1), zip around in snappy little snowmobiles!

1. _____

2. _____

3. _____

4. _____

5. _____

When the ice melts, an easy way to get around is to paddle a (2), a special boat.

The huge, snow-colored (3) looks at us as if to say, "Isn't the Arctic wonderful?"

This leaping (4) has a thick layer of fat called (5) that keeps it warm in cold water.

fur   tundra   walrus   caribou   seal

6. _____
7. _____
8. _____
9. _____
10. _____

The (6) has two huge teeth called tusks.

A sleek (7) tends to its pup.

The reindeer feeding on the grass is also called a (9)!

This girl will stay warm in a hood trimmed in animal (8).

The caribou stands on the treeless plain, called (10).

■ SPELL WELL

Rhyming Helpers   The rhyming helpers *meal* and *Mary Lou* can help you spell two list words. Write the list word that rhymes with each rhyming helper.

11. The polar bear
    Sniffs the air,
    Hoping for a meal.
    While diving for a codfish,

    It sees a lively _____.

12. "What are you doing,
    Mary Lou?"
    "Reading a book

    About _____."

TRY IT OUT

The Inuit are famous for their sculptures. They use soapstone, whalebone, and other material to carve animals or scenes from their environment. Try it yourself. Use clay or a bar of soap to carve something you see each day.

strengths
appreciate
weaknesses
decision
disagree
tears
result
psychologist
special
appearance

_____

_____

Know Yourself

You are one-of-a-kind. The list words celebrate that. Add your own words to the list. Use the Spelling Dictionary for help.

■ GETTING AT MEANING

Talking About You The friends in the comic strip are eager to share their wisdom with you, but the cartoonist left out words. Use the list words to complete their sentences.

1. _____   3. _____

2. _____   4. _____

strengths   appreciate   special   appearance   tears

The Walkie Talkies

You know, nobody else is quite like you. You are unique. You are (1).

That's right! For instance, your (2)-- what you look like. Your looks are yours alone.

Right! And what about your (3)? What do you do really well? What do people like about you and (4) you for?

Feelings are important too. What makes you smile? What brings (5) to your eyes?

5. _____ 8. _____

6. _____ 9. _____

7. _____ 10. _____

■ SPELL WELL

Problem Parts Some words cause problems because they are not spelled the way they sound. Write *psychologist* and *appreciate.* Underline any letters in these words that you think might cause spelling problems.

11. _____ 12. _____

decision psychologist disagree result weaknesses

And what makes you mad? An argument? It's okay to (<u>6</u>) with people. You can't agree all the time.

And, like all of us, you have faults. Be aware of your (<u>7</u>). What needs improvement? Once you've made a (<u>8</u>) to improve a fault, ask family and friends to help.

If a problem is bigger than you can handle, a professional (<u>9</u>) may help you.

The (<u>10</u>) may be a happier, healthier you!

crosswalks
first aid
pedestrians
rescue
reflector
bicycle
hand signal
jaywalking
emergency
helmet

_____

_____

Being Safe

You've heard the phrase "safety first." Understanding the words in the list can help you put safety first in your life. Add your own words to the list. Use the Spelling Dictionary if you need help.

■ GETTING AT MEANING

Labeling   Write a list word from the sign that identifies each numbered part of the picture.

reflector
bicycle
helmet
hand signal

1. _____

2. _____

3. _____

4. _____

186

Using Context Clues   As Sara rides to school, she is reviewing some of the safety rules she knows. Use the list words on the sign to complete Sara's thoughts.

- People who are walking, or (5), must follow safety rules.
- Pedestrians should cross streets only at (6), or specially marked places.
- Not crossing a street at a crosswalk is called (7).
- If someone is hurt in an accident, call the police and request an ambulance. A paramedic team will come to the (8).
- When driving a car or riding a bike, always pull over to the right side of the road and stop to allow an (9) vehicle to pass.
- Stand back and allow the paramedics to provide (10).

jaywalking
pedestrians
first aid
emergency
rescue
crosswalks

DETOUR

Did You Know?

Preventing accidents is the goal of safety engineers. These experts design structures and equipment to keep us safe at home, in school, on the job, and on the road.

5. _____

6. _____

7. _____

8. _____

9. _____

10. _____

■ **SPELL WELL**

Divide and Conquer   Sometimes it helps to study long words piece by piece. Study the following words syllable by syllable. Then write each one.

11. e • mer • gen • cy _____

12. pe • des • tri • an _____

bicuspid
cuspid
incisor
molar
enamel
epidermis
dermis
pore
sweat gland
oil gland

_____

_____

Your Body

■ GETTING AT MEANING

There's more to teeth than a dazzling smile, and more to skin than bone covering. Read about them below. Add more words to the list. Use your Spelling Dictionary for help.

Labeling Diagrams   Read about the teeth and skin. Then use list words to write the parts of each diagram.

The Teeth

The word **cuspid** means "tooth with a sharp point." A **bicuspid,** therefore, is a tooth with two sharp points. An **incisor** is a front tooth, and a **molar** is a back tooth. All of our teeth are protected by hard, white **enamel.**

1. _____

2. _____

3. _____

4. _____

5. _____
(the hard covering)

The Skin

The **epidermis** is the outer layer of the skin. The **dermis** is the inner layer. Each tiny opening in the skin is called a **pore.** Sweat is released through the **sweat gland,** and oil is released through the **oil gland.**

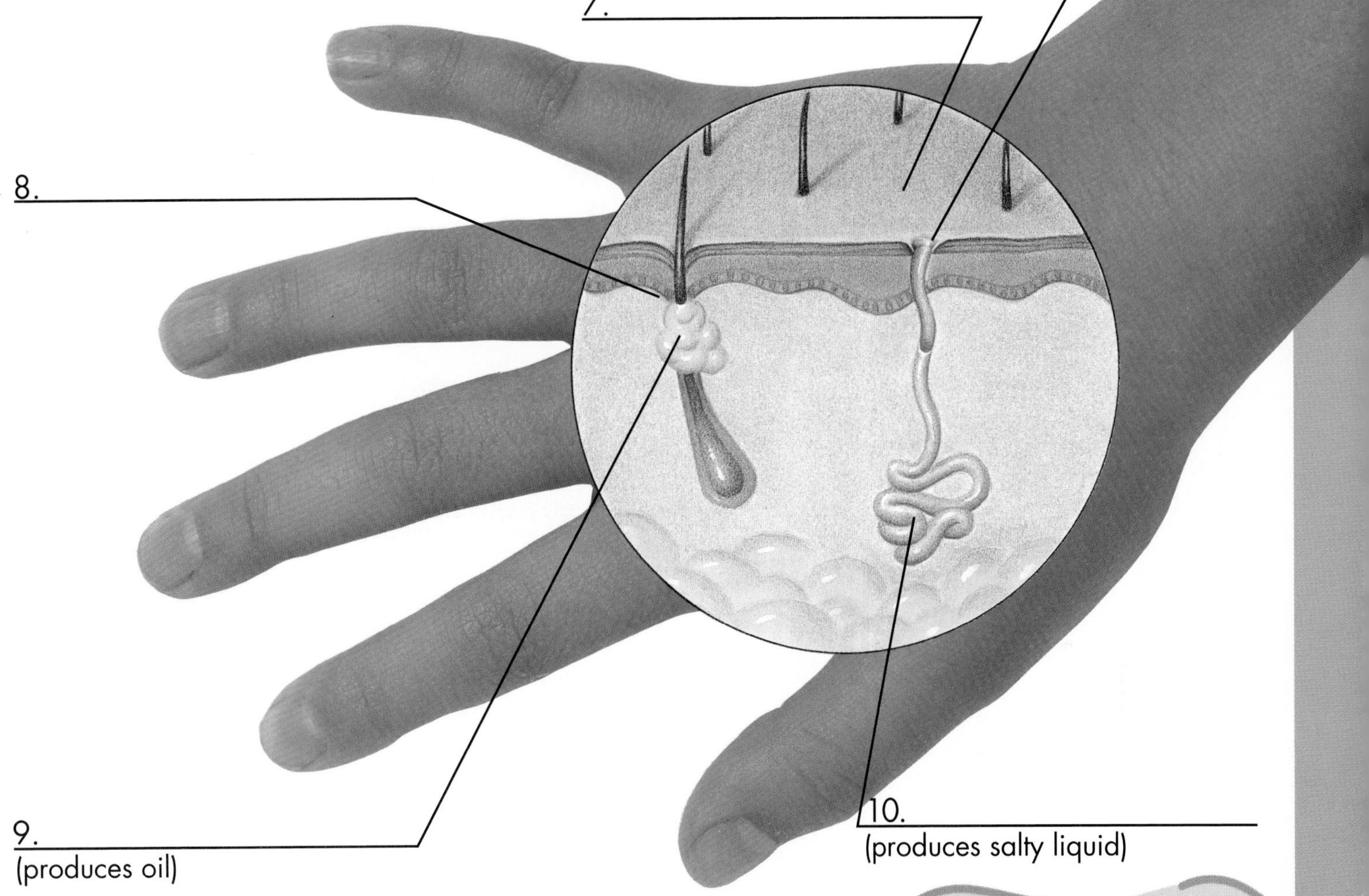

6. _____

7. _____

8. _____

9. _____
(produces oil)

10. _____
(produces salty liquid)

■ SPELL WELL

Root Awareness   Some of your list words come from Greek and Latin words. Often, a word is easier to understand and remember if you look at its root, the word it came from. Complete the chart to create two list words.

Prefix	Root Word	List Word
	derm (skin)	11. _____
epi (on, upon)	derm (skin)	12. _____

Try to Talk Without Teeth!

Not only do we need our teeth to eat, we need them to talk. Slowly read this sentence out loud: *The tiny worm sat upon a log.* Write down the words in which your tongue touches your teeth. Next to each word, also jot down where your tongue touches your teeth.

189

reproduce
seed
conifers
ferns
spores
pollen
stamen
pistil
fertilize
fruit

_____

_____

Plant Reproduction

How do plants reproduce—that is, make other plants?
Use the list words and the diagrams to find the answer.
Add your own words to the list. Use the Spelling Dictionary.

■ **GETTING AT MEANING**

Plants from Seeds   Many plants, like the cherry tree
below, reproduce by means of seeds. The diagram will
help you complete the sentences.

1. This flower will _____ by means of seeds.

2. The tiny grains made by the stamen are called _____ .

3. The flower's _____ makes these tiny grains.

4. Bees and butterflies carry pollen from the stamen to the _____ .

5. The pollen will _____ an egg at the bottom of the flower's pistil.

6. The fertilized _____ will grow inside the plant.

7. The _____ grows around the seed.
   It is the part we eat.

fertilize
bee carries pollen
from flower to flower

pollen
combines
with egg
to make
seed

stamen
makes tiny
grains of
pollen

fruit

seed

pistil
makes eggs
that combine
with pollen

190

Plants from Spores and Cones Ferns and mosses reproduce by means of **spores. Conifers** such as pine trees reproduce by means of cones. The male cone is smaller and softer. The female cone is larger and harder. Use the diagram to complete the sentences.

8. Unlike flowers, mosses and _____ have clusters of tiny cells under their leaves.

9. These cells are called _____.

10. Spruce and pine are both _____. They produce cones.

fern

spores
on the underside of a fern

■ SPELL WELL

Divide and Conquer

Long words are easy to spell if you divide them into smaller parts. Study each word below, syllable by syllable. Then write each word.

11. fer • ti • lize _____

12. re • pro • duce _____

13. con • i • fers _____

Plants Aplenty

What's your favorite plant? A garden flower? A wildflower? An exotic tree of the rain forest? Draw and paint or color your favorite plant on a big sheet of paper. Cut it out, and with your classmates' plants, create a classroom "botanical garden" on the wall. For fun, label your plant with its name, where it grows, and some interesting facts about it.

Living Together

producers
consumers
herbivore
carnivore
omnivore
food chain
food web
predator
prey
decomposer

_____

_____

Every living thing—plant and animal—depends in some way on other living things. The list words can help you find out how. Can you add others? Use your Spelling Dictionary.

■ GETTING AT MEANING

Looking at Pictures   Producers make their own food.
Consumers eat other living things.
Look at the picture below. Then answer the questions.

I'm an herbivore—I eat only plants.

YOUR BACKYARD

I'm an omnivore—I eat plants and meat.

1. The dog, boy, and squirrel all eat food.

   What are they called? _____

2. Are plants such as lettuce and carrots producers

   or consumers? _____

3. What do you call an animal who eats

   only beef and chicken? _____

4. What is an animal who eats only leaves, fruit,

   and nuts called? _____

5. What is an animal who eats both fish

   and rice called? _____

6. What do you call the tiny organism that causes
   dead plants and animals to crumble and rot?

   _____

I'm a decomposer—I break down dead plants and animals.

I'm a carnivore—I eat only meat.

Seeing Connections Animals that are hunted and eaten are called **prey.** Animals that do the hunting and eating are called **predators.** A **food chain** shows a direct link between an animal and the thing it eats and is eaten by. A **food web** is a complex arrangement of food chains. Label each picture below either **food chain** or **food web.** Answer the questions that follow.

7. _____

8. _____

9. Is the mouse in the food chain predator or prey?_____

10. Is the hawk in the food chain predator or prey?_____

■ **SPELL WELL**

Pronouncing Words Carefully We sometimes spell words wrong because we say them wrong. Say each word below. Be sure to pronounce the sounds of the underlined letters. Write the words.

11. her<u>b</u>ivore _____

12. carni<u>v</u>ore _____

13. omni<u>v</u>ore _____

Draw the Food Chain in Your Yard

Take a good look around your schoolyard or yard at home. Sketch some of the plant and animal life you see. Turn your sketches into an illustration of your yard's food chains. Does your yard also have a food web? Illustrate that too!

193

conduct
insulation
current
series circuit
parallel circuit
magnet
magnetism
poles
magnetic field
compass

_____

_____

Electricity and Magnetism

Electricity and magnetism are forces we use every day. The list words tell about each force. Look up unknown words in the Spelling Dictionary. Add other words to the list.

■ GETTING AT MEANING

Using Diagrams Write the words **current, conduct, insulation, series circuit,** and **parallel circuit** to complete the explanation below the diagrams.

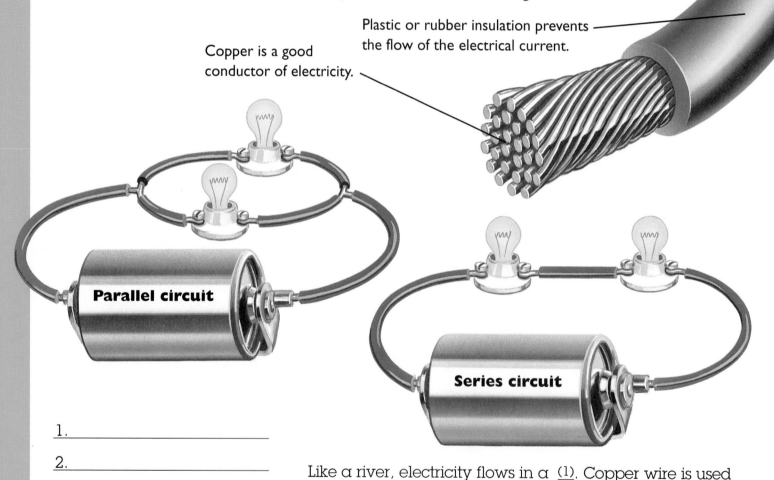

Plastic or rubber insulation prevents the flow of the electrical current.

Copper is a good conductor of electricity.

Parallel circuit

Series circuit

1. _____

2. _____

3. _____

4. _____

5. _____

Like a river, electricity flows in a (1). Copper wire is used to (2) the electricity. The wires are wrapped in plastic (3) so that they are safe to touch. When the electricity moves along one path, the circuit is a (4). When the electricity moves along two or more paths, the circuit is a (5).

Using Diagrams Use the words below to complete the sentences.

poles   magnetic field   magnetism   compass   magnet

A <u>(6)</u> is any piece of iron or steel that can pull iron or steel things to it. The magnet's power to attract is called <u>(7)</u>. The parts of a magnet where the magnetism is the strongest are called the <u>(8)</u>. The magnetic force curves out between a magnet's poles creating what is called a <u>(9)</u>. A magnetic <u>(10)</u> helps travelers to find directions. The arrow on the compass will point to the north because the north-seeking pole of the needle is attracted to the magnetic north pole of the earth.

6. _____

7. _____

8. _____

9. _____

10. _____

Magnet

Compass

magnetic field

poles

■ **SPELL WELL**

Related Words Write the two list words that are related in spelling and meaning to *magnet*.

11. _____

12. _____

Did You Know?

About 500 species of fish send out electric charges. Electric eels are the best known. They stun their prey with a 350–650 volt charge!

meteorologist
forecast
barometer
wind vane
rain gauge
humidity
air mass
front
Fahrenheit
Celsius

_____

_____

Weather

The weather's "behavior" tells us how to behave. What we wear and do often depends on the weather. The list words name ways we find out about weather. Look up unfamiliar words in the Spelling Dictionary. Add more weather words to the list.

■ GETTING AT MEANING

Weather Report Finish writing the newscaster's and weather forecaster's cue cards by writing these list words. Use the thermometer on the next page to help you.

humidity

meteorologist

forecast

Celsius

Fahrenheit

And now it's time for the weather (1). Here's Channel 2 (2), Connie Yu.

Thanks, Dave. Did you notice how damp the air was today? The (3) was so high! Watch out for the rain tonight— and it could freeze! That's because the temperature might drop to 32 degrees (4). That's the same as 0 degrees (5). Brrr!

1. _____

2. _____

3. _____

4. _____

5. _____

Related Words Complete each sentence by writing the list word that is related to the underlined word.

rain gauge

wind vane

barometer

6. A _____ measures the <u>barometric</u>, or air, pressure.

7. A _____ measures the amount of <u>rainfall</u>.

8. Both a _____ and a <u>wind sock</u> can show wind direction.

Reading a Weather Map An **air mass** is a large body of air pushing into an area. A **front** is where two different air masses meet. Look at the map key. Then label the symbols on the map for **air mass** and **front**.

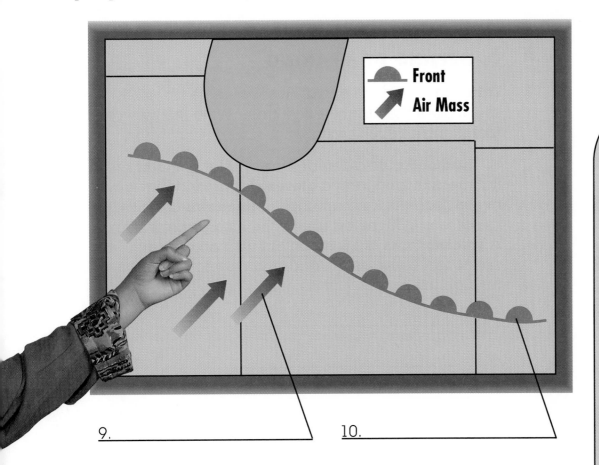

Front

Air Mass

9. _____   10. _____

100°C ─   ─ 212°F

Weather Records

What's the coldest recorded temperature in your hometown? What's the warmest recorded temperature? Find out and share your information with your classmates.

0°C ─   ─ 32°F

■ **SPELL WELL**

Divide and Conquer Study these long words syllable by syllable. Then cover the words and write them.

11. me • te • o • rol • o • gist _____

12. Fahr • en • heit _____

landforms
mountains
plains
plateau
plates
volcano
faults
earthquake
seismograph
Richter scale

_____

_____

Landforms

Can you describe your natural surroundings? Are there any mountains or plains nearby? The list words will help you talk about landforms and the forces that cause them. Look up unfamiliar words in the Spelling Dictionary. Add two words of your own.

■ GETTING AT MEANING

Labeling Read the explanations of these list words and look at the numbered pictures. Write the list word that identifies each picture.

Landforms are different shapes of land. **Plains** are flat areas of land, and a **plateau** is flat land that is higher than the land around it. **Mountains** are hills that rise at least 600 meters above the land around them. A **volcano** looks like a mountain with an opening on the top. Lava, ashes, and steam sometimes flow through this opening in the earth's crust.

1. _____

2. _____

3. _____

4. _____

5. These four shapes of land are called

_____ .

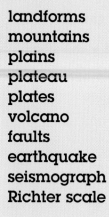

1

2

3

4

Scientific Vocabulary When writers use technical words, they often put clues in the sentences to help you understand what the terms mean. Using the underlined clues, write list words to complete this paragraph about earthquakes.

Earth Notes

When the earth shakes, it is called an (6). An earthquake is caused by the shifting of large sections of rock that make up the earth's surface called (7). The earth's surface has cracks called (8). Earthquakes usually begin along these fault lines. An instrument called a (9) records how strong the earthquake is by drawing lines on graph paper. Scientists report their results using the (10), a scale of measurement that goes from zero for the weakest quake, up to 9 for the very strongest.

6. ______________________
7. ______________________
8. ______________________
9. ______________________
10. ______________________

SPELL WELL

Divide and Conquer Study these long words syllable by syllable. Then cover the words and write them.

11. earth • quake ______________________

12. seis • mo • graph ______________________

Did You Know?

There are about 1,300 potentially active volcanoes in the world. Many of them lie in what is called "The Ring of Fire" around the Pacific Ocean.

pupil
iris
retina
optic nerve
lens
eardrum
ear canal
outer ear
middle ear
inner ear

_____

_____

The Eyes and Ears

Our eyes and ears provide us with two important senses—seeing and hearing. The list words tell about the parts that make up our eyes and ears. Add other related words. Use your Spelling Dictionary for help.

■ GETTING AT MEANING

Labeling Diagrams   Read the paragraphs describing the parts of the eye and the parts of the ear. Write the list word that identifies each numbered part in the diagram.

The Eyes   We can see only certain parts of the eye: the white of the eye and the colored part called the **iris.** The iris has an opening in the middle called the **pupil,** which controls the amount of light that enters the eye. Right behind the iris is the **lens.** The lens works to make sure that the eye gets a sharp picture. The **retina** is the eye's "back wall." The retina changes the light coming in into electric signals. Then the **optic nerve** carries the electric signals to the brain.

1. _____

2. _____

3. _____

4. _____

5. _____

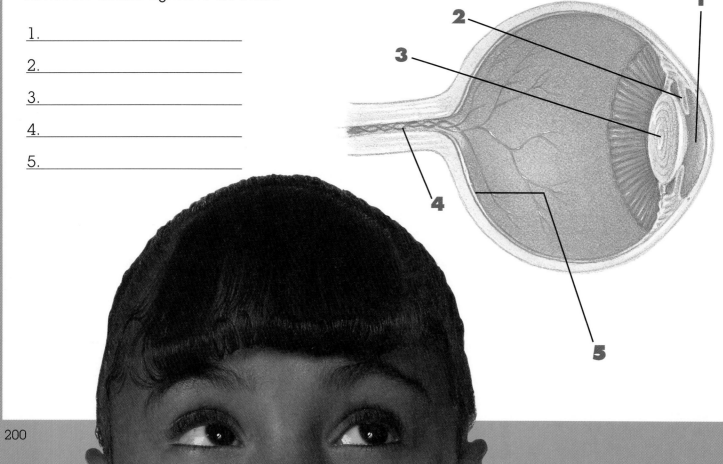

200

The Ears

Ears are the sense organs that let us hear. The part of the ear on the outside of the head is part of the **outer ear.** The other part of the outer ear is the **ear canal.** This little "tunnel" leads from the outer ear to the **eardrum,** which separates the outer ear from the **middle ear.** Sound waves make the eardrum vibrate. These vibrations move through the middle ear to the inner ear. The middle ear has three tiny bones that link the eardrum to the **inner ear** deep inside the head. The inner ear is the part of the ear that sends messages to the brain. The brain then "hears" the sounds.

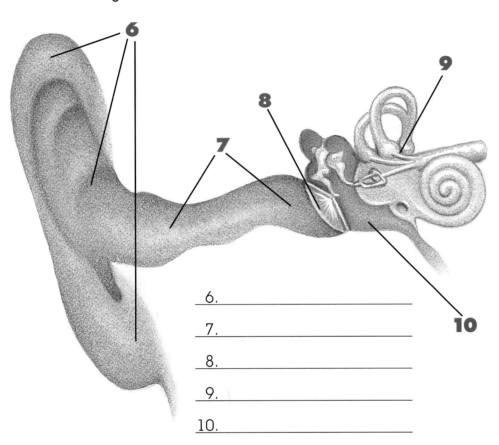

6. _____

7. _____

8. _____

9. _____

10. _____

■ SPELL WELL

Pronouncing Words Carefully

Some words are not spelled the way they're pronounced. Exaggerate the sounds of the underlined letters to help you remember them. Write the words.

11. retin̲a _____

12. pupi̲l _____

All Eyes and Ears

The animal kingdom is full of amazing eyes and ears. Check out eagles, owls, cats, insects, or lobsters to learn about their eyes. To learn about animals that "get an earful," check out foxes, bats, dogs, or elephants. Share what you find.

accomplishments
artist
celebrated
humor
confidence
determination
disappointment
expert
strategy
successful

_____

_____

Hopes, Dreams, and Wishes

What goals and achievements do you dream about and wish for? The words in the list will help you understand attitudes and actions that help make dreams come true. Look up unfamiliar words in the Spelling Dictionary. Add your own words to the list.

■ GETTING AT MEANING

Using Context Clues   Write the list words below to complete a recipe for success.

determination   1. _____

disappointment   2. _____

accomplishments   3. _____

humor   4. _____

expert   5. _____

HoPES, DREAMS, and WishEs

Start with your (1) —your talents and skills.

Add plenty of drive and (2) to help you focus on your goal.

Sprinkle in a few chuckles— (3) adds flavor to this dish.

Leave out (4) —so you won't give up.

Mix them all together to become an (5) at what you do—the very best.

Using Synonyms Write the list word that is similar in meaning to each group of words below.

successful   celebrated   strategy   artist   confidence

6. _____
painter, musician, sculptor

7. _____
famous, well-known

8. _____
method, plan

9. _____
self-trust, self-belief

10. _____
triumphant, fortunate,
well-off

■ SPELL WELL

Double Trouble Double letters can cause spelling problems. Write the words below. Underline the double letters in each word to help you remember them.

11. successful _____

12. accomplishments _____

13. disappointment _____

Did You Know?

Not all dreams come true overnight. Inventors Wilbur and Orville Wright experimented for about seven years before their first successful airplane flight!

assignments
collections
counselor
demonstrations
interview
experiment
exhibit
research
librarian
brainstorm

_____

_____

Many Ways of Learning

How do we learn new things? We learn in many different ways. The list words name just a few. Use the Spelling Dictionary to look up unknown words. Add your own words.

■ GETTING AT MEANING

Labeling Illustrations   Write the list word that identifies each picture.

interview	brainstorm
exhibit	assignments
experiment	

1. _____

2. _____

3. _____

4. _____

5. _____

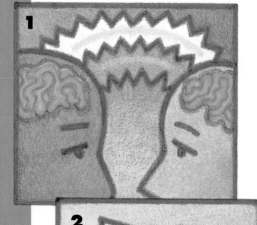

Completing Word Webs Use the following list words to finish the word webs.

librarian
demonstrations
counselor
research
collections

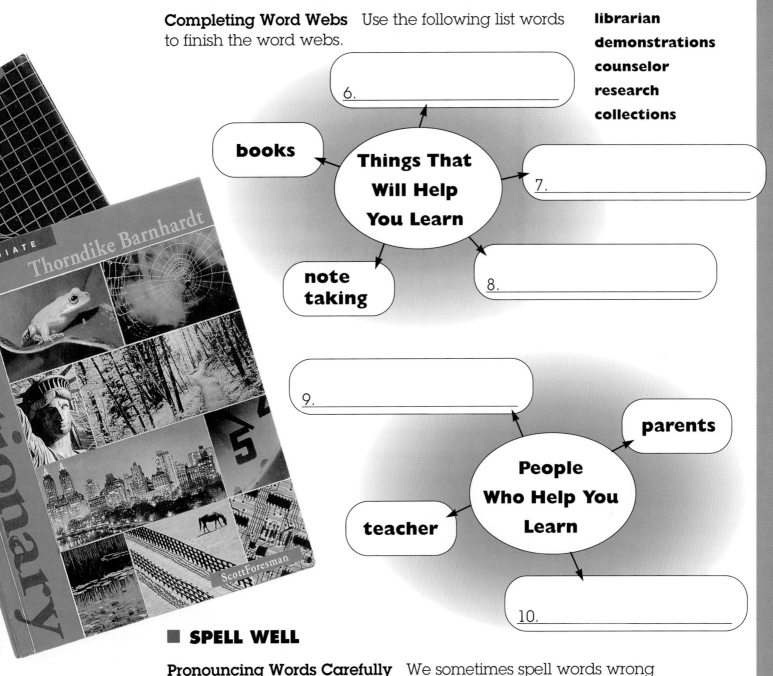

6. _____

books

Things That Will Help You Learn

7. _____

note taking

8. _____

9. _____

parents

People Who Help You Learn

teacher

10. _____

■ SPELL WELL

Pronouncing Words Carefully We sometimes spell words wrong because we say them wrong. Say each word carefully. Be sure to pronounce the sound of each underlined letter. Write each word.

11. experiment _____

12. counselor _____

Create the Perfect Learning Environment

Suppose you could create the perfect place where you could learn everything you wanted to know. Where would it be? What would it look like? What would you have there? Who would you have there? Draw or write a description of your "perfect learning place."

family
parents
children
home
shared
chores
love
childhood
memories
scrapbook

_____

_____

How Families Matter

What makes families special? Read the list of words, and look up unknown words in the Spelling Dictionary. Add your own family words to the list.

■ GETTING AT MEANING

Labeling Photographs   Everyone's family is different. Using what you know about families, write the list word that describes each photograph in John's scrapbook.

home   **family**   **chores**   **parents**   **children**

1. _____

2. _____   4. _____

3. _____   5. _____

Using Context Clues Use these list words to complete the note that John's parents wrote to him in the front of his scrapbook.

love   **shared**   **childhood**

memories   **scrapbook**

6. _____

7. _____

8. _____

9. _____

10. _____

Dear John,

We can't believe that you are nine years old already! Your (6) is going so quickly! For your birthday we would like you to have this (7). It is full of photos, and it holds (8) of many happy times we have (9) together. Happy 9th birthday! We (10) you!

Mom and Dad

Conduct Interviews

Interview the older members of your family. Ask them to tell you about their early memories of childhood. Take notes as they speak. Share these memories with the class.

■ **SPELL WELL**

Related Words
Write the two list words that are related in spelling and meaning to *child*.

11. _____

12. _____

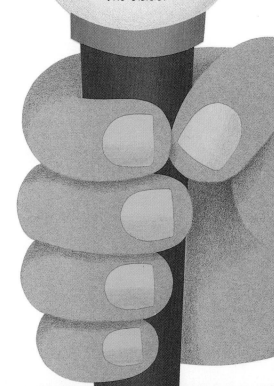

cafeteria
concert
curtains
furniture
office
library
orchestra
skateboarding
spider web
water fountain

_____

_____

Your Own Universe

The words in the list name just ten of the thousands of things that are part of your universe. Add your own words. Use the Spelling Dictionary if you need help.

■ GETTING AT MEANING

Context Clues   School is a big part of your universe. Look at the bulletin board notices from Maple School. Complete them with list words.

THANK YOU, P.T.A. PARENTS!

Thanks to a generous gift from the P.T.A., students will not go thirsty during recess. Take a sip from the new (1) on the playground.

You're Invited!

Enjoy an evening of music. The band and the (2) will have a combined (3) on Saturday, May 22, at 7:30 P.M.

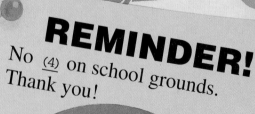

REMINDER!
No (4) on school grounds. Thank you!

1. _____

2. _____

3. _____

4. _____

HELP WANTED!

We still need help with the fourth-grade play, *Charlotte's Web*. These jobs are still open.

Stage Crew: Responsible for opening and closing the (5) between acts.

Set Design: Responsible for building a (6) for Charlotte the spider.

5. _____

6. _____

7. _____

8. _____

9. _____

10. _____

FOR SALE

Used art table $10.00
File Cabinets $15.00
Money from the sale of the (7) will be used to buy new books for the (8).

$10.00

$15.00

HOT DOG HEAVEN

The Student Council will be selling hot dog lunches every Wednesday. Tickets are $1.75 each and may be purchased in the principal's (9) before school or in the (10) during the lunch hour.

home

music

Take a Look at Your Universe

School is only one part of your universe. Create word webs to show other parts of it—home, sports, hobbies, fashion, and so on. Share your webs with friends or display them on a bulletin board.

nature

sports

■ SPELL WELL

Pronouncing for Spelling Some words are not spelled the way they're pronounced. Exaggerate the sounds of the underlined letters in each word below. Then write the words.

11. or<u>ch</u>estra _____

12. furnit<u>u</u>re _____

fashion

cathedral
Chartres
church
temple
Parthenon
marble
jewels
tomb
Taj Mahal
honor

_____

_____

Looking at the World in New Ways

Imagine that you are at the Parthenon, the Cathedral of Notre Dame, or the Taj Mahal. What would you notice about it? The list words tell about these three monuments. Add words about other world-famous buildings. Use your Spelling Dictionary for help.

■ GETTING AT MEANING

Using Photographs   Complete the caption under each postcard. Use the words in the brick.

The (1) is in Athens, Greece. The ancient Greeks built this beautiful (2) to honor Athena, the goddess of wisdom. The Greeks built the entire structure of white (3). Inside stood a huge gold-and-ivory statue of Athena.

temple   marble
Parthenon

1. _____

2. _____

3. _____

210

cathedral	Chartres
church	jewels

4. _____

5. _____

6. _____

7. _____

The city of (4) in France is world famous for its (5), called the Cathedral of Notre Dame. The great (6) has more than 100 stained-glass windows so richly colored that they shine like (7).

The (8) is in Agra, India. The Indian ruler Shah Jahan had this beautiful (9) built in the mid-1600s. It was constructed in (10) of his wife, Mumtaz Mahal. It has a domed roof and four prayer towers.

tomb	honor
Taj Mahal	

8. _____

9. _____

10. _____

■ SPELL WELL

Capital Letters Three of your list words are proper nouns. Write them. Remember to capitalize the words.

11. _____

12. _____

13. _____

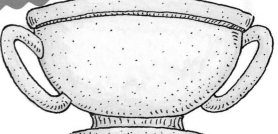

Design a Monument

The Parthenon was erected to honor Athena. Farmers in Enterprise, Alabama, erected a monument to the boll weevil in 1919. By destroying their crops, the insect forced them to grow new and different crops. As a result, the farmers became richer. Think of someone you'd like to design a monument to honor. Draw the monument and write an inscription.

compassionate
debris
devastate
emergency
extraordinary
panic
pressure
recover
siren
tremendous

_____

_____

Tales of Courage

Many situations call for courage. The words in the list bring to mind some sounds, sights, and feelings of such situations. Add some of your own words of courage.

■ GETTING AT MEANING

Using Context Clues   Use the list words at the right to complete the phone call.

siren
pressure
emergency
panic
recover

Hi, Aunt Betty! Guess what?
I'm a heroine, but I hardly remember what happened!
When I saw Gram fall on the stairs and hit her head,
I knew it was an (1). I managed not to (2). I ran to the phone
and dialed 911. Giving my name and address helped me (3)
my control. But until I heard the (4) and saw the paramedics
pull up in the fire truck, I really felt the (5). I couldn't do
anything for Gram—just wait and hold her hand. Anyhow,
the doctor said I saved her life. And our newspaper gave
me a commendation. Say hello to Uncle Jack.
Bye for now!

1. _____

2. _____

3. _____

4. _____

5. _____

More Context Clues Complete the paragraph with these list words. The underlined words may help you.

debris compassionate extraordinary tremendous devastate

A powerful earthquake can <u>destroy</u>, or (6), a city. The <u>awesome</u>, (7) force of the earth moving can topple buildings. <u>Building materials, crushed automobiles, broken pipes, and other</u> (8) can block the streets. At times like this, <u>ordinary</u> citizens show (9) courage to help their neighbors. And <u>concerned</u> people from all over the country show their (10) nature by sending food, clothing, and money to aid the victims of an earthquake.

6. _____

7. _____

8. _____

9. _____

10. _____

■ SPELL WELL

Divide and Conquer Study the words below syllable by syllable. Then cover them and write them.

11. com • pas • sion • ate _____

12. ex • traor • di • nar • y _____

Did You Know?

Courage comes from a Latin word that means "heart."

213

operation key
number keys
display
memory recall
memory plus
memory minus
key sequence
error
clear key
equals key

_____

_____

1. _____

2. _____

3. _____

4. _____

5. _____

6. _____

7. _____

The Calculator

Do you, your parents, or your friends use calculators? The words in the list tell all about these small, remarkable machines. Add your own words. Use the Spelling Dictionary for help.

■ GETTING AT MEANING

Understanding a Calculator   Read the paragraphs below. Then write list words to complete the sentences.

The **number keys** and each **operation key** are used to give information to the calculator. The order in which you press the keys is the **key sequence.** The answer to the problem appears in the **display** after you press the **equals key.**

Press the **clear key** once if you make a mistake entering numbers. An "E" will appear in the display if you make an **error** like trying to divide by zero.

Marta wanted to add the number of muffins she sold on Monday and Tuesday. She pressed the (1) 3 and 5, and the number 35 appeared in the (2). She pressed the "+" (3) before she entered 27. When 24 appeared in the display, she realized that she had pressed the 4 by mistake. She pressed the (4) once and then entered the correct numbers. The answer appeared after she pressed the (5). 35 ⊞ 27 ⊟ is the (6) Marta entered to solve her problem. If the answer to her problem had been greater than eight digits long, or she had tried to divide by zero, an "E" in the display would have told her that she had made an (7).

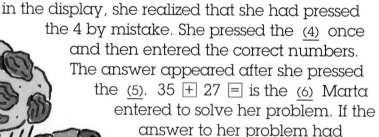

muffins 25¢

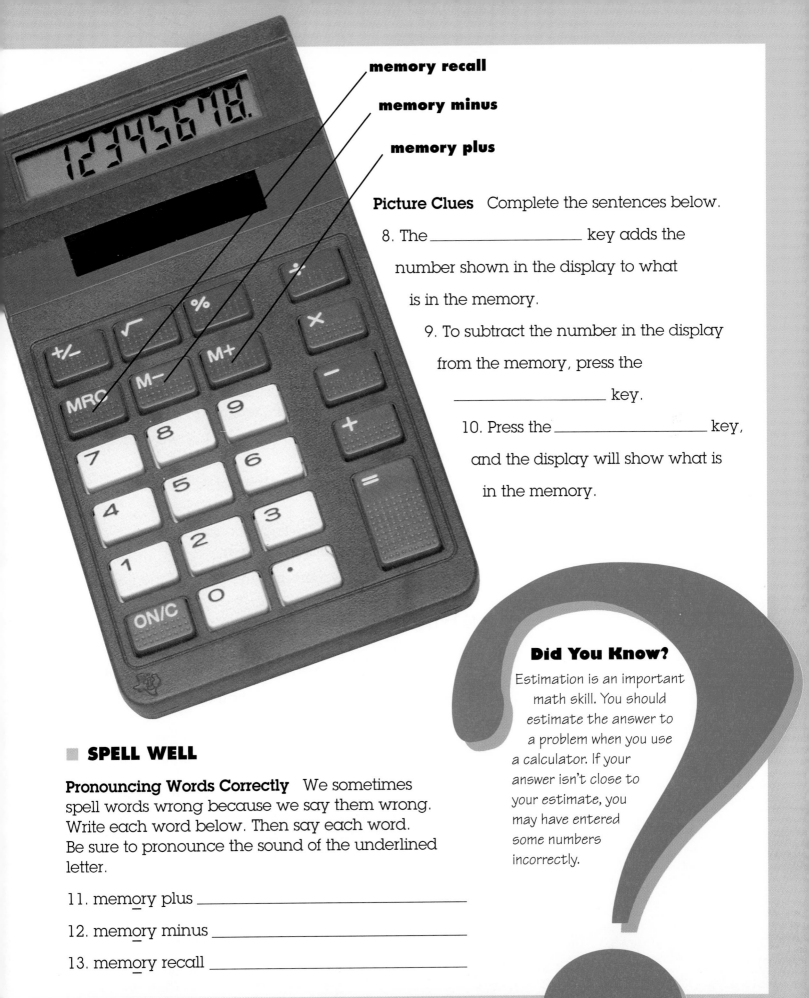

memory recall

memory minus

memory plus

Picture Clues Complete the sentences below.

8. The _____ key adds the number shown in the display to what is in the memory.

9. To subtract the number in the display from the memory, press the _____ key.

10. Press the _____ key, and the display will show what is in the memory.

■ SPELL WELL

Pronouncing Words Correctly We sometimes spell words wrong because we say them wrong. Write each word below. Then say each word. Be sure to pronounce the sound of the underlined letter.

11. mem<u>o</u>ry plus _____

12. mem<u>o</u>ry minus _____

13. mem<u>o</u>ry recall _____

Did You Know?

Estimation is an important math skill. You should estimate the answer to a problem when you use a calculator. If your answer isn't close to your estimate, you may have entered some numbers incorrectly.

length
width
height
weight
capacity
volume
area
perimeter
distance
temperature

_____

_____

1. _____

2. _____

3. _____

4. _____

5. _____

6. _____

7. _____

8. _____

Measurement

How would you describe the size and shape of a soccer field? Words of measurement, like the ones in the word list, help you describe places or objects.

■ GETTING AT MEANING

Context Clues   Complete each sentence with the correct list word from those given in parentheses.

1. In youth soccer, the field is usually 100 yards in length and 50 yards in _____. **(width, length)**

2. The _____ of the field is divided by a halfway line. **(width, length)**

3. The _____ from one goal to the other is 100 yards. **(distance, area)**

4. The entire _____ of the field covers about 5,000 square yards. **(distance, area)**

5. White lines are drawn around the _____ of the field. **(perimeter, volume)**

6. Modern soccer shoes are light in _____ . **(height, weight)**

7. In soccer, the _____ and weight of a player are not as important as the player's speed and fitness. **(height, width)**

8. Soccer can be played outside whether the _____ is warm or cool. **(volume, temperature)**

Understanding Measurements   Study the figure to the right. Complete each sentence with the correct list word.

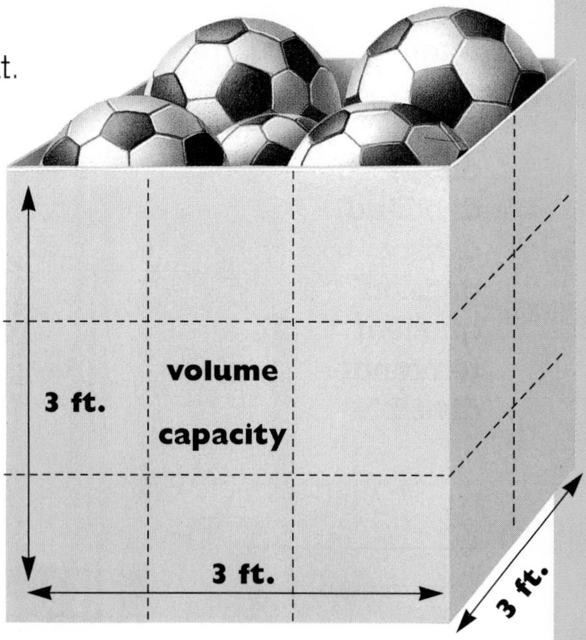

9. To measure volume, multiply length x width x height.

    The _____ of the box is 27 cubic feet.

10. When the box is filled to its _____

    it holds about ten soccer balls.

volume

capacity

3 ft.

3 ft.

3 ft.

■ **SPELL WELL**

Pronouncing Words Correctly   We sometimes spell words wrong because we say them wrong. Write each word below. Then say each word. Be sure to pronounce the sound of the underlined letter.

11. temperature _____

12. width _____

Measure Up

With a partner, measure the size of your classroom. Measure to the nearest foot. On a separate sheet of paper, write your measurements on a chart like the one below. Assume the height is 9 feet.

length: _____ feet

width: _____ feet

height: __9__ feet

area (length x width): _____ square feet

volume (length x width x height): _____ cubic feet

Division

family of facts
grouping
number sentence
divide
dividend
divisor
division
quotient
remainder
divisible

_____

_____

Division is one of the four basic math operations. Read the list of words that talk about division and add your own words. Look up unfamiliar words in the Spelling Dictionary.

■ **GETTING AT MEANING**

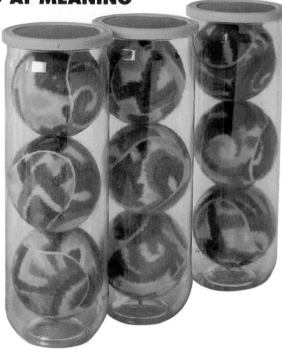

Understanding Math Terms When you have 12 tennis balls and want to put them into groups of 3, you **divide** to find the number of groups you can make. You may show the **division** problem in two ways.

$$3 \overline{)\ 12}^{\,4} \qquad\qquad \text{divisor} \overline{)\ \text{dividend}}^{\,\text{quotient}}$$

$$12 \div 3 = 4 \qquad \text{dividend} \div \text{divisor} = \text{quotient}$$

A **family of facts** can be used to represent the groupings of the tennis balls. Each **number sentence** in a family of facts tells about the **grouping.** Two of the number sentences show related multiplication facts and two of the number sentences show the related division facts.

Write the list word that describes each item.

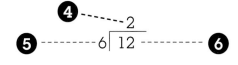

2. _____

3. _____

4. _____

5. _____

1. _____

6. _____

A number is **divisible** by another if it can be divided by that number with no remainder. When a number cannot be divided exactly by another number, the number left over is called a **remainder.**

Look at the examples below. Complete the sentences with list words.

$$\frac{4}{2\overline{)8}}$$
$$\frac{2R1}{2\overline{)5}}$$

7. Eight is _____ by two.

8. One is the _____ in the second problem.

9. When you _____ eight by two, the quotient is four.

10. The symbol ÷ represents the operation of _____ .

SPELL WELL

Problem Parts Say the words below. Notice that the last syllables of the two words sound alike but are spelled differently. Write each word and underline the last two letters.

11. divis<u>or</u> _____

12. remaind<u>er</u> _____

Did You Know?
Division is repeated subtraction. To find how many groups of 3 are in 12 you can subtract 3 from 12 until your answer is zero. You can subtract 4 times, so there are 4 groups of 3 in 12.

angle
vertex
endpoint
intersecting
line
parallel
point
ray
segment
perpendicular

_____

_____

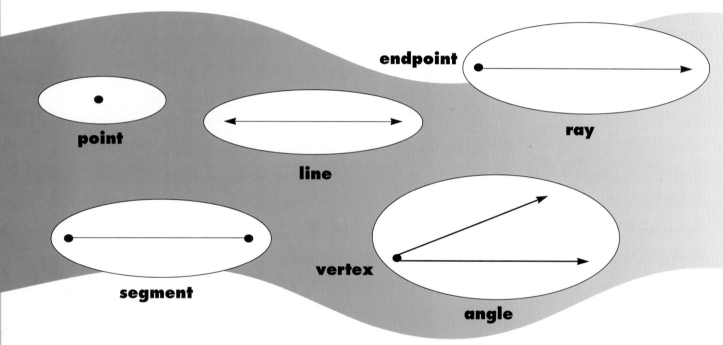

Geometry

Geometry is the branch of mathematics that studies and measures lines, angles, and shapes. The words in the list will tell you about geometry. Look up unknown words in the Spelling Dictionary. Add more words.

■ GETTING AT MEANING

Picture Clues Use the illustrations to help you write the list words that complete the sentences.

1. _____

2. _____

3. _____

4. _____

5. _____

6. _____

7. _____

A (1) continues without end in both directions.

A (2) is part of a line. It has two endpoints.

A (3) is part of a line that has one (4) and goes on and on in one direction.

An (5) is formed by two rays with the same endpoint. The endpoint is its (6).

The sharpened end of your pencil could be thought of as a (7).

220

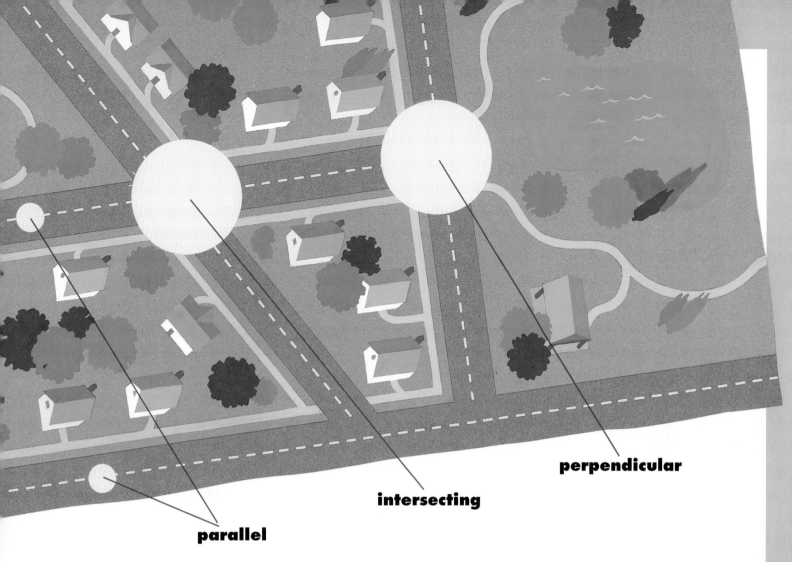

perpendicular

intersecting

parallel

Sometimes lines meet, or intersect. Two lines that cross each other at one point are <u>(8)</u> lines.

Lines that do not meet and remain the same distance apart are called <u>(9)</u> lines.

Intersecting lines that form square corners are called <u>(10)</u> lines.

8. _____

9. _____

10. _____

■ SPELL WELL

Divide and Conquer Long words are easier to spell when they are divided into syllables. Say the syllables in each word. Then write the words.

11. par • al • lel _____

12. in • ter • sect • ing _____

Did You Know?

The word *geometry* comes from two ancient Greek words that mean "to measure" and "earth." The ancient Egyptians used geometry to figure out the boundaries of their farms every year after the Nile River's flooding washed away or covered landmarks!

kicks
stroke
breathe
floats
treads
dive
dog paddle
backstroke
butterfly
freestyle

_____

_____

1. _____

2. _____

3. _____

4. _____

5. _____

6. _____

Swimming

Swimming is a sport that people of every age enjoy. What swimming skills do you have? Which are you working on? Add your own words about swimming to the list. Check unknown words in the Spelling Dictionary.

■ GETTING AT MEANING

Using Picture Clues Look at the illustration. Complete the sentences using list words.

treads   floats   stroke   kicks   breathe   dog paddle

Jamal is practicing (1), moving his legs and feet.

An instructor shows students a new (2) with his arms.

As Sal raises his arm, he brings his head out of the water to (3).

Mailee does the (4). Just like a swimming dog, she keeps her head above water and moves her arms in circles.

Robert (5) quietly nearby.

Julie (6) water by moving her feet up and down as if she were walking underwater!

222

freestyle   dive   butterfly   backstroke

A good (7) will give Alma a super start.

Janice likes the (8) because it's easy to breathe swimming on her back.

Abe works on his (9) stroke. Moving both arms and legs together is tough!

Abe, Janice, and Alma compete in (10) meets. In these races swimmers are free to choose any swimming style.

7. _____

8. _____

9. _____

10. _____

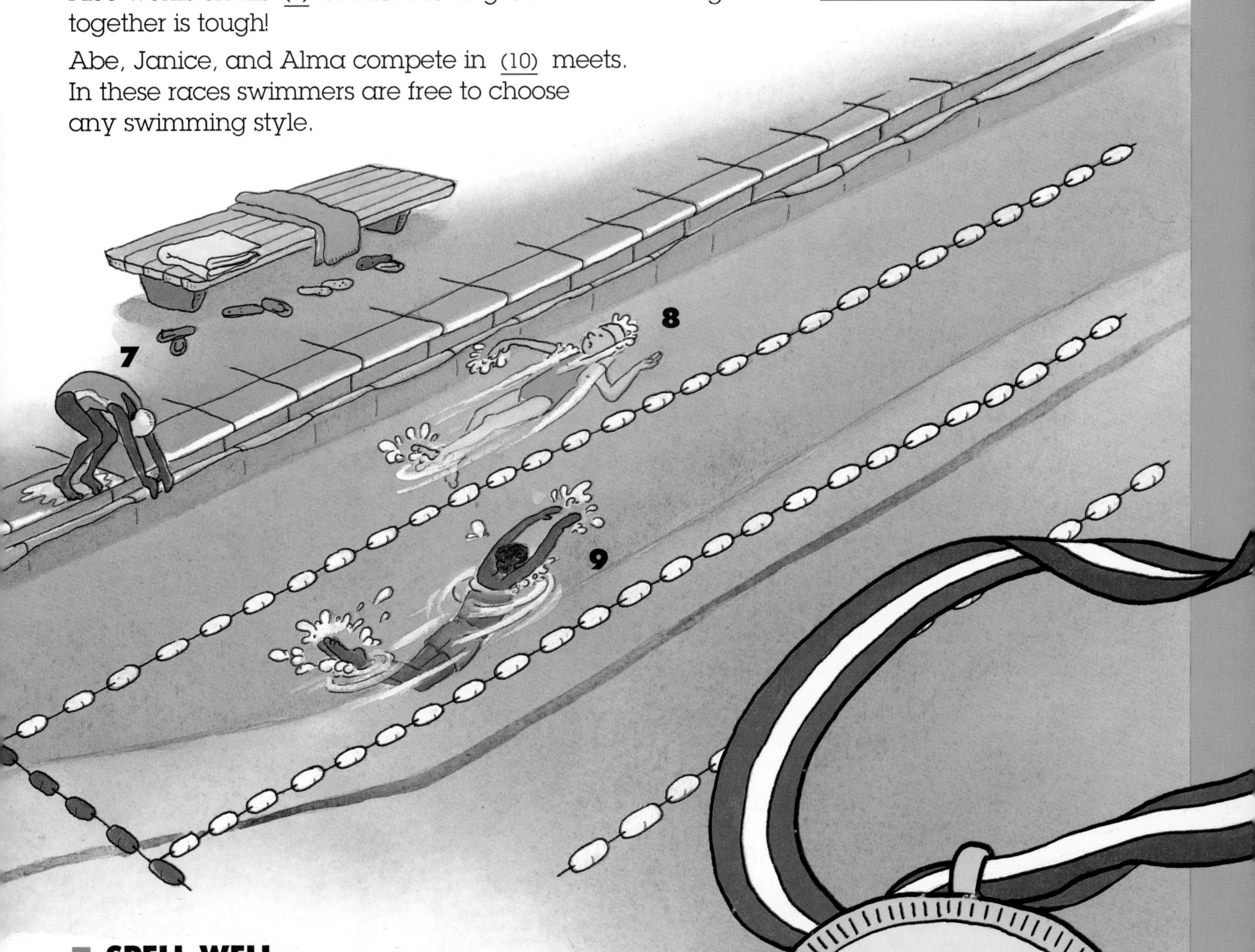

■ **SPELL WELL**

Double Consonants The double consonants in the words below have only one sound. Remember to include both consonants when you write these words.

11. butterfly_____

12. dog paddle_____

Did You Know?
American swimmer Mark Spitz has won more Olympic medals in swimming events than any other swimmer. Spitz has eleven medals: nine gold, one silver, and one bronze. He won seven of his nine gold in 1972.

Basketball

Basketball is a fun, fast, and entertaining game. Knowing the list words can help you enjoy the game more. Read the sentences below. Add your own related words to the list. Check unknown words in the Spelling Dictionary.

backboard	A **backboard** with a basket hangs over each end of the court.
rim	A basket is made of a net hung from a metal **rim.**
dribble	Players can **dribble** the ball on the floor past an opponent.
rebound	A **rebound** is a ball that bounces off the backboard or rim.
foul	Hitting or pushing another player is a **foul.**
free throw	A player shoots a **free throw** from behind a free throw line.
field goal	A player can score a **field goal** from anywhere on the court.
lay-up	A player close to the basket can shoot a **lay-up** to score.
jump shot	A player jumps straight up to shoot a **jump shot.**
slam-dunk	In a **slam-dunk,** a player slams the ball through the basket from above.

_____   _____

_____   _____

■ GETTING AT MEANING

Rhyming Clues   Complete these rhyming basketball cheers with list words.

Just (1) that basketball
down the floor!
Make a (2)
for two points more!

The ball bounces off the (3)
And rolls around the (4).
Get that (5) and put it in!

We'll all howl
If you (6).

1. _____

2. _____

3. _____

4. _____

5. _____

6. _____

Picture Clues What kind of shot is each player trying to make?
Write the list word that matches each picture.

lay-up   slam-dunk   jump shot   free throw

7. _____   9. _____

8. _____   10. _____

■ **SPELL WELL**

Divide and Conquer It helps to study some
words piece by piece. Study the words
syllable by syllable. Then cover them and
write them.

11. re • bound _____

12. drib • ble _____

Did You Know?
The first game
of basketball was
played with two
peach baskets and
a soccer ball.

articles
headline
deadline
byline
lead
details
interview
verify
sources
editors

_____

_____

Reporter

Newspapers and magazines employ thousands of reporters. Knowing the list words will help you understand a reporter's job. Use your Spelling Dictionary to learn the exact meaning of the words or to find other words to add to the list.

■ GETTING AT MEANING

Using Picture Clues Look at the illustration below to help you finish each sentence with the correct list word.

Newspapers and magazines contain many (1) about important events and people.

A (2) in big, dark print tells about the article in a few words.

Many articles have a (3) that gives the writer's name.

1. _____

2. _____

3. _____

byline **headline** **articles**

WALKER★SCHOOL
NEWS

Who's That Shaggy-Looking New Kid?

by Erin Gates

Ms. Maggie Sullivan's kindergarten had an unusual visitor last week. New student Eliot Greenwald's dog Dexter decided to follow him to sch Dexter ran behind the schoo bus all the way to Walker S Then he wouldn't stay outs on the playground. Ms. Su kindly allowed Dexter to in the kindergarten room Eliot until Mr. Greenwa

Just Reuse It!

by Jason Nevin

Walker School students have joined the community effort to recycle. First of all, the entire student body has pledged to carry their lunches in reusabl or b

bring from home. Also, recycling bins have been placed in the cafeteria for collecting used milk cartons, aluminum cans, and aluminum foil.

In addition, recycling bins for paper products have been

Using Definitions Use the definitions to help you complete
the news article on the computer screen.

details	the facts of a news story that give more information about the news
editors	people who often write the headlines and add or rewrite the details of articles
sources	people, places, or written materials where reporters and editors get information
lead	the opening paragraph of a news story
verify	to be sure that a fact is true
interview	to ask people about their activities or opinions
deadline	latest time by which articles must be finished

4. _____

5. _____

6. _____

7. _____

8. _____

9. _____

10. _____

GETTING THE STORY TAKES WORK

Newspaper reporters get their stories from many (4).
Some have a regular route called a beat. Some investigate
politics or crime. Others report the news from overseas.
Reporters sometimes (5) people to get their opinions.
Once reporters "get the story," they quickly write it and give
it to one of the (6). The most important information goes
in the (7), or opening paragraph. The editors must (8)
the (9) in the stories. They call people whom reporters
have interviewed or check the details in books or magazines
or special news services. All this work must be done quickly
so that the newspaper can meet its daily (10). At deadline
time, a story must go to the printing presses.

Be a Reporter
Grab a pad and pencil and
cover your school's beat!
Look for something unusual
or funny or mysterious that's
happening. Interview the people
involved to get the details.
Be sure to verify them! Then
write your story. Have your
teacher or another student
edit it. Ask if you can read it
over your school's P.A. system.

■ SPELL WELL

Problem Parts Sometimes the vowel sounds you hear in a word
give you no clue as to its spelling. Pay special attention to the
underlined letters below. Then write the words.

11. articles _____   12. editors _____

camera
film
lens
shutter
focus
portrait
snapshot
develops
negative
print

_____

_____

Photography

Photographs surround us everywhere we go. In newspapers, in magazines, on billboards, and in brochures, photographs give us glimpses of people, places, and events. The list words tell about photography. Look up unfamiliar words in the Spelling Dictionary. Add your own related words.

■ GETTING AT MEANING

Diagrams Complete the sentences with words from the labels and captions of the diagram.

film shutter camera lens focus

film

Load **film** here.

shutter **lens**

camera

Use the lens to **focus** the picture.

1. A_____ is a photographer's tool.

2. The glass_____ is the camera's "eye." You see your subject through the lens.

3. The lens also helps to_____ the picture so that it will appear sharp and clear.

4. The_____opens to let light through the lens. The shutter works like an eyelid.

5. As the shutter clicks, a picture is recorded on the_____ inside.

Analogies Use the words in dark type in the following sentences to finish the analogies.

- A special process **develops** the photographs on film.
- A **negative** photograph is developed first. A negative shows dark objects as light and light objects as dark.
- A **print** is made from each negative.
- A **portrait** is a photograph of a person's face.
- A **snapshot** is a photograph taken quickly with a small camera.

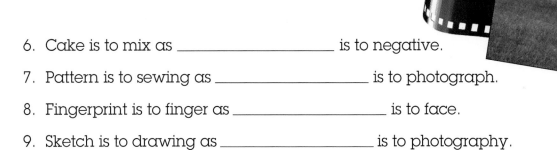

6. Cake is to mix as _____ is to negative.

7. Pattern is to sewing as _____ is to photograph.

8. Fingerprint is to finger as _____ is to face.

9. Sketch is to drawing as _____ is to photography.

10. Bakes is to cake mix as_____ is to film.

■ SPELL WELL

Divide and Conquer Some words are easier to study in smaller parts. Study each word syllable by syllable. Then cover the words and write them.

11. cam • er • a _____

12. neg • a • tive _____

Writer's Handbook

INTRODUCTION

You can speak and even read well without knowing how to spell. However, knowing how to spell well is a skill that every good writer needs. This handbook will help you with some of the other skills good writers need.

CONTENTS

The Writing Process

This section answers questions that you might ask about the five steps of the writing process: prewriting, drafting, revising, proofreading, and presenting.

1. PREWRITING

What should I do before I start to write?

Think about and plan your writing before you actually put sentences on paper. Time you spend prewriting is time well spent. Follow these steps and suggestions.

- **Select a topic** by listing ideas; by browsing through books, magazines, or newspapers for ideas; or by reviewing a personal journal or diary.
- **Determine your purpose and audience**. Your purpose may be to express feelings, describe or explain, give or get information, persuade, or tell a story. Your audience could be classmates, your aunt in Tennessee, or a friend.
- **Narrow your topic.** To focus on one specific idea, you might brainstorm questions about the topic, create a word web or cluster, or list and classify key words to explore.
- **Find details** about your topic from a variety of sources and make notes. Make personal observations, interview people, or look up information in books and magazines.
- **Organize your information** to best accomplish your purpose for writing. Use time order, spatial order, or order of importance.

2. DRAFTING

How do I actually begin to write the paper?

Take your writing materials and prewriting notes to a comfortable, well-lighted place. Plan on writing for at least twenty minutes. Try some of these strategies to get started.

- **Ignore** distractions like the telephone, and television.
- **Set a goal.** Decide how much that you *will* write now.
- **Review** your notes to find an idea for the first paragraph.
- **Start** with a direct, interesting sentence that states the main idea of the composition. Then let your ideas flow.
- **Push ahead** without worrying about perfect spelling, punctuation, or capitalization.

3. REVISING

How do I start revising?

Revising means to review what you've written and find ways to improve it. To begin, you might do the following:

- **Read your draft to yourself** to catch obvious errors such as unclear sentences.
- **Have a conference** with other students or your teacher.

What kinds of changes should I make?

You might do any or all of the following:

- **Add** words or ideas.
- **Take out** unnecessary words, sentences, or paragraphs.
- **Move** words, sentences, or paragraphs.
- **Substitute** words or ideas to improve your draft.

What kinds of questions should I ask myself?

The questions you'll ask depend on your purpose, audience, and type of writing. Here are some basic questions:

Ask yourself these questions!

- Did I say what I wanted to say?
- Are my details in the best possible order?
- Do I have a clear beginning, middle, and end?
- Does each paragraph have a topic sentence and stick to one idea?
- Can I take out extra words or choose better ones?
- Are all facts and figures correct?

4. PROOFREADING

Why should I proofread, and when and how should I do it?

Proofreading a paper means reading it carefully to find any mistakes in grammar, punctuation, and spelling. Proofread after you have completed revising your first draft to be sure that you have included all corrections. Proofread your final copy too.

Use proofreading symbols such as those at the right to clearly mark the corrections that are needed.

=	Make a capital.
/	Make a small letter.
∧	Add something.
ℓ	Take out something.
⊙	Add a period.
¶	New paragraph

What kinds of things should I look for when I proofread?

Use the following questions as a proofreading checklist:

- Do subjects and verbs agree?
- Is each sentence correctly punctuated?
- Have I avoided fragments and run-on sentences?
- Did I capitalize the first word of each sentence?
- Did I capitalize proper nouns and adjectives?
- Did I check spelling and meaning of unfamiliar words?
- Is my handwriting clear and easy to read?

Check for these possible errors!

5. PRESENTING

How should I present my final work?

Publishers have certain guidelines for writers. Teachers do too. The guidelines will vary depending on the assignment.

Here are some suggestions for **regular assignments.**

- Write neatly on the front side only of white lined paper. If you're typing your final copy on a computer, use plain white paper.
- Put your name, the class, and the date in the top right-hand corner of the first page.
- Center the title of your composition on the second line.
- Leave a one-inch margin on the sides of the paper and leave the last line blank.

Special ways to present writing include displaying it on a bulletin board, sharing it in a young author's conference, binding it in an illustrated book, publishing it in a newspaper, and reading it aloud.

Taking Writing Tests

Writing under pressure can be difficult. Improve your performance on writing tests by following these guidelines.

GENERAL GUIDELINES FOR WRITING TESTS

- **Listen carefully to test instructions.** Note how much time you have. Listen for whether to use pen or pencil.
- **Read the assignment and identify the key words.** Be certain that you are writing the correct type of answer. Look for key words like these and know what they mean.

Look for these key words!

Categorize or *Classify:* Sort ideas or facts into groups.
Compare or *Contrast:* Point out similarities (compare) or differences (contrast).
Defend: Give evidence to show why a view is right.
Define: Tell what something is or means.
Describe: Create a word picture with details and examples.
Discuss: State your ideas about what something means.
Evaluate: Give your opinion, with support, on whether an idea is good or bad, right or wrong.
Explain: Make something clear by giving reasons, examples, or steps.
Summarize: State main points, or retell important parts of a story or article.

- **Plan how you'll use your time.** Allow time for prewriting activities, actual writing, and revision.
- **Write a strong opening** to catch your reader's attention. It should address the topic directly.
- **Use specific facts, details, or incidents** to develop your topic.
- **Write an interesting conclusion** that sums up your ideas or brings your story to a satisfying end.

WRITING A PERSONAL NARRATIVE

When you write about something you did or something that happened to you, you are writing a personal narrative.

KEY WORDS IN ASSIGNMENTS

- "Tell **what happened** to you. . ."
- "Write about how you **felt** when. . ."
- "What did you **do** when. . ."

SAMPLE ASSIGNMENTS

- Write about an experience you had when you were a child. Tell what you did and how you felt about your experience.
- Write about something you have done that makes you feel proud of yourself. Be sure to tell where you were when it happened and why it made you feel proud.

A PLAN OF ATTACK

- For both assignments, choose an occasion to write about that will be interesting and entertaining for the reader. If your topic seems too broad, narrow it.
- Jot down the details describing the event you are writing about. Think of strong verbs and colorful adjectives and adverbs to use to relate your story.
- Organize your story in **time order.** Make notes on what happened at the beginning, middle, and end of your experience. Then, when you write, use your time-order notes and list of details as a guide.

FOLLOW-UP CHECKLIST

- Did you tell your story in time order, from beginning to end?
- Did you tell both what happened and how you felt about what happened?
- Did you leave your readers with a clear sense of what kind of person you are?
- Is all capitalization, punctuation, and spelling correct?

WRITING A DESCRIPTION

Descriptive writing allows a reader to experience a scene by appealing to the senses of sight, sound, smell, touch, and taste.

KEY WORDS IN ASSIGNMENTS

- "**Tell** what you **see** (or **hear, smell, feel, taste**). . ."
- "**Describe** what it **looks** (or **sounds, smells, feels, tastes**) **like**. . ."

SAMPLE ASSIGNMENTS

- Thanksgiving is an American holiday celebrated with a traditional dinner. Describe a Thanksgiving dinner.
- Many people wear uniforms for their jobs. Visualize yourself wearing a uniform for a job you might enjoy. Describe what you are wearing.

A PLAN OF ATTACK

- Know exactly what you must write about. In the first assignment describe the sights, sounds, smells, and tastes of a Thanksgiving dinner. In the second, tell only about the uniform, not the job itself.
- Jot down specific details that tell about the color, shape, feel, sounds, smells, and tastes. Think of colorful, precise words. What comparisons can you use?
- Choose an order to use to describe details. You might use **time order** for the first assignment, describing the first course through dessert. Many descriptions use **spatial order.** You might describe the uniform from top to bottom.

FOLLOW-UP CHECKLIST

- Does the topic sentence state what you're describing in an interesting way?
- Do all the details focus on your topic?
- Do you follow the order you've decided upon?
- Does your ending tie your description together?
- Is all capitalization, punctuation, and spelling correct?

WRITING INSTRUCTIONS

Instructions tell a reader how to do or make something. Good instructions are written in step-by-step order.

KEY WORDS IN ASSIGNMENTS

- "**Explain how to. . .** "
- "**Describe the steps** you would take to. . ."
- "**Tell how you would**. . ."

SAMPLE ASSIGNMENTS

- Mmmm good! Explain how to make the best-ever ice cream sundae.
- Recycle it! Describe the steps you would take to make a book cover from a brown paper grocery bag.

A PLAN OF ATTACK

- Before you write, list the materials needed and the steps in the process.
- Organize the steps in time order, beginning with the first step and ending with the last.
- When you write, use time-order words like *first, next, then,* and *last* to show the correct order of steps.

FOLLOW-UP CHECKLIST

- Does the topic sentence state what the reader will learn to make or do?
- Are the steps arranged in correct order, and are all the steps there?
- Have you stuck to the topic—or have you put in extra information that you ought to get rid of?
- Are time-order words used to help the reader understand the order of the steps?
- Is all capitalization, punctuation, and spelling correct?

WRITING A FABLE

A fable is a very short story. The characters are usually animals, and the story states a moral, or lesson.

KEY WORDS IN ASSIGNMENTS

- "Write a modern **fable**. . ."
- "Choose a **moral,** or **lesson,** to **illustrate**. . ."

SAMPLE ASSIGNMENTS

- Choose a moral from this list. Then write a modern fable to illustrate it.

  Think how you will get out before you get in.
  Better safe than sorry.
  One good turn deserves another.
- We sometimes think of animals as having human traits—the fox as sly, the owl as wise, and so on. Choose several animals. What morals or lessons might they teach by their actions? Write an original fable that features one or more of these animals.

A PLAN OF ATTACK

- For either assignment, think carefully until you choose or decide upon the moral you will develop into a fable. Visualize animal characters that will teach the lesson well.
- Develop the plot of the fable. List what happens in the beginning, the middle, and the end. Organize the details of the plot in time order.
- Jot down possible dialogue that the animals might use to develop the story and to show character traits.
- End your fable with your moral.

FOLLOW-UP CHECKLIST

- Have you told your story in time order, with a beginning, a middle, and an ending?
- Are the animal characters well-chosen to teach the lesson you've chosen to illustrate?
- Does your fable really teach the moral that ends it?
- Is all capitalization, punctuation, and spelling correct?

WRITING COMPARISON/CONTRAST

Comparison tells a reader how two or more people or things are alike. Contrast tells how two or more things are different from each other.

KEY WORDS IN ASSIGNMENTS

- "**Compare** (or **contrast**) these two things (or people, places, ideas, and so on)."
- "Describe the **similarities** (or **differences**) between. . ."
- "How are . . . **alike?** How are . . .**different?**"

SAMPLE ASSIGNMENTS

- Like mother, like daughter. Like father, like son. Write a paragraph explaining how you and one of your family members are alike.
- What's that you're reading? Contrast the differences between reading for pleasure and reading a textbook.

A PLAN OF ATTACK

- Know the purpose of your paragraph. In the first assignment, you will tell about likenesses. In the second, you will tell about differences.
- List the likenesses or differences. Think of vivid, descriptive words to use for the comparison or contrast.
- Decide what order you will use to describe details. You may want to use **order of importance**—from the most important likeness or difference to the least important. If you are making a physical comparison or contrast, you may want to use **spatial order**—from head to toe, for example.

FOLLOW-UP CHECKLIST

- Does the topic sentence state what things are being compared or contrasted?
- Are the points of comparison or contrast arranged in the order you planned?
- Are words like *same* and *different* used to signal comparisons and contrasts?
- Is all capitalization, punctuation, and spelling correct?

WRITING A PERSUASIVE PARAGRAPH

When you write a persuasive paragraph, your goal is to make the reader agree with your opinion. To do this, you must support your opinion with good reasons.

KEY WORDS IN ASSIGNMENTS

- "**Persuade** your parents. . ."
- "Write a paragraph to **convince** your principal. . ."

SAMPLE ASSIGNMENTS

- You have been eyeing the iguana in the pet store for months, and you are sure it would be a perfect pet. Write a paragraph for your parents to persuade them to let you buy it.
- Your home town's baseball team is playing in a championship game in a nearby town. Convince your teacher to allow your class to watch the championship game, which will be played on a school day.

A PLAN OF ATTACK

- Clearly state the opinion you intend to support.
- List at least three good reasons to support your opinion.
- Organize your reasons in **order of importance.** Usually writers save their strongest reason for last.
- Jot down convincing words to use to persuade your reader.

FOLLOW-UP CHECKLIST

- Does the topic sentence clearly state your opinion?
- Are the supporting reasons organized from least important to most important?
- Are the reasons logical and sensible?
- Does the conclusion summarize the opinion and reasons?
- Is all capitalization, punctuation, and spelling correct?

Models and Guidelines

FRIENDLY LETTER FORM

Study the five parts of the friendly letter below. Notice the capitalization and punctuation in the greeting and the closing. If you know the person you are writing well, omit your address from the heading, but include the date.

> 21 Juneway Terrace
> Glenview, IL 60025
> February 13, 19—
>
> Dear Julie,
>
> Thanks for inviting me to your Mardi Gras party! I'm really upset that I can't be there. We're going to be out of town that weekend. Take pictures so I can see all the costumes. Maybe we can get together over summer vacation.
>
> Your friend,
>
> Lizzie

Heading

Greeting

Body

Closing

Signature

State abbreviations:

AL (Alabama)	**LA** (Louisiana)	**OH** (Ohio)
AK (Alaska)	**ME** (Maine)	**OK** (Oklahoma)
AZ (Arizona)	**MD** (Maryland)	**OR** (Oregon)
AR (Arkansas)	**MA** (Massachusetts)	**PA** (Pennsylvania)
CA (California)	**MI** (Michigan)	**RI** (Rhode Island)
CO (Colorado)	**MN** (Minnesota)	**SC** (South Carolina)
CT (Connecticut)	**MS** (Mississippi)	**SD** (South Dakota)
DE (Delaware)	**MO** (Missouri)	**TN** (Tennessee)
FL (Florida)	**MT** (Montana)	**TX** (Texas)
GA (Georgia)	**NE** (Nebraska)	**UT** (Utah)
HI (Hawaii)	**NV** (Nevada)	**VT** (Vermont)
ID (Idaho)	**NH** (New Hampshire)	**VA** (Virginia)
IL (Illinois)	**NJ** (New Jersey)	**WA** (Washington)
IN (Indiana)	**NM** (New Mexico)	**WV** (West Virginia)
IA (Iowa)	**NY** (New York)	**WI** (Wisconsin)
KS (Kansas)	**NC** (North Carolina)	**WY** (Wyoming)
KY (Kentucky)	**ND** (North Dakota)	

CAPITALIZATION

Besides letter parts, capitalize the following:

Names, initials, and titles used with names:

Dr. Martin S. Alvarez, Jr.   Lieutenant Ann Jones

Proper adjectives:

Midwestern values   Canadian bacon   African art

The pronoun *I*:

Laura and I will interview the principal.

Names of cities, states, countries, continents:

Glenview   Utah   Mexico   Australia

Names of lakes, rivers, mountains, structures:

Fish Lake   Po River   Ural Mountain   Navy Pier

Names of streets and street abbreviations:

Fir Street   Locust Ave.   Crown Rd.   East Spruce

Days, months, holidays, special events:

Monday   Wed.   June   Dec.
Labor Day   Olympics

First, last, and all important words in movie, book, story, play, and TV show titles:

Tom Sawyer   The Cat in the Hat   "The Gold Bug"

First word in a sentence:

We'll try harder.

First word inside quotation marks:

Marcus said, "He's allergic to cats."

PUNCTUATION

Use **periods**

- to end declarative and imperative sentences:

Susan likes sunflowers.   Please listen carefully.

- after most **abbreviations**:

Ms.   Jan.   Sat.   Jr.   Ave.   P.M.   Dr.

Use **exclamation marks**

- after sentences that show strong feeling:

    We won the championship!

Use **question marks**

- after interrogative sentences:

    Where are the stamps?

Use **commas**

- between the day and the year in a date:

    April 15, 1994

- between the name of a city and state:

    Mendocino, California

- between series of words in a sentence:

    Mr. Lee grows tomatoes, peppers, and beans.

- before the word that joins a compound sentence:

    The sun is out, and the air is warm.

- to separate a noun after a direct address:

    Mom, where's my key?   It's on the desk, Amy.

- before quotation marks or inside the end quotation marks:

    Bob said, "I like soup."   "I prefer salads," said Zoe.

Use **quotation marks**

- around the exact words someone used when speaking:

    Vera asked, "What time is it?"

- around titles of stories, poems, and songs:

    "The Cat's in the Cradle"   "The Pit and the Pendulum"

Underline titles of books and movies:

    Anne of Green Gables   Aladdin

Use **apostrophes**

- to form the possessive of a noun:

    nurse's   brothers'   men's

- in contractions in place of dropped letters:

    wasn't (was not)   don't (do not)   I'm (I am)

Use **colons** between hours and minutes to indicate time:

    2:20   4:45

Spelling Dictionary

Parts of a Dictionary Entry

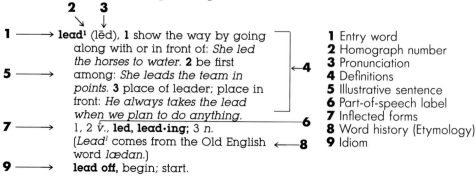

2 **3**

1 ⟶ **lead¹** (lēd), **1** show the way by going along with or in front of: *She led the horses to water.* **2** be first among: *She leads the team in points.* **3** place of leader; place in front: *He always takes the lead when we plan to do anything.*

5 ⟶

7 ⟶ 1, 2 *v.*, **led, lead·ing**; 3 *n.* (*Lead¹* comes from the Old English word *lædan.*)

9 ⟶ **lead off,** begin; start.

1 Entry word
2 Homograph number
3 Pronunciation
4 Definitions
5 Illustrative sentence
6 Part-of-speech label
7 Inflected forms
8 Word history (Etymology)
9 Idiom

Full Pronunciation Key

a	hat, cap	**i**	it, pin	**p**	paper, cup	**v**	very, save
ā	age, face	**ī**	ice, five	**r**	run, try	**w**	will, woman
ä	father, far			**s**	say, yes	**y**	young, yet
âr	care, hair	**j**	jam, enjoy	**sh**	she, rush	**z**	zero, breeze
		k	kind, seek	**t**	tell, it	**zh**	measure, seizure
b	bad, rob	**l**	land, coal	**th**	thin, both		
ch	child, much	**m**	me, am	**ŦH**	then, smooth		
d	did, red	**n**	no, in			**ə**	represents:
		ng	long, bring	**u**	cup, butter		a in about
e	let, best			**ů**	full, put		e in taken
ē	equal, be	**o**	hot, rock	**ü**	rule, move		i in pencil
ėr	term, learn	**ō**	open, go				o in lemon
		ȯ	all, saw				u in circus
f	fat, if	**ô**	order, store				
g	go, bag	**oi**	oil, voice				
h	he, how	**ou**	house, out				

The contents of the dictionary entries in this book have been adapted from the *Scott, Foresman Intermediate Dictionary,* Copyright © 1993, 1988, 1979, 1974 by Scott, Foresman and Company or from the *Scott, Foresman Advanced Dictionary,* Copyright © 1993, 1988, 1983, 1979 by Scott, Foresman and Company.

Spellings of English Sounds*

Symbol	Spellings
a	at, plaid, half, laugh
ā	able, aid, say, age, eight, they, break, vein, gauge, crepe, beret
ä	father, ah, calm, heart, bazaar, yacht, sergeant
âr	dare, aerial, fair, prayer, where, pear, their, they're
b	bad, rabbit
ch	child, watch, future, question
d	did, add, filled
e	end, said, any, bread, says, heifer, leopard, friend, bury
ē	equal, eat, eel, happy, cities, vehicle, ceiling, receive, key, these, believe, machine, liter, people
ėr	stern, earth, urge, first, word, journey
f	fat, effort, laugh, phrase
g	go, egg, guest, ghost, league
gz	example, exhaust
h	he, who, jai alai, Gila monster
hw	wheat
i	it, England, ear, hymn, been, sieve, women, busy, build, weird
ī	I, ice, lie, sky, type, rye, eye, island, high, eider, aisle, height, buy, coyote
j	jam, gem, exaggerate, schedule, badger, bridge, soldier, large, allegiance
k	coat, kind, back, echo, ache, quit, account, antique, excite, acquire
l	land, tell
m	me, common, climb, solemn, palm
n	no, manner, knife, gnaw, pneumonia

Symbol	Spellings
ng	long, ink, handkerchief, tongue
o	odd, honest
ō	open, oak, toe, own, home, oh, folk, though, bureau, sew, brooch, soul
ȯ	all, author, awful, broad, bought, walk, taught, cough, Utah, Arkansas
ô	order, board, floor, tore
oi	oil, boy
ou	out, owl, bough, hour
p	pay, happy
r	run, carry, wrong, rhythm
s	say, miss, cent, scent, dance, tense, sword, pizza, listen
sh	she, machine, sure, ocean, special, tension, mission, nation
t	tell, button, two, Thomas, stopped, doubt, receipt, pizza
th	thin
ŦH	then, breathe
u	up, oven, trouble, does, flood
u̇	full, good, wolf, should
ü	food, junior, rule, blue, who, move, threw, soup, through, shoe, two, fruit, lieutenant
v	very, have, of, Stephen
w	will, quick
y	yes, opinion
yü	use, few, cue, view, vacuum
z	zero, has, buzz, scissors, xylophone
zh	measure, garage, division
ə	alone, complete, moment, authority, bargain, April, cautious, circus, pageant, physician, oxygen, dungeon, tortoise

*Not all English spellings of these sounds are included in this list.

A

a·bil·i·ty (ə bil′ə tē), **1** power to do some special thing; skill: *He has great ability in making jewelry.* **2** special natural gift; talent: *Musical ability often shows itself early in life. n., pl.* **a·bil·i·ties.**

a·ble (ā′bəl), having enough power, skill, or means to do something; capable: *A cat is able to see in the dark. adj.*

ac·ci·dent (ak′sə dent), something harmful or unlucky that happens: *automobile accidents. n., pl.* **ac·ci·dents.**

ac·com·plish·ment (ə kom′plish ment), something that has been done with knowledge, skill, or ability; achievement: *The teachers were proud of their pupils' accomplishments. n., pl.* **ac·com·plish·ments.**

ac·tion (ak′shən), process of acting; doing something: *The quick action of the firemen saved the building from being burned down. n.*

a·do·be (ə dō′bē), **1** brick made of sun-dried clay. **2** building made of sun-dried clay. **3** built or made of adobe. 1,2 *n.,* 3 *adj.* (*Adobe* was borrowed from Spanish *adobe,* which came from Arabic *at-tūb,* meaning ''the brick.'')

ad·van·tage (ad van′tij), anything that is in one's favor, or is a benefit; a help in getting something desired: *Good health is always a great advantage. n.*

a·gain (ə gen′), another time; once more: *Come again to play. Say that again. adv.*

air mass (âr mas), a large amount of air with the same temperature and humidity.

aisle (īl), passage between rows of seats in a hall, theater, school, etc.: *The teacher walked down the aisle between the rows of desks. n.*

a·lign (ə līn′), bring into line; arrange in a straight line: *The mechanic aligned the front wheels of our car. v.*

al·ley (al′ē), a narrow back street in a city or town. *n., pl.* **al·leys.**

adobe (definition 3)
an **adobe** village

almond blossom
The **almond blossom** is the national flower of Israel.

al·low·ance (ə lou′əns), a sum of money given or set aside for expenses: *a household allowance for groceries of $50 a week. My weekly allowance is $1. n.*

al·mond blos·som (ä′mend *or* am′ənd blos′əm), flower, especially of a plant that produces a peachlike fruit from a tree growing in Israel. *n.*

al·most (ȯl′mōst), very near to; all but; nearly: *It is almost ten o'clock. I almost missed the train. adv.*

a lot (ə lot), **1** a great deal; much: *I feel a lot better.* **2** often, a great many; a great deal: *a lot of books.*

al·pha·bet (al′fə bet), the letters of a language arranged in their usual order, not as they are in words. *n.* (*Alphabet* can be traced back to the names of the first two letters of the Greek alphabet: *alpha* A and *beta* B.)

al·ways (ȯl′wiz *or* ȯl′wəz), at all times; every time: *Night always follows day. adv.*

a·mus·ing (ə myü′zing), causing laughter or smiles: *an amusing joke. adj.*

an·a·con·da (an′ə kon′də), a very large South American snake related to the boa that crushes its prey in its coils. Anacondas live in tropical forests and rivers and are the longest snakes in America, sometimes over 30 feet (9 meters). *n., pl.* **an·a·con·das.**

an·gel (ān′jel), **1** messenger from God. **2** person as good or as lovely as an angel. **3** a replica used as a statue on a tree. *n.*

an·gle (ang′gəl), **1** the space between two lines or surfaces that meet. **2** the figure formed by two such lines or surfaces. *n.*

an·gry (ang′grē), feeling or showing anger: *I was angrier when you disobeyed me again. adj.,* **an·gri·er, an·gri·est.**

an·i·mal (an′ə məl), any living thing that is not a plant. Most animals can move about, feed upon other animals or plants, and have a nervous system. A dog, a bird, a fish, a snake, a fly, and a worm are animals. *n., pl.* **an·i·mals.**

an·nounce (ə nouns′), give public or formal notice of: *The teacher announced that there would be no school tomorrow. v.*, **an·nounced, an·nounc·ing.**

an·nounce·ment (ə nouns′mənt), what is announced or made known: *The principal made two announcements. The announcement was published in the newspapers. n.*

an·oth·er (ə nuᴛʜ′ər), **1** one more: *Have another glass of milk (adj.). I ate a candy bar and then asked for another (pron.).* **2** a different: *Show me another hat.* 1,2 *adj.*, 1 *pron.*

an·ten·na (an ten′ə), one of the long, slender feelers on the head of an insect, scorpion, lobster, etc. *The antennas of the grasshopper can be long or short. n., pl.* **an·ten·nae** (an ten′ē) or **an·ten·nas.**

an·y·way (en′ē wā), in any case; at least: *I am coming anyway, no matter what you say. adv.*

an·y·where (en′ē hwer), in, at, or to any place: *I'll meet you anywhere you say. adv.*

a·pol·o·gize (ə pol′ə jīz), make an apology; say one is sorry; offer an excuse: *I apologized for being late. v.* **a·pol·o·gized, a·pol·o·giz·ing.**

a·pos·tro·phe (ə pos′trə fē), sign (') used: **1** to show the omission of one or more letters in contractions. **2** to show the possessive forms of nouns or indefinite pronouns. **3** to form plurals of letters and numbers. *n.*

ap·pear·ance (ə pir′əns), outward look: *a pleasing appearance. n.*

ap·point·ment (ə point′mənt), meeting with someone at a certain time and place; engagement: *an appointment to see the doctor at four o'clock. n.*

ap·pre·ci·ate (ə prē′shē āt), think highly of; recognize the worth or quality of; value; enjoy: *Almost everyone appreciates good food. v.* **ap·pre·ci·at·ed, ap·pre·ci·at·ing.**

A·pril (ā′prəl), the fourth month of the year. It has 30 days. *n.*

are (är; *unstressed* ər), form of the verb **be** used with *we, you,* and *they* and any plural noun to indicate the present tense. *We are ready. You are next. They are waiting. v.*

ar·e·a (âr′ē ə), amount of surface; extent of surface: *The area of this floor is 600 square feet. n., pl.* **ar·e·as.**

ar·gue (är′gyü), discuss with someone who disagrees: *He argued with his sister about who should wash the dishes. v.* **ar·gued, ar·gu·ing.**

ar·rive (ə riv′), come to; reach: *You should arrive at school before nine o'clock. v.* **ar·rived, ar·riv·ing.**

ar·thri·tis (är thrī′tis), inflammation of a joint or joints of the body. *n.*

ar·ti·cle (är′tə kəl), a written composition on a special subject, complete in itself, but forming part of a magazine, newspaper, or book: *This newspaper has a good article on gardening. n., pl.* **ar·ti·cles.**

art·ist (är′tist), person who is skilled in any of the fine arts, such as sculpture, music, or literature. *n.*

ash·es (ash′iz), what remains of a thing after it has thoroughly burned: *Ashes have to be removed from the fireplace to make room for more wood. n. pl.*

ask (ask), try to find out by words; inquire: *Why don't you ask? She asked about our health. Ask the way. v.*

antenna
Snails have slender
antennae.

							ə stands for	
a	hat	**ī**	ice	**u̇**	put		**ə**	in about
ā	age	**o**	not	**ü**	rule		**a**	in taken
ä	far, calm	**ō**	open	**ch**	child		**e**	in taken
âr	care	**ȯ**	saw	**ng**	long		**i**	in pencil
e	let	**ô**	order	**sh**	she		**o**	in lemon
ē	equal	**oi**	oil	**th**	thin		**u**	in circus
ėr	term	**ou**	out	**ᴛʜ**	then			
i	it	**u**	cup	**zh**	measure			

astronaut

An **astronaut** is trained to travel in space.

barometer

A **barometer** predicts changes in weather.

as·sign (ə sīn′), **1** appoint (to a post or duty): *We were assigned to decorate the room for the party.* **2** name definitely; fix; set: *The judge assigned a day for the trial.* *v.*

as·sign·ment (ə sīn′mənt), something assigned, especially a piece of work to be done: *Today's assignment in arithmetic consists of ten examples. n., pl.* **as·sign·ments.**

as·tro·naut (as′trə nȯt), pilot or member of the crew of a spacecraft. *n.*

At·lan·tic O·cean (at lan′tik ō′shən), ocean east of North and South America, west of Europe and Africa.

at·tack (ə tak′), **1** use force or weapons against; set upon to hurt; begin fighting: *The dog attacked the cat. The enemy attacked at dawn.* **2** act harmfully on: *Locusts attacked the crops. v.*

Au·gust (ȯ′gəst), the eighth month of the year. It has 31 days. *n.*

aunt (ant), **1** sister of one's father or mother. **2** wife of one's uncle. *My aunt's name is Sarah. n.*

au·to·graph (ȯ′tə graf), **1** a person's signature: *Many people collect the autographs of celebrities.* **2** write one's name in or on: *The movie star autographed my program.* **1** *n.,* **2** *v.*

Ave. or **ave.,** Avenue; avenue.

a·while (ə hwīl′), for a short time: *Stay awhile. adv.*

B

ba·by (bā′bē), **1** child too young to walk or speak; infant: *The babies' mothers took them to the park.* **2** the youngest of a family or group. *n., pl.* **ba·bies.**

back·board (bak′bôrd′), (in basketball) the upright, rectangular surface of wood, glass, or plastic, to which the basket is fastened. *n.*

back·pack (bak′pak′), a pack, often supported by a frame, that is worn on the back by hikers and campers to carry food, clothes, and equipment. *n.*

back·stroke (bak′strōk′), a swimming stroke made by a swimmer lying on his back. *n.*

ba·con (bā′kən), salted and smoked meat from the back and sides of a hog. *n.*
bring home the bacon, succeed; win; earn a living.

band (band), group of musicians performing together, especially on wind and percussion instruments: *The school band played several marches. n.*

bare·foot (bâr′fùt′ or bar′fùt), without shoes and stockings on: *A barefoot child played in the puddles (adj.). If you go barefoot, watch out for broken glass (adv.). adj., adv.*

ba·rom·e·ter (bə rom′ə tər), instrument for measuring the pressure of air, used in determining height above sea level and in predicting probable changes in the weather. *n.*

bar·rel (bar′əl), container with a round, flat top and bottom and sides that curve out slightly. Barrels are usually made of boards held together by hoops. *n.*

base·ball (bās′bȯl′), **1** game played with bat and ball by two teams of nine players each, on a field with four bases. A player who touches all the bases, under the rules, scores a run. **2** ball used in this game. *n.*

bas·ket·ball (bas′kit bȯl′), **1** game played with a large, round ball by two teams of five players each. The players try to toss the ball through a ring into a net shaped like a basket but open at the bottom. **2** ball used in this game. *n.*

beach (bēch), an almost flat shore of sand or pebbles over which water washes when high. *n., pl.* **beach·es.**

beat (bēt), **1** stroke or blow made again and again: *the beat of a drum.* **2** get the better of; defeat; overcome: *Their team beat ours by a huge score.* **3** mix by stirring rapidly with a fork, spoon, or other utensil: *I helped make the cake by beating the eggs.* 1 *n.*, 2,3 *v.*, **beat, beat·en** or **beat, beat·ing.**

beau·ti·ful (byü/tə fəl), very pleasing to see or hear; delighting the mind or senses. *adj.*

be·cause (bi kòz/), for the reason that; since: *Because we were late, we ran the whole way home. conj.*

beet (bēt), the thick, fleshy root of a garden plant. Red beets and their green leaves are eaten as vegetables. Sugar is made from white beets. *n.*

be·gin (bi gin/), do the first part; make a start: *begin on one's work. When shall we begin? Begin at the third chapter. v.*, **be·gan, be·gun, be·gin·ning.**

be·go·nia (bi gō/nyə), a tropical plant often grown for its large, richly colored leaves and waxy flowers. *n., pl.* **be·go·nias.** (*The begonia* was named after Michel *Bégon*, 1638-1710, a French patron of botany.)

be·hav·ior (bi hā/vyər), manner of behaving; way of acting: *Her sullen behavior showed that she was angry. n.*

be·hind (bi hīnd/), **1** not on time; late: *The class is behind in its work.* **2** farther back: *The rest of the bikers are still behind. adv.*

be·lieve (bi lēv/), **1** think (somebody) tells the truth: *Her friends believe her.* **2** think; suppose: *I believe I will go. v.*

bev·y (bev/ē), a small group or flock: *a bevy of quail. n., pl.* **bev·ies.**

bib (bib), cloth worn under the chin, especially by babies and small children, to protect clothing during meals. *n.*

bi·cus·pid (bī kus/pid), a double-pointed tooth that tears and grinds food. Adult human beings have eight bicuspids. *n.*

bi·cy·cle (bī/sik/əl), a lightweight vehicle with two wheels, one behind the other, that support a metal frame on which there is a seat. The rider pushes two pedals and steers with handlebars. *n.*

big (big), great in amount or size; large: *a big room, a big book. Making automobiles is a big business. An elephant is a big animal. adj.* **big·ger, big·gest.**

blan·ket (blang/kit), a soft, heavy covering woven from wool, cotton, nylon, or other material, used to keep people or animals warm. *n.*

bleach·ers (blē/chərz), section of wooden or plastic benches for spectators at baseball or other outdoor events. Bleachers are not roofed, and are the lowest priced seats. *n., pl.*

bliss·ful (blis/fəl), very happy; joyful: *blissful memories of a summer vacation. adj.*

block (blok), space in a city or town enclosed by four streets; square. *n.*

bloom·ers (blü/mərz), loose trousers, gathered at the knee, formerly worn by women and girls for physical training: *In the old days girls wore bloomers when playing sports. n. pl.* (*Bloomers* were named for Amelia J. *Bloomer*, 1818-1894, an American magazine publisher who popularized their use.)

blub·ber (blub/ər), fat of whales and some other sea animals. The oil obtained from whale blubber was formerly burned in lamps. *n.*

bicycle
riding **bicycles** in the park

a	hat	**ī**	ice	**u̇**	put	**ə** stands for	
ā	age	**o**	not	**ü**	rule	**a**	in about
ä	far, calm	**ō**	open	**ch**	child	**e**	in taken
âr	care	**ȯ**	saw	**ng**	long	**i**	in pencil
e	let	**ô**	order	**sh**	she	**o**	in lemon
ē	equal	**oi**	oil	**th**	thin	**u**	in circus
ėr	term	**ou**	out	**ᴛʜ**	then		
i	it	**u**	cup	**zh**	measure		

bridge

a **bridge** over the bay

broccoli

two stalks of **broccoli**

Blvd., boulevard.

bo·lo·gna (bə lō′nē *or* bə lō′nə), a large sausage usually made of beef, veal, and pork. *n., pl.* **bo·lo·gnas.** (*Bologna* was named for *Bologna,* Italy, where it was first made.)

boom (büm), a deep hollow sound like the roar of cannon or of big waves: *The big bell tolled with a loud boom. n.*

bor·row (bor′ō), get (something) from another person with the understanding that it must be returned: *I borrowed his book and promised to return it in a week. v.*

boss (bȯs), person who hires workers or watches over or directs them; foreman; manager: *It was the boss's decision to hire the new construction worker. n., pl.* **boss·es.**

bot·tle (bot′l), container for holding liquids, made of glass, plastic, etc. Bottles often have narrow necks fitted with caps or stoppers: *drink a bottle of milk. n.*

bow¹ (bou), **1** to stoop; bend: *The old man was bowed by age.* **2** submit; yield: *She bowed to her parents' wishes. v.*
bow out, withdraw.
take a bow, accept praise or applause for something done.

bow² (bō), **1** weapon for shooting arrows. A bow usually consists of a strip of flexible wood bent by a string. **2** a slender rod with horsehairs stretched on it, for playing a violin, cello, etc. *n.*

bow³ (bou), the forward part of a ship, boat, or aircraft. *n.*

boy (boi), a male child from birth to about eighteen: *I forgot the boy's name. n.*

brain·storm (brān′stôrm′), INFORMAL. a sudden idea or inspiration. *n.*

brake (brāk), **1** anything used to slow or stop the motion of a wheel or vehicle by pressing or scraping or by rubbing against. **2** slow or stop by using a brake: *The driver braked the speeding car and it slid to a stop.* 1 *n.,* 2 *v.*

break (brāk), **1** come apart or make come apart; smash: *The plate broke into pieces when it fell on the floor.* **2** fail to keep; act against: *to break a promise. People who break the law are punished. v.,* **broke, bro·ken, break·ing.**

breathe (brēᴛʜ), stop for breath; rest; allow to rest and breathe. *v.,* **breathed, breath·ing.**

breath·less (breth′lis), out of breath: *Running upstairs very fast made me breathless. adj.*

bridge (brij), something built over a river, road, railroad, or other obstacle, so that people, cars, trains, etc., can get across. *n.*

bright (brīt), lively or cheerful: *There was a bright smile on his face. adj.* —**bright′ly,** *adv.* —**bright′ness,** *n.*

bring (bring), come with or carry (a thing or person) from another place; take along to a place or person: *The bus brought us home. Bring me a clean plate. v.,* **brought, bring·ing.**

broad·leaf (brȯd′lēf), a type of tree with broad, flat leaves. An oak is a broadleaf tree. *adj.*

broc·co·li (brok′ə lē), vegetable with green branching stems and flower heads. It belongs to the cabbage family. *n. pl.* **broc·co·li.** (*Broccoli* comes from Italian *broccoli,* meaning "sprouts.")

broke (brōk), See **break.** *I broke my watch. v.*

bro·ken (brō′kən), separated into parts by a break; in pieces: *a broken leg, a broken cup. adj.*

brook (brůk), a small stream; creek. *n.*

broth·er (bruᴛʜ′ər), son of the same parents. A boy is a brother to the other children of his parents. *I knocked on my brother's door. n.*

brought (brȯt), See **bring.** *I brought my lunch yesterday. They were brought to school in a bus. v.*

bruise (brüz), injury to the body, caused by a fall or a blow, that breaks blood vessels without breaking the skin: *The bruise on my arm turned black and blue. n.*

bub·ble (bub′əl), **1** a thin, round film of liquid enclosing air or gas. The surface of boiling water is covered with bubbles. **2** plan or idea that looks good, but soon falls apart. *n.*

buf·fa·lo (buf′ə lō), the bison of North America. *n., pl.* **buf·fa·loes, buf·fa·los,** or **buf·fa·lo.**

build (bild), make by putting materials together; construct: *People build houses, bridges, and machines. Birds build nests. v.,* **built, build·ing.**

bunch (bunch), group of things of the same kind growing, fastened, placed, or thought of together: *a bunch of grapes, a bunch of flowers, a bunch of sheep. n., pl.* **bunch·es.**

bush (bush), a woody plant smaller than a tree, often with many separate branches starting from or near the ground. *n., pl.* **bush·es.**

bus·y (biz′ē), having plenty to do; working; active; not idle: *a busy person. adj.,* **bus·i·er, bus·i·est.**

busi·ness (biz′nis), thing that one is busy at; work; occupation: *A carpenter's business is building. n.*

butch·er (buch′ər), person who cuts up and sells meat. *n.*

but·ter·fly (but′ər flī′), **1** an insect with a slender body and two pairs of large, often brightly colored, overlapping wings. **2** a swimming stroke, a type of breast stroke, in which both arms are pulled upward out of the water and forward while the feet are kicking up and down. *n., pl.* **but·ter·flies.**

but·ton (but′n), **1** a round, flat piece of metal, bone, glass, or plastic, fastened on garments to hold them closed or to decorate them. **2** fasten the buttons of; close with buttons: *Button your coat.* 1 *n.,* 2 *v.*

by-line (bī′līn′), line at the beginning of a newspaper or magazine article giving the name of the writer. *n.*

C

cab·i·net (kab′ə nit), piece of furniture with shelves or drawers, used to hold articles for use or display: *a medicine cabinet, a filing cabinet for letters. We keep our very best dishes in the china cabinet. n.*

ca·ble (kā′bəl), an insulated bundle of wires which carries an electric current. *n.*

cac·tus (kak′təs), plant with a thick, fleshy stem that usually has spines but no leaves. Most cactuses grow in very hot, dry regions of America and often have brightly colored flowers. *n., pl.* **cac·tus·es, cac·ti** (kak′tī).

caf·e·ter·i·a (kaf′ə tir′ē ə), restaurant where people serve themselves. *n., pl.* **caf·e·ter·i·as.**

cam·er·a (kam′ər ə), machine for taking photographs or motion pictures. A camera lens focuses light rays through the dark inside part of the camera onto film which is sensitive to light. *n.*

Can·a·da (kan′ə də), country in the N part of North America, consisting of ten provinces and two territories and extending from the Atlantic to the Pacific. *Capital:* Ottawa. *n.*

ca·nal (kə nal′), waterway dug across land for ships or small boats to go through or to carry water to places that need it. *n.*

ca·noe (kə nü′), **1** a light boat pointed at both ends and moved with a paddle. **2** paddle a canoe; go in a canoe. 1 *n.,* 2 *v.,* **ca·noed, ca·noe·ing.**

butterfly (definition 1)
three colorful
butterflies

α	hat	ī	ice	u̇	put	ə *stands for*	
ā	age	o	not	ü	rule	α	in about
ä	far, calm	ō	open	ch	child	e	in taken
âr	care	ȯ	saw	ng	long	i	in pencil
e	let	ô	order	sh	she	o	in lemon
ē	equal	oi	oil	th	thin	u	in circus
ėr	term	ou	out	ŦH	then		
i	it	u	cup	zh	measure		

catcher

a **catcher** kneeling behind home plate

ca·pac·i·ty (kə pas′ə tē), amount of room or space inside; largest amount that can be held by a container. *n., pl.* **ca·pac·i·ties.**

care (kãr), **1** a troubled state of mind because of fear of what may happen; worry: *Few people are completely free from care.* **2** be concerned; feel interest: 1 *n.,* 2 *v.,* **cared, car·ing.**
take care of, watch over; be careful with: *Take care of your money.*

care·ful (kãr′fəl), showing care; done with thought or effort; exact; thorough: *Arithmetic requires careful work. adj.* —**care′ful·ly,** *adv.*

care·less (kãr′lis), not thinking what one says; not watching what one does; not careful: *I was careless and broke the cup. adj.*

car·i·bou (kãr′ə bü), the North American reindeer. *n., pl.* **car·i·bous** or **car·i·bou.**

car·ni·vore (kär′nə vôr), any animal that feeds chiefly on flesh. Carnivores have large, strong teeth with sharp cutting edges. *n.*

cash (kash) money in the form of coins and bills. *n.*

cat (kat), a small, furry, flesh-eating mammal, often kept as a pet or for catching mice and rats: *The cat meowed for food. n.*

catch (kach), **1** grab or seize (something in flight): *Catch the ball with both hands.* **2** come upon suddenly; surprise; *Mother caught me just as I was hiding her birthday present. v.,* **caught, catch·ing.**

catch·er (kach′ər), a baseball player positioned behind the batter to catch the ball thrown by the pitcher. *n.*

ca·the·dral (kə thē′drəl), a large or important church. *n.*

cat·tle·ya or·chid (kat′lē ə ôr′kəd), a tropical South American plant with showy flowers. (The *cattleya orchid* was named for William *Cattley,* died 1832, English patron of botany.)

cattleya orchid

The **cattleya orchid** is the national flower of Costa Rica.

caught (kót), See **catch.** *I caught the ball. v.*

cause (kóz), **1** person, thing, or event that makes something happen: *The flood was the cause of much damage.* **2** make happen; make do; bring about: *The fire caused much damage.* 1 *n.,* 2 *v.,* **caused, caus·ing.**

cel·e·brat·ed (sel′ə brā′tid), much talked about; famous; well-known: *a celebrated author. adj.*

cel·er·y (sel′ər ē), vegetable related to parsley, with long, crisp stalks. Celery is eaten either raw or cooked. *n.*

Cel·si·us (sel′sē əs), of, based on, or according to the Celsius scale; centigrade. *adj.* (The *Celsius* scale was named for Anders *Celsius,* 1701-1744, a Swedish astronomer who invented it in 1742.)

ce·ment (sə ment′), a fine, gray powder made by burning clay and limestone. Cement is used to make concrete and mortar. *n.*

cer·e·mo·ny (sâr′ə mō′nē), a special act or set of acts to be done on special occasions such as weddings, funerals, graduations, or holidays: *The graduation ceremony was held in the gymnasium. n., pl.* **cer·e·mo·nies.**

cer·tain (sėrt′n) without a doubt; sure: *It is certain that 2 and 3 do not make 6. I am certain that these are the facts. adj.*

chalk·board (chók′bôrd), a smooth, hard surface, used for writing or drawing on with crayon or chalk. *n.*

cham·pi·on (cham′pē ən), person, animal, or thing that wins first place in a game or contest: *He is the swimming champion of our school. n.*

change (chānj), **1** make or become different: *She changed the room by painting the walls green. The wind changed from east to west.* **2** change one's clothes; *After swimming we went to the cabin and changed. v.,* **changed, chang·ing.**

Cha·nu·kah (hä′nə kə), Hanukkah. *n.*

chap·ter (chap/tər), main division of a book or other writing, dealing with a particular part of the story or subject. *n.*

charge (chärj), **1** put down as a debt to be paid: *We charged the entire dinner, so the restaurant will send a bill for it.* **2** a task, a responsibility: *The charge of the baby was given to my sister.* 1 *v.,* **charged, charg·ing;** 2 *n.*

Char·tres (shär/trə), city in N France. Its Gothic cathedral is over 700 years old. *n.*

chase (chās), run or follow after to catch or kill: *The cat chased the mouse.* *v.,* **chased, chas·ing.**

check (chek), stop suddenly. *v.*

cheer·ful (chir/fəl), full of cheer; joyful; glad: *She is a smiling, cheerful girl.* *adj.*

child (chīld), **1** a young boy or girl: *games for children.* **2** son or daughter: *Parents love their children.* *n., pl.* **chil·dren.**

child·hood (child/hud), time during which one is a child. *n.*

Chi·nese New Year (chī nēz/ nü yir), a yearly event that begins between the dates of January 21 and February 19. It lasts four days, and on the last day people dress as dragons.

choc·o·late (chok/lit *or* chok/ə lit), **1** candy made of chocolate. **2** made of or flavored with chocolate: *chocolate cake.* 1 *n.,* 2 *adj.*

chop (chop), cut by hitting with something sharp: *You can chop wood with an ax. We chopped down the dead tree.* *v.,* **chopped, chop·ping.**

chore (chôr), an odd job; small task: *Feeding the dog is my daily chore.* *n., pl.* **chores.**

Christ·mas (kris/məs), the yearly celebration of the birth of Christ; December 25. *n., pl.* **Christ·mas·es.**

church (chėrch), building for public Christian worship. *n.*

cin·na·mon (sin/ə mən), spice made from the dried inner bark of a small tree of the East Indies: *Put cinnamon into the apple cider and heat it up.* *n.*

cir·cus (sėr/kəs), a traveling show of acrobats, clowns, horses, riders, and wild animals. The performers who give the show and the performances they give are both called the circus. *n., pl.* **cir·cus·es.**

cit·i·zen (sit/ə zen), person who by birth or by choice is a member of a nation. A citizen owes loyalty to that nation and is given certain rights by it. *Many immigrants have become citizens of the United States.* *n.*

class (klas), group of students taught together: *The art class meets in room 202.* *n., pl.* **classes.**

class·mate (klas/māt/), member of the same class in school. *n.*

class·room (klas/rüm/ *or* klas/rum/), room in which classes are held; schoolroom. *n.*

clat·ter (klat/ər), a confused noise like that of many plates being struck together: *The clatter in the cafeteria made it hard for us to hear one another talk.* *n.*

clear key (klir kē), the computer key that enables the user to remove the number in the display window from the calculator's memory.

climb (klīm), **1** go up, especially by using the hands or feet, or both; ascend: *She climbed the stairs quickly.* **2** go in any direction, especially with the help of hands: *climb over a fence, climb down a ladder.* *v.*

cinnamon
different forms of the
spice **cinnamon**

a	hat	**ī**	ice	**u̇**	put	**ə**	_stands for_
ā	age	**o**	not	**ü**	rule	**a**	in about
ä	far, calm	**ō**	open	**ch**	child	**e**	in taken
âr	care	**ȯ**	saw	**ng**	long	**i**	in pencil
e	let	**ô**	order	**sh**	she	**o**	in lemon
ē	equal	**oi**	oil	**th**	thin	**u**	in circus
ėr	term	**ou**	out	**ᵀH**	then		
i	it	**u**	cup	**zh**	measure		

collection

a baseball card
collection

compass

Compasses show
directions.

close¹ (klōz), bring together or move the parts of so as to leave no opening; shut: *Close the door. The sleepy child's eyes are closing.* v., **closed, clos·ing.**

close² (klōs), intimate; dear: *We are close friends. adj.,* **clos·er, clos·est.**

clos·et (kloz'it), a small room for storing clothes or household supplies. *n.*

clothes (klōz *or* klōᴛʜz), coverings for a person's body: *I bought some new clothes for my trip. n.pl.*

cloud (kloud), 1 mass of tiny drops of water, water vapor, or ice particles floating in the air high above the earth. Clouds may be white, rounded heaps, streamers, or dark, almost black, masses. 2 mass of smoke or dust in the air. *n.*

coal (kōl), a black mineral that burns and gives off heat, composed mostly of carbon. It is formed from partly decayed vegetable matter under great pressure in the earth. Anthracite and bituminous coal are two kinds of coal. *n.*

col·lapse (kə laps'), fall in; shrink together suddenly: *Sticking a pin into the balloon made it collapse. v.,* **col·lapsed, col·laps·ing.**

col·lec·tion (kə lek'shən), group of things gathered from many places and belonging together: *Our library has large collections of books. n., pl.* **col·lec·tions.**

co·logne (kə lōn'), a fragrant liquid, not so strong as perfume. *n.*

col·o·ny (kol'ə nē), group of animals or plants of the same kind, living or growing together: *a colony of ants. Coral grows in colonies. n., pl.* **col·o·nies.**

col·or (kul'ər), any color except black, white, or gray; red, yellow, blue, or any combination of them. The color green is a mixture of yellow and blue. *n.*

comb (kōm), take out tangles with a comb. *v.*

come (kum), move toward: *Come this way. v.,* **came, come, com·ing.**

com·mer·cial (kə mėr'shəl), 1 having to do with trade or business: *a store or other commercial establishment.* 2 an advertising message on radio or television, broadcast between or during programs. 1 *adj.,* 2 *n.*

com·mon (kom'ən), 1 from all; by all; to all; general: *By common consent of the class, she was chosen president.* 2 often met with; ordinary; usual. *adj.*

com·mute (kə myüt'), 1 travel regularly to and from work by train, bus, automobile, etc. 2 the distance or trip ordinarily traveled by a commuter: *a long commute, an easy commute.* 1 *v.,* **com·mut·ed, com·mut·ing;** 2 *n.*

com·pass (kum'pəs), instrument for showing directions, especially one consisting of a needle that points to the North Magnetic Pole. *n., pl.* **com·pass·es.**

com·pas·sion·ate (kəm pash'ə nit), wishing to help those that suffer; sympathetic; pitying. *adj.*

com·plete (kəm plēt'), 1 with all the parts; whole; entire: *We have a complete set of garden tools.* 2 make whole or entire; make up the full number or amount of: *I completed the set of dishes by buying the cups and saucers.* 1 *adj.,* 2 *v.,* **com·plet·ed, com·plet·ing.** —**com·plete'ly,** *adv.*

com·pose (kəm pōz'), 1 make up; form: *The ocean is composed of salt water.* 2 put together. To compose a story or poem is to construct it from words. To compose a piece of music is to invent the tune and write down the notes. *v.,* **com·posed, com·pos·ing.**

com·po·si·tion (kom'pə zish'ən), thing composed. A symphony, poem, a school exercise, or painting is a composition. *n.*

con·cert (kon'sərt), a musical performance in which several musicians or singers take part: *The school orchestra gave a concert last night. n.*

con·duct (kən dukt'), transmit; be a channel for: *Those pipes conduct steam to the radiators upstairs. v.*

con·fes·sion (kən fesh′ən), act of confessing; owning up; telling one's mistakes or sins. *n.*

con·fi·dence (kon′fe dens), firm belief in oneself; self-confidence: *Years of work at school have given her great confidence. n.*

con·fuse (kən fyüz′), **1** throw into disorder; mix up; bewilder: *So many people talking to me at once confused me.* **2** be unable to tell apart; mistake (one thing or person for another): *People often confuse this girl with her twin sister. v.,* **con·fused, con·fus·ing.**

con·i·fer (kon′ə fer *or* kō′nə fer), plant that bears cones. The pine, fir, spruce, hemlock, and larch are conifers. *n., pl.* **con·i·fers.**

con·scious·ness (kon′shes nis), condition of being conscious; awareness: *The injured woman did not regain consciousness for two hours. n.*

con·sti·tu·tion (kon′stə tü′shən *or* kon′stə tyü′shən), **1** way in which a person or thing is organized; nature; makeup: *A person with a good constitution is strong and healthy.* **2** system of fundamental principles according to which a nation, state, or group is governed: *The United States has a written constitution.* **3 the Constitution,** the written set of fundamental principles by which the United States is governed. *n.*

con·sum·er (kən sü′mer), person who uses food, clothing, or anything grown or made by producers: *A low price for wheat should reduce the price of flour to the consumer. n., pl.* **con·sum·ers.**

con·test (kon′test *for 1,2;* kən test′ *for 3*), **1** trial of skill to see which can win. A game or race is a contest.

2 a fight, struggle, or dispute. **3** argue against; dispute about: *The decision was not contested.* 1,2 *n.,* 3 *v.*

con·test·ant (kən tes′tənt), person who takes part in a contest: *My sister was a contestant in the 100-yard dash. n.*

cool (kül), somewhat cold; more cold than hot: *a cool, cloudy day. adj.*

co·or·di·nate (kō ôrd′n it), any of a set of numbers that give the position of a point by reference to fixed lines or axes. *n., pl.* **co·or·di·nates.**

corn (kôrn), kind of grain that grows on large ears; Indian corn. *n.*

cor·rect (kə rekt′), **1** free from mistakes; right: *give the correct answer.* **2** change to what is right; remove mistakes or faults from: *Correct any misspellings that you find.* 1 *adj.,* 2 *v.*

cor·rec·tion (kə rek′shən), a change to correct an error or mistake: *Write in your corrections neatly. n.*

couch (kouch), a long seat, usually upholstered and having a back and arms; sofa: *She sat on the couch and read the newspaper. n., pl.* **couch·es.**

could've (kůd′uv), could have.

coun·se·lor *or* **coun·sel·lor** (koun′se lər), person who gives advice; adviser. *The counselor helped my brother select some courses for college. n.*

cou·ple (kup′əl), **1** INFORMAL. a small number; a few: *Give me a couple of those apples—about four of them.* **2** man and woman who are married, engaged, partners in a dance, etc. *n.*

constitution
(definition 3)
the **Constitution** of
the United States

a	hat	ī	ice	u̇	put	ə	*stands for*
ā	age	o	not	ü	rule	a	in about
ä	far, calm	ō	open	ch	child	e	in taken
âr	care	ȯ	saw	ng	long	i	in pencil
e	let	ô	order	sh	she	o	in lemon
ē	equal	oi	oil	th	thin	u	in circus
ėr	term	ou	out	ŦH	then		
i	it	u	cup	zh	measure		

courtroom

hearing a case in the
courtroom

crocodile

A **crocodile** is a large
reptile.

cou·ra·geous (kə rä′jəs), full of
courage; brave; fearless. *adj.*

course (kôrs), **1** regular order: *the
course of nature.* **2** a series of
studies in a school, college, or
university. A student must complete
a certain course in order to
graduate: *Biology is the course I
will take to become a science
teacher. n.*

court (kôrt), place marked off for a
game: *a tennis court, a basketball
court. n.*

court·room (kôrt′rüm′ or kôrt′rúm′),
room where a court of law is held.
n.

cous·in (kuz′n), son or daughter of
one's uncle or aunt. First cousins
have the same grandparents;
second cousins have the same
great-grandparents. *n.*

cov·er (kuv′ər), **1** put something over:
I covered the child with a blanket.
2 anything that covers. Books have
covers. A box, can, or jar usually
has a cover. A blanket is a cover.
3 be enough for; provide for: *My
allowance covers my lunch at
school.* 1,3 *v.,* 2 *n.*

cov·er·let (kuv′ər lit), a covering,
especially a covering for a bed. *n.*

cov·ey (kúv′ē), a small flock of
partridges, quail, etc. *n., pl.*
cov·eys.

cow·ard (kou′ərd), person who lacks
courage or is easily made afraid;
person who runs from danger,
trouble, etc. *n.*

crash (krash) a sudden, loud noise
like many dishes falling and
breaking: *The lightning was
followed by a crash of thunder. n.,
pl.* **crash·es.**

cra·zy (krā′zē), unwise or senseless;
foolish: *It was a crazy idea to jump
out of such a high tree. adj.,*
cra·zi·er, cra·zi·est.

cred·it (kred′it), a trust in a person's
ability and intention to pay: *This
store will extend credit to you by
opening a charge account in your
name. n.*

cried (krīd), See **cry.** *The baby cried
until its mother picked it up. v.*

croc·o·dile (krok′ə dīl), a large,
lizardlike reptile with thick skin,
similar to the alligator, but having
a long narrow head and webbed
feet. Crocodiles live in the rivers
and marshes of the warm parts of
Africa, Asia, Australia, and
America. *n.*

cross·walk (krȯs′wȯk′), area marked
with lines, used by pedestrians in
crossing a street. *n., pl.* **cross·walks.**

crowd (kroud) a large number of
people together: *A crowd
gathered at the scene of the fire. n.*

cruise (krüz), **1** sail about from place
to place on pleasure or business;
sail over or about: *Freighters and
tankers cruise the oceans of the
world.* **2** a voyage from place to
place for pleasure: *We went for a
cruise on the Great Lakes last
summer.* 1 *v.,* **cruised, cruis·ing;**
2 *n.*

crumb (krum), a very small piece of
bread, cake, etc., broken from a
larger piece: *I fed crumbs to the
birds. n.*

crum·ble (krum′bəl), fall to pieces;
decay: *The old wall was crumbling
away at the edges. v.*

crutch (kruch), a support to help a
lame or injured person walk. It is a
stick with a padded crosspiece at
the top that fits under a person's
arm and supports part of the
weight in walking. *n., pl.* **crutch·es.**

cry (krī), call loudly; shout: *"Wait!"
she cried from behind me. v.,*
cried, cry·ing.

cuck·oo clock (kü′kü klok), clock with
a little toy bird that makes a sound
like that of the European cuckoo to
mark intervals of time.

cue card (kyü kärd), words written
out as to what to do or when to act:
*He held up the cue cards to the
actor so he could continue the
play. n., pl.* **cue cards.**

cur·few (kėr′fyü), rule requiring
certain persons to be off the streets
or at home before a fixed time:
*There is a 10 p.m. curfew for
children in our city. n.*

cur·rent (kėr′ent), **1** flow of electricity through a wire, etc.: *The current went off when lightning hit the power lines.* **2** of the present time: *We discuss current events in social studies class.* 1 *n.,* 2 *adj.*

cur·tain (kėrt′n), the fall or closing of the curtain at the end of an act or scene. *n., pl.* **cur·tains.**

cush·ion (kùsh′en), a soft pillow or pad used to sit, lie, or kneel on: *I rested my head on a cushion. n.*

cuspid (kus′pid), the kind of tooth with a sharp point used to tear food. Adults have four cuspids. *n.*

cute (kyüt), pretty and dear: *a cute baby. adj.,* **cut·er, cut·est.**

D

dad (dad), INFORMAL. father: *Dad's new car n.*

dahl·ia (dal′ye), a tall plant with large, showy flowers of many colors and varieties that bloom in autumn. It is related to the aster. *n., pl.* **dahl·ias.** (The *dahlia* was named for Anders *Dahl,* 1751-1789, a Swedish botanist.)

dai·ly (dā′lē), done, happening, or appearing every day, or every day but Sunday, day by day: *a daily newspaper, a daily visit. adj.*

dair·y (dâr′ē, der′ē), room or building where milk and cream are kept and made into butter and cheese. *n., pl.* **dair·ies.**

dance (dans), move in rhythm, usually in time with music: *She can dance very well. v.,* **danced, danc·ing.**

dan·ger (dān′jer), chance of harm; nearness to harm; risk; peril: *The trip through the jungle was full of danger. n.*

dark (därk), **1** absence of light; darkness: *Don't be afraid of the dark.* **2** night; nightfall: *The dark comes on early in the winter. n.* —**dark′ness,** *n.*

dead·line (ded′līn′), the latest possible time to do something: *The teacher made Friday afternoon the deadline for handing in all book reports. n.*

deal (dēl), distribute playing cards: *It's your turn to deal. v.,* **dealt, deal·ing.**

dealt (delt), See **deal.** *The cards have been dealt. v.*

de·bris (de brē′), scattered fragments; ruins; rubbish: *The street was covered with debris from the explosion. n.*

Dec., December.

De·cem·ber (di sem′ber), the 12th and last month of the year. It has 31 days. *n.*

de·cide (di sīd′), make up one's mind; resolve: *She decided to be a scientist. v.,* **de·cid·ed, de·cid·ing.**

de·ci·sion (di sizh′en), **1** a making up of one's mind; deciding: *I have not yet come to a decision about buying the property.* **2** judgment reached or given: *The jury brought in a decision of not guilty. n.*

de·com·pos·er (dē′kem pō′zer), a consumer that puts materials from dead plants and animals back into soil, air, and water. *n.*

deed (dēd), thing done; act; action: *a good deed. Deeds, not words, are needed. n.*

deep (dēp), **1** going a long way down from the top or surface: *the deepest well. The pond is deeper in the middle.* **2** in depth: *a tank 8 feet deep. adj.,* **deep·er, deep·est.**

dance
dancing in a ballet

a	hat	**ī**	ice	**u̇**	put	**ə** stands for	
ā	age	**o**	not	**ü**	rule	**a**	in about
ä	far, calm	**ō**	open	**ch**	child	**e**	in taken
âr	care	**ȯ**	saw	**ng**	long	**i**	in pencil
e	let	**ô**	order	**sh**	she	**o**	in lemon
ē	equal	**oi**	oil	**th**	thin	**u**	in circus
ėr	term	**ou**	out	**ᵺ**	then		
i	it	**u**	cup	**zh**	measure		

desert[1]

exploring the dry
desert

diary

A **diary** is for writing
personal thoughts.

de·gree (di grē′), **1** unit for measuring temperature: *The freezing point of water is 32 degrees (32°) Fahrenheit, or 0 degrees (0°) Celsius.* **2** unit for measuring an angle or an arc of a circle. A degree is ¹⁄₉₀ of a right angle or ¹⁄₃₆₀ of the circumference of a circle. 45 degrees (45°) is half a right angle. *n., pl.* **de·grees.**

de·lay (di lā′), **1** put off till a later time: *We will delay the party for a week and hold it next Saturday.* **2** a putting off till a later time: *The delay upset our plans.* **3** be late; go slowly; stop along the way: *Do not delay on this errand.* 1,3 *v.,* 2 *n., pl.* **delays.**

de·liv·er·y (di liv′ər ē), a carrying and giving out of letters, goods, etc.: *There is one delivery of mail a day in our city. n., pl.* **de·liv·er·ies.**

dem·o·crat·ic (dem′ə krat′ik), of a democracy; like a government run by the people who live under it. *adj.*

dem·on·stra·tion (dem′ən strā′shən), a showing or explaining something by carrying out experiments or by using samples: *A compass was used in a demonstration of the earth's magnetism. n., pl.* **dem·on·stra·tions.**

den·im (den′əm), a heavy, coarse cotton cloth with a diagonal weave, used for overalls, sports clothes, etc. *n.* (*Denim* comes from French *serge de Nimes,* meaning "serge from Nimes," a town in France where the fabric was made.)

der·mis (dėr′mis), the sensitive layer of skin beneath the outer skin; derma. *n.*

de·scrip·tion (di skrip′shən) a telling in words how a person, place, thing, or an event looks or behaves; describing: *The reporter's description of the hotel fire made me feel as if I were right at the scene. n.*

des·ert[1] (dez′ərt), a dry, barren region that is usually sandy and without trees. The Sahara Desert is a great desert in northern Africa. *n.*

de·sert[2] (di zert′), go away and leave a person or a place, especially one that should not be left; forsake: *She deserted her old friends when she became famous. v.*

de·sign (di zīn′), **1** arrangement of details, form, and color in painting, weaving, building, etc.: *a wallpaper design in tan and brown.* **2** make a first sketch of; arrange form and color of; draw in outline: *design a dress.* 1 *n.,* 2 *v.*

de·tail (di tāl′ *or* dē′tāl), a small or unimportant part: *Her report was complete: it didn't leave out a single detail. n., pl.* **de·tails.**

de·ter·mi·na·tion (di tėr′mə nā′shən), great firmness in carrying out a purpose; fixed purpose: *His determination was not weakened by the difficulties he met. n.*

de·ter·mine (di tėr′mən), make up one's mind very firmly; resolve: *He determined to become the best player on the team. v.*

dev·as·tate (dev′ə stāt), lay waste; destroy; ravage: *A long war devastated the country. v.,* **dev·as·tat·ed, dev·as·tat·ing.**

de·vel·op (di vel′əp), **1** come into being or activity; grow: *Plants develop from seeds.* **2** treat (a photographic film or plate) with chemicals to bring out the picture: *A photographer develops film and makes prints.* **3** make or become known: *The lawyer's investigation did not develop any new facts. v.*

di·ar·y (dī′ər ē), a book for writing down each day of what has happened to one, or what one has done or thought, during that day. *n., pl.* **di·ar·ies.**

dic·tion·ar·y (dik′shə när′ē), book that explains the words of a language or of some special subject. It is arranged alphabetically. You can use this dictionary to find out the meaning, spelling, or pronunciation of a word. *n., pl.* **dic·tion·ar·ies.**

did·n't (did′nt), did not: *I didn't hear you.*

dif·fer·ent (dif′ər ənt), **1** not alike; not like: *People have different names. A boat is different from an automobile.* **2** not like others or most others; unusual. *adj.*

di·rect (də rekt′ *or* dī rekt′). have authority or control over; manage or guide: *The teacher directs the work of the class. v.*

di·rec·tion (də rek′shən *or* dī rek′shən), a directing; managing or guiding: *the direction of a play or movie. The school is under the direction of the principal. n.*

dirt·y (dėr′tē) soiled by dirt; not clean: *Children playing in the mud get dirty. adj.*

dis·a·gree (dis′ə grē′), have unlike opinions; differ: *Doctors sometimes disagree about the proper method of treating a patient. Your account of the accident disagrees with hers. v.*

dis·ap·pear (dis′ə pir′), pass from sight; from existence; stop being seen: *The dog disappeared around the corner. When spring comes, the snow disappears. v.*

dis·ap·point·ment (dis′ə point′mənt), a being disappointed; the feeling you have when you do not get what you expected or hoped for: *When she did not get a new bicycle her disappointment was very great. n.*

dis·cov·er (dis kuv′ər), see or learn of for the first time; find out: *discover a new drug, discover a secret. v.*

dis·hon·est (dis on′ist), ready to cheat; not upright: *A person who lies or steals is dishonest. adj.*

dis·like (dis līk′), not like; object to; have a feeling against: *He dislikes studying and would rather play football. v.,* **dis·liked, dis·lik·ing.**

dis·o·be·di·ence (dis′ə bē′dē əns), refusal to obey; failure to obey: *The child was punished for disobedience. n.*

dis·play (dis plā′), a showing of information in visual form, as on the screen of a computer or calculator. *n.*

dis·tance (dis′təns), space in between: *The distance from the farm to the town is five miles. n.*

dis·trust (dis trust′), have no confidence in; not trust; be suspicious of; doubt: *Many people distrust statements made in advertisements. v.*

dive (dīv), **1** plunge headfirst into water. **2** act of diving: *The crowd applauded the girl's graceful dive.* **1** *v.,* **dived** *or* **dove, dived, div·ing;** **2** *n.*

di·vide (də vid′), to find how a total amount can be separated into an equal number of groups, or into groups of equal size. *v.,* **di·vid·ed, di·vid·ing.**

div·i·dend (div′ə dend), number or quantity to be divided by another: *In 728 ÷ 16, 728 is the dividend. n.*

di·vis·i·ble (də viz′ə bəl), able to be divided without leaving a remainder: *12 is divisible by 1, 2, 3, 4, 6, and 12. adj.*

di·vi·sion (də vizh′ən), operation of dividing one number by another: *26 ÷ 2 = 13 is a simple division. n.*

di·vi·sor (də vī′zər), number or quantity by which another is to be divided: *In 728 ÷ 16, 16 is the divisor. n.*

doc·tor (dok′tər), person trained in treating diseases or injuries. Physicians, surgeons, dentists, and veterinarians are doctors. *n.*

does·n't (duz′nt), does not.

dive (definition 1)

a	hat	**ī**	ice	**u̇**	put	**ə**	stands for
ā	age	**o**	not	**ü**	rule	**a**	in about
ä	far, calm	**ō**	open	**ch**	child	**e**	in taken
âr	care	**ȯ**	saw	**ng**	long	**i**	in pencil
e	let	**ô**	order	**sh**	she	**o**	in lemon
ē	equal	**oi**	oil	**th**	thin	**u**	in circus
ėr	term	**ou**	out	**ᴛʜ**	then		
i	it	**u**	cup	**zh**	measure		

dog pad·dle (dȯg pad′l), a downward swimming stroke in which the arms and legs stay under the water and each limb paddles by turns, first one and then the other: *The child did the dog paddle in the pool.*

dol·phin (dol′fen) a sea mammal related to the whale, but smaller. It has a beaklike snout and remarkable intelligence. *n.*

don·key (dong′kē) a small animal somewhat like a horse but with longer ears and a shorter mane. *n., pl.* **don·keys.**

door·bell (dôr′bel′), bell that a caller may ring by pressing a button or pulling a handle on the outside of a door to a house. *n.*

down·stairs (doun′sterz′ *or* doun′starz′), on or to a lower floor: *Look downstairs for my glasses* (*adv.*) *The downstairs rooms are dark* (*adj.*).

Dr., Doctor.

drib·ble (drib′el), **1** move (a ball) along by bouncing it or giving it short kicks: *dribble a basketball, dribble a soccer ball.* **2** act of dribbling a ball. 1 *v.,* **drib·bled, drib·bling;** 2 *n.*

dried (drīd), See **dry.** *I dried my hands. The dishes have already been dried. v.*

drive (drīv), **1** go or carry in an automobile or carriage: *We want to drive through the mountains on the way home. She drove us to the station.* **2** (in sports) hit very hard and fast: *drive a golf ball.* **3** make by drilling, boring: *drive a well. v.,* **drove, driv·en, driv·ing.**

drive·way (drīv′wā′), a privately owned road to drive on, usually leading from a house or garage to the road. *n.*

drove (drōv), See **drive.** *We drove two hundred miles today. v.*

drown (droun), die under water or other liquid because of lack of air to breathe: *We almost drowned when our sailboat suddenly overturned. v.,* **drowned, drown·ing.**

dolphin
a **dolphin** enjoying the water

dry (drī), make or become dry: *We washed and dried the dishes after dinner. Clothes dry in the sun. v.,* **dried, dry·ing.**

dry cleaner (drī klē′ner), person or business that does dry cleaning.

dry dock (drī dok), dock built watertight so that the water may be pumped out or kept high. Dry docks are used for building or repairing ships.

dry run (drī run), a practice test or session.

dud (dud), shell or bomb that fails to explode. *n.*

dune (dün *or* dyün), mound or ridge of loose sand heaped up by the wind. *n.*

dur·ing (dúr′ing *or* dyúr′ing), through the whole time of; throughout: *The children played inside during the storm. prep.*

E

ear (ir), part of the body by which people and animals hear. It consists of the external ear, the middle ear, and the inner ear. *n.*
be all ears, INFORMAL. listen eagerly; pay careful attention: *The children were all ears while their teacher read them the exciting story.*
play by ear, play (a piece of music or a musical instrument) without using written music: *She can't read notes but she can play any tune on the piano by ear.*

ear ca·nal (ir ke nal′), tunnel sound travels through to the eardrum.

ear·drum (ir′drum′), a thin membrane across the middle ear that vibrates when sound waves strike it. *n.*

ear·ring (ir′ring′), ornament for the ear. *n., pl.* **ear·rings.**

earth·quake (ėrth′kwāk′), a shaking or sliding of a portion of the earth's crust. It is caused by the sudden movement of masses of rock far beneath the earth's surface. Earthquakes are often related to volcanic activity. *n.*

e·del·weiss (ā′dil vīs), a small plant that grows in high places, such as the mountains in Austria and Switzerland. It has heads of very small, white flowers in the center of star-shaped leaf clusters. *n., pl.* **e·del·weiss** or **e·del·weiss·es.**

edge (ej), **1** line or place where something ends or begins; side: *This page has four edges. We walked to the edge of the water.* **2** rim; brink: *The stag stood on the edge of the cliff. n.*

ed·i·tor (ed′ə tər), person who edits: *She is the editor of our school paper. n., pl.* **ed·i·tors.**

e·lect (i lekt′), choose or select for an office by voting: *We elect our class officers every autumn. v.,* **elect·ed, elect·ing.**

e·lec·tion (i lek′shən), a choosing or selecting for an office by vote: *In our city we have an election for mayor every four years. n.*

e·lec·tric·i·ty (i lek′tris′ə tē), form of energy which can produce light, heat, motion, and magnetic force. Electricity makes light bulbs shine, televisions play, and cars start. *n.*

el·e·phant (el′ə fənt), a huge, heavy mammal, the largest living land animal, with ivory tusks and a long, muscular snout called a trunk. *n.*

e·lev·en (i lev′ən), **1** one more than ten; 11. **2** a football or cricket team. 1,2 *n.,* 1 *adj.*

e·mer·gen·cy (i mėr′jən sē), **1** a sudden need for immediate action: *I keep a box of tools in my car for use in an emergency.* **2** for a time of sudden need: *The surgeon did an emergency operation.* 1 *n., pl.* **e·mer·gen·cies;** 2 *adj.*

e·nam·el (i nam′əl), the smooth, hard, glossy outer layer of the teeth. *n.*

end·point (end point), the point at the end of a line segment or ray. *n., pl.* **end·points.**

en·e·my (en′ə mē), a force, nation, army, fleet, or air force that opposes another; person, ship, etc., of a hostile nation. *n., pl.* **en·e·mies.**

en·er·gy (en′ər jē), capacity for doing work, such as lifting or moving an object. Light, heat, and electricity are different forms of energy: *A steam engine changes heat into mechanical energy. n., pl.* **en·er·gies.**

en·er·vate (en′ər vāt), lessen the vigor or strength of; weaken: *A hot, damp climate enervates people who are not used to it. v.,* **en·er·vat·ed, en·er·vat·ing.**

en·gine (en′jən), machine that changes energy from fuel, steam, water pressure, etc., into motion and power. An engine is used to apply power to some work, such as a car engine. *n.*

Eng·lish (ing′glish), the language of England. English is also spoken in the United States, Canada, Australia, New Zealand, the Republic of South Africa, and many other countries. *n. sing.*

e·nough (i nuf′), quantity or number needed or wanted; sufficient amount: *I had enough to eat. n.*

ep·i·der·mis (ep′ə dėr′mis), the outer layer of the skin. *n.*

ep·i·gram (ep′ə gram), a short, pointed or witty saying. EXAMPLE: "Speech is silver, but silence is golden." *n.*

e·qual (ē′kwəl), **1** the same in amount, size, number, value, or rank: *Ten dimes are equal to one dollar. All persons are considered equal before the law.* **2** the same throughout; even; uniform: *equal pieces. adj.*

edelweiss
The **edelweiss** is the national flower of Austria.

elephant
The **elephant** is the largest four-footed animal.

a	hat	ī	ice	u̇	put	ə stands for	
ā	age	o	not	ü	rule	a	in about
ä	far, calm	ō	open	ch	child	e	in taken
âr	care	ȯ	saw	ng	long	i	in pencil
e	let	ô	order	sh	she	o	in lemon
ē	equal	oi	oil	th	thin	u	in circus
ėr	term	ou	out	ŦH	then		
i	it	u	cup	zh	measure		

e·qual·ly (ē′kwə lē), in equal shares; in an equal manner: *Divide the pie equally. My sister and brother are equally talented. adv.*

e·quals key (ē′kwəlz kē), supplies a result of a calculator's next calculation.

e·qua·tion (i kwā′zhən), statement of the equality of two quantities. EXAMPLES: $(4 \times 8) + 12 = 44$. $C = 2\pi r$. *n.*

e·qua·tor (i kwā′tər), an imaginary circle around the middle of the earth, halfway between the North Pole and the South Pole. The United States is north of the equator; Australia is south of it. *n.*

Er·ie (ir′ē), **Lake,** one of the five Great Lakes that borders Ohio, Pennsylvania, New York, and Canada. *n.*

er·ror (âr′ər), a message that appears on a calculator when more digits are generated than can be displayed. *n.*

e·rup·tion (i rup′shən) a bursting or throwing forth: *There was an eruption of glowing melted rock from the mountain top. n.*

es·cape (e skāp′), get out and away; get free: *The bird escaped from its cage. v.,* **es·caped, es·cap·ing.**

es·pe·cial·ly (e spesh′ə lē), more than others; specially; particularly; principally; chiefly. *adv.*

etc., et cetera. *Etc.* is usually read ''and so forth.'' *Etc.* shows that the definition applies to many similar items in addition to the ones mentioned.

eve (ēv), the evening or day before a holiday or some other special day: *New Year's Eve, Christmas Eve, the eve of my birthday. n.*

eve·ning (ēv′ning), the last part of day and early part of night; time between sunset and bedtime. *n.*

ev·er·green (ev′ər grēn′), a plant that has green leaves or needles all year round. *n., pl.* **ev·er·greens.**

eve·ry·bod·y (ev′rē bud′ē *or* ev′rē bod′ē), every person; everyone: *Everybody likes the principal. pron.*

evergreen

the majestic **evergreen**

experiment

working on an

experiment with light

eve·ry·one (ev′rē wun *or* ev′rē wən), each one; everybody: *Everyone in the class is here. pron.*

ex·act·ly (eg zakt′lē), accurately; precisely; just so; quite right. *adv.*

ex·cel·lent (ek′sə lənt), of unusually good quality; better than others; superior: *Excellent work deserves high praise. adj.*

ex·cept (ek sept′) leaving out; other than: *He works every day except Sunday. prep.*

ex·cess (ek ses′), part that is too much; more than enough: *The tailor trimmed off the excess from the cloth being measured for the two sleeves. n.*

ex·cite (ek sīt′), **1** stir up the feelings of: *News of the wedding excited the entire family.* **2** arouse: *Plans for a field trip excited the students' interest. v.,* **ex·cit·ed, ex·cit·ing.**

ex·cuse (ek skyüs′), reason, real or pretended, that is given; explanation: *Sickness was his excuse for being absent from school. n.*

ex·hib·it (eg zib′it), an exhibiting; public showing: *The village art exhibit drew 10,000 visitors. n.*

ex·pect (ek spekt′), think something will probably come or happen; look forward to: *I expect to take a vacation in May. v.*

ex·per·i·ment (ek spâr′ə mənt), trial or test to find out something: *a chemistry experiment. Scientists test out theories by experiments. n.*

ex·pert (ek′spėrt′ ek spėrt′ *or* ek′spėrt′), a very skillful person; person who knows a great deal about some special thing: *She is an expert at fishing. n.*

ex·plain (ek splān′), make plain or clear; tell the meaning of: *The teacher explained long division to the class. Will you explain this poem to me? v.*

ex·plo·sion (ek splō′zhən), a bursting with a loud noise; a blowing up: *The explosion shook the whole neighborhood. n.*

ex·tra (ek′strə), beyond what is usual, expected, or needed; additional: *extra fare, extra pay, extra favors.* *adj.* (*Extra* was probably shortened from *extraordinary.*)

ex·traor·di·nar·y (ek strôr′də när′ē, ek strôr′də ner′ē), beyond what is ordinary; very unusual; very remarkable: *Eight feet is an extraordinary height for a person.* *adj.*

eye (ī), the organ of the body by which people and animals see. *n.*
an eye for an eye, punishment as severe as the injury.
catch one's eye, attract one's attention: *The bright red sign caught my eye.*
see eye to eye, agree entirely: *My parents and I do not see eye to eye on my weekly allowance.*

eye·lash (ī′lash′), **1** one of the hairs on the edge of the eyelid. **2** fringe of such hairs. *n., pl.* **eye·lash·es.**

F

Fahr·en·heit (far′ən hīt), a scale for measuring temperature on which 32 degrees marks the freezing point of water and 212 degrees marks the boiling point. *adj.* (The *Fahrenheit* scale was named for Gabriel D. *Fahrenheit*, 1686-1736, a German physicist who introduced it.)

fair·ness (fâr′nis *or* far′nis), a being fair: *Our teacher is known for fairness in grading pupils.* *n.*

fam·i·ly (fam′ə lē), **1** a father, mother, and their children: *Our town has about a thousand families.* **2** all of a person's relatives: *His family's reunion is an annual event.* *n., pl.* **fam·i·lies.**

fam·i·ly of facts, (faks), related number sentences for addition and subtraction (or multiplication and division) that contain all the same numbers.

fat (fat), **1** having much flesh; fleshy; plump; well-fed: *a fat baby, a fat pig.* **2** large or larger than usual: *a fat contract, a fat salary.* *adj.,* **fat·ter, fat·test.**

fa·ther (fä′ᴛʜər), a male parent. *n.*

fault (fôlt), a break in the earth's crust, with the mass of rock on one side of the break pushed up, down, or sideways. *n., pl.* **faults.**

fa·vor·ite (fā′vər it), liked better than others. *adj.*

fear·less (fir′lis), without fear; afraid of nothing; brave; daring. *adj.*

Feb., February.

Feb·ru·ar·y (feb′rü âr′ē *or* feb′yü er′ē), the second month of the year. It has 28 days except in leap years, when it has 29. *n.*

fed·er·al (fed′ər əl), formed by an agreement between states establishing a central government to handle their business while the states keep separate their own affairs: *Switzerland and the United States both became nations by federal union.* *adj.*

feel·ing (fē′ling), **1** emotion. Joy, sorrow, fear, and anger are feelings. *The loss of the ball game stirred up much feeling.* **2** feelings, *pl.* tender or sensitive side of one's nature: *You hurt my feelings when you yelled at me.* *n., pl.* **feel·ings.**

fence (fens), railing, wall, put around a yard, garden, field, farm, etc., to show where it ends or to keep people or animals out or in. Most fences are made of wood, wire, or metal. *n.*

Fahrenheit
The **Fahrenheit** scale is used on these thermometers.

a	hat	**ī**	ice	**u̇**	put	**ə** stands for	
ā	age	**o**	not	**ü**	rule	**a**	in about
ä	far, calm	**ō**	open	**ch**	child	**e**	in taken
âr	care	**ȯ**	saw	**ng**	long	**i**	in pencil
e	let	**ô**	order	**sh**	she	**o**	in lemon
ē	equal	**oi**	oil	**th**	thin	**u**	in circus
ėr	term	**ou**	out	**ᴛʜ**	then		
i	it	**u**	cup	**zh**	measure		

fern
two Boston **ferns**

fern (fėrn), kind of plant that has roots, stems, and feathery leaves, but does not have flowers or seeds. The plant reproduces by means of spores which grow in little brown clusters on the backs of the leaves. *n., pl.* **ferns.**

fer·ti·lize (fėr′tl īz), unite with (an egg cell) in fertilization; impregnate. *v.,* **fer·ti·lized, fer·ti·liz·ing.**

few (fyü), not many: *Few people attended the meeting. adj.*

field (fēld), piece of land used for crops or for pasture. *n.*

field goal (fēld gōl), (in basketball) a basket scored while the ball is in play, counting two points.

fil·i·gree (fil′ə grē), very delicate, lacelike, ornamental work of gold or silver wire. *n.*

film (film), roll or sheet of thin, flexible material covered with a coating that is sensitive to light, used in taking photographs. *n.*

fi·nal·ly (fī′nl ē), at the end; at last. *adv.*

fin·ger (fing′ger), one of the five slender divisions that end the hand, especially the four besides the thumb. *n.*
put one's finger on, point out exactly: *The inspector was able to put his finger on the weak point in the suspect's alibi.*

fire·proof (fīr′prüf′), very resistant to fire; almost impossible to burn: *A building made entirely of steel and concrete is fireproof. adj.*

football (definition 2)

first (fėrst), **1** coming before all others: *She is first in her class.* **2** person, thing, place, etc., that is first: *We were the first to get here.* 1 *adj.,* 2 *n.*

first aid (fėrst ād), emergency treatment given to an injured or sick person before a doctor sees the person.

flash·light (flash′līt′), a portable electric light, operated by batteries. *n.*

flaw (flò), defective area: *There is a flaw in this shirt. n.*

flawed (flòd), having a defect: *a flawed diamond. adj.*

float (flōt), stay on top of or be held up by air, water, or other liquid. A cork will float, but a stone sinks. *v.*

Flo·ri·da (flôr′ə də), one of the southeastern states of the United States. *Abbreviation:* Fla. or FL *Capital:* Tallahassee. *n.*

flow·er (flou′er), part of a plant that produces the seed; blossom. It has modified leaves called petals. Flowers are often beautifully colored or shaped. *n., pl.* **flow·ers.**

fly (flī), any of a large group of insects that have two wings and make a buzzing sound, especially the housefly. *n., pl.* **flies.**

fo·cus (fō′kəs), bring (rays of light, heat, etc.) to a focus: *The lens focused the sun's rays on a piece of paper. v.* **fo·cused, fo·cus·ing,** or **fo·cussed, fo·cus·sing.**

food chain (füd chān), several kinds of living things that are linked because each uses another as food. Cats, birds, caterpillars, and plants eat the one named next.

food web (füd web), the flow of energy and materials through connected food chains.

foot (fút), *n., pl.* **feet** the end part of a leg; part that a person, animal, or thing stands on. *n.*
put one's best foot forward, INFORMAL. do one's best.

foot·ball (fút′bòl′), **1** game played with an inflated leather ball by two teams of eleven players each, on a field with a goal at each end. A player scores by carrying the ball over the goal line by a run or pass, or by kicking it through the goal posts. **2** ball used in this game. *n.*

fore·cast (fôr′kast′), what is coming; prophecy; prediction: *What is the forecast for the weather today? n.* **—fore′cast′er,** *n.*

fo·rest (fôr′ist), a large piece of land covered with trees; thick woods. *n.*

for·get (fer get′), fail to think of; fail to do, take, notice, etc.: *I forgot to call the dentist. v.,* **for·got, for·got·ten** or **for·got, for·get·ting.**

for·got (fər got′), See **forget**. *She was so busy that she forgot to eat her lunch.* v.

form (fôrm), **1** be formed; take shape: *Clouds form in the sky.* **2** piece of printed paper with blank spaces to be filled in: *We filled out a form to get a license for our dog.* 1 *v.,* 2 *n.*

foul (foul), **1** (in football, basketball, etc.) an unfair play; thing done against the rules. **2** make an unfair play against. 1 *n.,* 2 *v.*

four·teen (fôr′tēn′), four more than ten; 14. *n., adj.*

fourth (fôrth), next after the third; last in a series of 4. *adj., n.*

Fourth of July, Independence Day.

fran·tic (fran′tik), very much excited; wild with rage, fear, pain, or grief. *adj.*

freck·le (frek′əl), a small, light-brown spot on the skin, often caused by exposure to the sun. *n., pl.* **freck·les.**

free·style (frē′stīl′), a freestyle race or figure-skating contest. *n.*

free throw (frē thrō), (in basketball) an unblocked shot from a line **(free-throw line)** about 15 feet (4.5 meters) away from the basket, awarded to a player fouled by a member of the opposing team, and worth one point.

friend (frend), **1** person who knows and likes another. *My friend's companionship is priceless.* **2** person who favors and supports: *She was a generous friend to the poor.* n.

front (frunt), the line where two air masses meet. *n.*

fruit (früt), a juicy or fleshy product of a tree, bush, shrub, or vine which consists of the seed and its covering and is usually sweet and good to eat. Apples and pears are fruits. *n.*

fuch·sia (fyü′shə), shrub with handsome pink, red, or purple flowers that droop from the stems. *n., pl.* **fuch·sias.** (The *fuchsia* was named for Leonhard *Fuchs,* 1501-1566, a German botanist.)

fudge (fuj), a soft candy made of sugar, milk, chocolate, butter, etc. *n.*

fu·el (fyü′əl), **1** anything that can be burned to produce useful heat or power. Coal, wood, and oil are fuels. **2** supply with fuel. **3** get fuel: *The ship will have to fuel at the nearest port.* 1 *n., pl.* **fu·els,** 2,3 *v.*

fun·ny (fun′ē), **1** causing laughter; amusing: *The clown's funny jokes and antics kept us laughing.* **2** INFORMAL. strange; queer; odd. *adj.,* **fun·ni·er, fun·ni·est.**

fur (fėr), **1** the soft hair covering the skin of many animals. **2** skin with such hair on it. Fur is used to make, cover, trim, or line clothing. *n.*

fur·ni·ture (fėr′nə chər), movable articles needed in a room or house. Beds, chairs, tables, and desks are furniture. *n.*

fruit
Fresh **fruit** is good for your health.

G

gag (gag), **1** something put in a person's mouth to prevent talking or crying out. **2** INFORMAL. joke; amusing remark or trick. *n.*

gal·lant (gal′ənt), noble in spirit or in conduct; brave: *King Arthur was a gallant knight.* adj.

gal·lon (gal′ən), measure for liquids equal to 4 quarts. *n.*

gang (gang), group of people acting or going around together: *A whole gang of us went swimming.* n.

gallon
a **gallon** of milk

a	hat	ī	ice	u̇	put	ə stands for	
ā	age	o	not	ü	rule	a	in about
ä	far, calm	ō	open	ch	child	e	in taken
âr	care	ȯ	saw	ng	long	i	in pencil
e	let	ô	order	sh	she	o	in lemon
ē	equal	oi	oil	th	thin	u	in circus
ėr	term	ou	out	ᵺ	then		
i	it	u	cup	zh	measure		

gas·o·line (gas′ə lēn′ *or* gas′ə lēn′), a colorless, liquid mixture of hydrocarbons which evaporates and burns very easily. It is made from petroleum or from gas formed in the earth and is used as a fuel to run automobiles, airplanes, etc. *n.*

gen·tle (jen′tl), not severe, rough, or violent; mild and soft: *a gentle tap. a gentle sound. adj.*, **gen·tler, gen·tlest.**

ghost (gōst), spirit of a dead person, supposed to appear to living people as a pale, dim, shadowy form: *A ghost was said to haunt the house. n.*

gi·ant (jī′ənt), like a giant; huge: *a giant potato. adj.*

gi·gan·tic (jī gan′tik), very large; huge: *a gigantic elephant. adj.*

gi·raffe (jə raf′), a large African mammal that chews its cud and has hoofs, a very long neck, long legs, and a spotted skin. Giraffes are the tallest living animals. *n.*

giraffe
Giraffes are the tallest animals in the world.

girl (gėrl), **1** a female child from birth to about eighteen: *The girl's face was young and pretty.* **2** a young, unmarried woman. *n.*

girl·friend (gėrl′frend′), INFORMAL. **1** boy's sweetheart or steady female companion. **2** a female friend. *n.*

glass (glas), **1** container to drink from made of glass: *I filled the glass with water.* **2 glasses,** *pl.* eyeglasses. *n., pl.* **glass·es.**

go (gō), move along. *v.* **went, gone, going.**

good·ness (gud′nis), a being good; kindness. *n.*

grand·ma (grand′mä′ *or* gram′ə), INFORMAL. grandmother: *My grandma's cookies are delicious. n.*

grand·pa (grand′pä′ *or* gram′pə), INFORMAL. grandfather: *My grandpa's stories are very funny. n.*

grasshopper
a **grasshopper** and its surroundings

grand·par·ent (grand′pâr ent *or* grand′par′ent), grandfather or grandmother: *Both sets of grandparents' letters arrived today. n.*

grass·hop·per (gras′hop′ər), a winged insect with strong hind legs for jumping. Locusts and katydids are grasshoppers. *n.*

grate·ful (grāt′fəl), feeling kindly because of a favor received; wanting to do a favor in return: *I am grateful for your help. adj.*

great·ness (grāt′nis), great mind or character. *n.*

group (grüp), number of persons or things together: *A group of children were playing tag. n.*

group·ing (grüp′ing), putting a known number of objects into each group and making as many groups as you can. *v.*

guess (ges), form an opinion of something without really knowing. *v.,* **guessed, guess·ing.**

guest (gest), person who is received and entertained at another's home or staying at a hotel or motel. *n.*

H

ham·burg·er (ham′bėr′gər), ground beef, usually shaped into round, flat cakes and fried or broiled and placed in a roll or bun. *n.* (*Hamburger* comes from German *Hamburger,* meaning "of Hamburg.")

ham·mer (ham′ər), hit again and again. *v.*

ham·ster (ham′stər), a small rodent with a short tail and large cheek pouches. Hamsters are used in scientific research and are often kept as pets. *n.*

hand (hand), the end part of the arm, below the wrist, which takes and holds objects. Each hand has four fingers and a thumb. *n.*
at first hand, from direct knowledge or experience.
by hand, by using the hands, not machinery: *embroidered by hand.*
lend a hand, help.
wash one's hands of, have no more to do with; refuse to be responsible for: *I washed my hands of that job when I discovered what I had done.*

hand sig·nal (hand sig′nəl), help giving a sign, a notice, warning, or pointing out something: *The girl gave a hand signal when she turned.*

Ha·nuk·kah (hä′nə kə), a yearly Jewish festival celebrated in November or December. Candles are lighted on each of the eight days of Hanukkah. *n.* Also, **Chanukah.**

hap·pen (hap′ən), 1 come about; take place; occur: *What happened at the party yesterday?* 2 be or take place by chance: *Accidents will happen. v.*, **hap·pened, hap·pen·ing.**

hap·pen·ing (hap′ə ning), something that happens; event; occurrence: *The evening newscast reviewed the happenings of the day. n.*

hap·py (hap′ē), feeling as you do when you are well and are having a good time; glad; pleased; contented: *She is happy in her new work. adj.,* **hap·pi·er, hap·pi·est.**

head (hed), the top part of the human body containing the brain, eyes, nose, ears, and mouth. *n.*
lose one's head, get excited; lose one's self-control.

head·line (hed′līn′), words printed in heavy type at the top of a newspaper article telling what it is about. *n.*

head·phone (hed′fōn′), earphone held against one or both ears by a band over the head. *n., pl.* **head·phones.**

heal (hēl), 1 make whole, sound, or well; bring back to health; cure. 2 become whole or sound; get well; return to health; be cured: *My cut finger healed in a few days. v.*

health (helth), condition of body or mind: *be in excellent health. n.*

hear (hir), 1 take in a sound or sounds through the ear: *We couldn't hear in the back row.* 2 receive news or information: *I heard from my parents. v.,* **heard, hear·ing.**

heart (härt), 1 the part of the body that pumps the blood. 2 the part that feels, loves, hates, and desires: *a heavy heart, a kind heart.* 3 figure shaped like this: ♥ *n.*

heart·bro·ken (härt′brō′kən), crushed by sorrow or grief. *adj.*

he'd (hēd; *unstressed* ēd), 1 he had: *He'd had an accident.* 2 he would: *He'd come if he could.*

height (hīt), measurement from top to bottom; how tall a person is; how high a thing is; how far up a thing goes: *the height of a mountain. n.*

he'll (hēl; *unstressed* hil), he will: *He'll tell us the story.*

hel·met (hel′mit), covering made of steel, leather, plastic, or some other sturdy material, worn to protect the head. *n.*

help·less (help′lis), not able to help oneself: *A little baby is helpless. adj.*

hem·i·sphere (hem′ə sfir), half of a sphere or globe, half of the earth's surface. The earth has four hemispheres: western, eastern, northern, and southern. *n., pl.* **hem·i·spheres.**

her·bi·vore (hėr′bə vôr), any animal that feeds mainly on plants. *n.*

her·self (hər self′), form of *she* or *her* used to make a statement stronger: *She did it herself. pron.*

hide (hīd), hide oneself, keep out of sight; conceal: *I'll hide, and you find me. v.*

high·way (hī′wā′), a main public road or route. *n.*

headphone
listening to music through
the **headphones**

herbivore
A rabbit is a
herbivore.

a	hat	ī	ice	u̇	put	ə stands for	
ā	age	o	not	ü	rule	a	in about
ä	far, calm	ō	open	ch	child	e	in taken
âr	care	ȯ	saw	ng	long	i	in pencil
e	let	ô	order	sh	she	o	in lemon
ē	equal	oi	oil	th	thin	u	in circus
ėr	term	ou	out	ᵀH	then		
i	it	u	cup	zh	measure		

hippopotamus

hip·po·pot·a·mus (hip′ə pot′ə məs), a huge, thick-skinned, almost hairless mammal found in and near the rivers of Africa that eats plants and can stay under water for a long time. *n., pl.* **hip·po·pot·a·mus·es, hip·po·pot·a·mi** (hip′ə pot′ə mī).

hob·by (hob′ē), something a person especially likes to work at or study which is not the person's main business or occupation; favorite pastime. *n., pl.* **hob·bies.**

hock·ey (hok′ē), game played by two teams on ice or on a field. The players hit a puck or ball with curved sticks to drive it across a goal. *n.*

ho·gan (hō′gän′), dwelling used by the Navajos. Hogans are built with logs and covered with earth. *n., pl.* **ho·gans.** (*Hogan* was borrowed from a Navajo word.)

hol·i·day (hol′ə dā), **1** day when one does not work; day of pleasure and enjoyment: *Labor Day and the Fourth of July are holidays in the United States.* **2** Often, **holidays,** *pl.* vacation. *n.*

home (hōm), place where a person or family lives; one's own house; where a person was born or brought up. *Her home is at 25 South Street. n.*

home·less (hōm′lis), without a home: *a stray, homeless dog. adj.* —**home′less·ness,** *n.*

hon·ey (hun′ē), a thick, sweet, yellow or golden liquid that bees make out of the nectar they collect from flowers. *n.*

hon·or (on′ər), great respect; high regard; *held in honor. n.*

hope·ful (hōp′fəl), feeling and giving or showing hope; expecting to receive what one desires: *a hopeful attitude. adj.* —**hope′ful·ly,** *adv.*

hope·less (hōp′lis), feeling or giving no hope: *He was disappointed so often that he became hopeless. adj.*

horn (hôrn), a hard, hollow, permanent growth, usually curved and pointed and in pairs, on the heads of cattle, sheep, goats, and certain other animals. *n.*
blow one's own horn or **toot one's own horn,** INFORMAL, praise oneself; boast.

hos·pi·tal (hos′pi təl), place for the care of the sick or injured. *n.*

hot (hot), having much heat; very warm: *Fire is hot. The sun is hot today. adj.,* **hot·ter, hot·test.**

ho·tel (hō tel′), house or large building that supplies rooms and food for pay to travelers and others. *n.*

house (hous), building in which people live. *n.*

how·ev·er (hou ev′ər), in spite of that; nevertheless; yet: *We were very late for dinner; however, there was plenty left for us. adv.*

huge (hyüj), very big; extremely large or great: *A whale is a huge animal. adj.*

hu·mid·i·ty (hyü mid′ə tē), moisture in the air: *On a hot, sultry day the humidity is high. The humidity today is worse than the heat. n.*

hu·mor (hyü′mər), funny or amusing quality: *I see no humor in your tricks. n.*

hu·mor·ous (hyü′mər əs), full of humor; funny; amusing: *We all laughed at the humorous story. adj.*

Hur·on (hyür′ən), **Lake,** one of the five Great Lakes that borders Michigan and Canada. *n.*

hy·dro·e·lec·tric (hī′drō i lek′trik), developing electricity from water power. *adj.*

I

I'd (īd), **1** I would: *I'd enjoy a vacation right now.* **2** I had: *I'd just finished dinner when she called.*

ig·nore (ig nôr′), pay no attention to; disregard: *The driver ignored the traffic light and almost hit another car. v.,* **ig·nored, ig·nor·ing.**

i·gua·na (i gwä′nə), a large tropical American lizard having a spiny crest along its back. *n., pl.* **i·gua·nas.**

hogan

A **hogan** is a type of house.

I'll (īl), I will: *I'll call you tomorrow.*

I'm (īm), I am: *I'm going to the concert tonight.*

i·mag·ine (i maj′ən), suppose; guess: *I cannot imagine what you mean.* v., **i·mag·ined, i·mag·in·ing; i·mag·i·na·ble,** *adj.*

im·pos·si·ble (im pos′ə bəl), not capable of being, being done, or happening; not possible: *It is impossible for two and two to be six. adj.*

in·ac·tive (in ak′tiv), not active; idle; slow: *Bears are inactive during the winter. adj.*

in·ci·sor (in sī′zər), tooth having a sharp edge for cutting; one of the front teeth between the canine teeth in either jaw. Humans have eight incisors. *n.*

in·com·plete (in′kəm plēt′), not complete; lacking some part; unfinished. *adj.*

in·con·ven·ient (in′kən vē′nyənt), not convenient; causing trouble, difficulty, or bother; troublesome: *Shelves that are too high to reach easily are inconvenient. adj.*

in·cor·rect (in′kə rekt′), containing errors or mistakes; not correct; wrong: *The newspaper gave an incorrect account of the accident. adj.*

in·cred·i·ble (in kred′ə bəl), hard to believe; seeming too extraordinary to be possible; unbelievable: *The racing car rounded the curve with incredible speed. adj.*

in·de·pend·ent (in′di pen′dənt), **1** not influenced by others; thinking or acting for oneself: *an independent voter, an independent thinker.* **2** person who is independent in thought or behavior. 1 *adj.* 2 *n.*

in·jur·y (in′jər ē), hurt or loss caused to or endured by a person or thing; harm; damage: *She escaped from the train wreck without injury. n., pl.* **in·jur·ies.**

inner ear (in′ər ir), the fluid-filled part of the ear that sends messages to the brain.

in·stru·ment (in′strə mənt), **1** a mechanical device that is portable, and usually operated by hand; tool: *a dentist's instruments.* **2** device for producing musical sounds: *wind instruments. n.*

in·su·late (in′sə lāt), keep from losing or transferring electricity, heat, sound, etc., especially by covering, packing, or surrounding with a material that does not conduct electricity, heat, etc.: *Telephone wires are often insulated by a covering of rubber. v.*

in·ten·si·ty (in ten′sə tē), extreme degree; great vigor; violence: *intensity of thought, intensity of feeling. n., pl.* **in·ten·si·ties.**

in·ter·est·ing (in′tər ə sting *or* in′tə res′ting), arousing interest; holding one's attention: *Stories about travel and adventure are interesting. adj.*

in·ter·sect·ing (in′tər sekt′ing), crossing each other at a point: *intersecting lines. adj.*

in·ter·view (in′tər vyü), a meeting between a reporter and a person from whom information is sought for publication or broadcast. *n.*

in·to (in′tü; *before consonants often* in′tə), to the inside of; toward and inside: *Come into the house. We drove into the city. I will look into the matter. prep.*

In·u·it (in′ü it *or* in′yü it), the people living mainly in the arctic regions of the world; the Eskimo people. *n.*

instrument
(definition 2)
types of brass
instruments

a	hat	**ī**	ice	**u̇**	put	**ə** stands for	
ā	age	**o**	not	**ü**	rule	**a**	in about
ä	far, calm	**ō**	open	**ch**	child	**e**	in taken
âr	care	**ȯ**	saw	**ng**	long	**i**	in pencil
e	let	**ô**	order	**sh**	she	**o**	in lemon
ē	equal	**oi**	oil	**th**	thin	**u**	in circus
ėr	term	**ou**	out	**ᴛ͟ʜ**	then		
i	it	**u**	cup	**zh**	measure		

jai alai
playing the game of
jai alai

in·vade (in vād′), enter with force or as an enemy; attack: *Soldiers invaded the country to conquer it.* *v.,* **in·vad·ed, in·vad·ing.**

in·va·sion (in vā′zhen), an invading; entering by force or as an enemy; attack. *n.*

in·ven·tion (in ven′shen), something new, thing invented: *Television is a modern invention. n.*

in·vis·i·ble (in viz′e bel), not visible; not capable of being seen: *Thought is invisible. Germs are invisible to the naked eye. adj.*

in·vite (in vīt′), ask (someone) politely to come to some place or to do something: *I invited some friends to a party. We invited them to join our club. v.,* **in·vit·ed, in·vit·ing.**

i·ris (ī′ris), the colored part of the eye around the pupil. *n., pl.* **i·ris·es.**

i·ron (ī′ern), **1** a silver-gray, easily shaped, heavy metallic element. Iron is the most useful metal and is used to make steel. **2** smooth or press (cloth, etc.) with a heated iron. 1 *n.,* 2 *v.*

is·land (ī′lend), body of land smaller than a continent and completely surrounded by water: *Cuba is a large island. n.*

is·sue (ish′ü), send out; put forth: *This magazine is issued every week. v.,* **is·sued, is·su·ing.**

it'll (it′l), it will: *It'll be better soon.*

it's (its), **1** it is: *It's my turn.* **2** it has: *It's been a beautiful day.*

J

jai a·lai (hī′ lī′), game similar to handball, played on a walled court with a hard ball. The ball is caught and thrown with a kind of curved wicker basket fastened to the arm.

James (jāmz), a boy's name. *James's house is next door to mine. n.*

Jan·u·ar·y (jan′yü âr′ē), the first month of the year. It has 31 days. *n.*

jewel
This **jewel** is a sapphire.

jay·walk (jā′wȯk′), walk across a street without paying attention to traffic rules. *v.* —**jay·walk·ing,** *n.*

jer·sey (jer′zē), a close-fitting, pullover sweater made of this cloth. *n.* (*Jersey* gets its name from the island of *Jersey,* where this cloth had been made for a long time.)

jew·el (jü′el), a precious stone; gem. *n., pl.* **jew·els.**

juice (jüs), the liquid part of fruits, vegetables, and meats: *the juice of a lemon, meat juice. n.*

Ju·ly (jů lī′), the seventh month of the year. It has 31 days. *n.*

jum·bo (jum′bō), INFORMAL. a big person, animal, or thing; something unusually large of its kind: *a jumbo ice-cream cone. adj.* (*Jumbo* comes from the name of a large circus elephant.)

jump shot (jump shot), (in basketball) shot made while jumping, especially at the highest point of the jump.

June (jün), the sixth month of the year. It has 30 days. *n.*

jur·y (jůr′ē), group of persons chosen to give a judgment in a court of law or to decide who is the winner in a contest: *The jury gave her poem the first prize. n., pl.* **jur·ies.**

K

Kan·sas (kan′zes), one of the midwestern states of the United States. *Abbreviation:* Kans. or KS *Capital:* Topeka. *n.*

kay·ak (kī′ak), an Eskimo canoe made of skins stretched over a light frame of wood or bone with an opening in the middle for a person. *n.* Also, **kaiak.**

key se·quence (kē sē′kwens), a connected series of keys on a calculator used in order to obtain a result.

kick (kik), strike out with the foot: *The boy kicked the soccer ball. v.*

kin·der·gar·ten (kin′dər gärt′n), school or class for children from about 4 to 6 years old that educates them by games, toys, and pleasant occupations. *n.* (*Kindergarten* is from German *Kindergarten,* which comes from *Kinder,* meaning "children," and *Garten,* meaning "garden.")

kitch·en (kich′ən), room or area where food is cooked. *n.* (*Kitchen* comes from Old English *cycene,* and can be traced back to Latin *coquere,* meaning "to cook.")

knee (nē), the joint between the thigh and the lower leg. *n.*

kneel (nēl), go down on one's knee or knees: *She knelt down to pull a weed. He kneels in prayer.* *v.,* **knelt** or **kneeled, kneel·ing.**

knit (nit), make (cloth or an article of clothing) by looping yarn or thread together with long needles, or by machinery which forms loops instead of weaving: *knit a pair of socks.* *v.,* **knit·ted** or **knit, knit·ting.**

knob (nob), handle on a door, drawer, etc.: *the knob on the dial of a television set.* *n.*

knot (not), **1** a fastening made by tying or twining together pieces of one or more ropes, cords, strings, etc.: *a square knot, a slip knot.* **2** tie or twine together in a knot: *He knotted two ropes together.* **3** group; cluster: *A knot of students stood talking outside the classroom.* 1,3 *n.,* 2 *v.,* **knot·ted, knot·ting.**

know (nō), have knowledge, have facts: *I know from experience how to drive on icy roads. She knows the poem.* *v.,* **knew, known, know·ing.**

known (nōn), See **know.** *George Washington is known as the father of his country.* *v.*

Kwan·za or **Kwan·zaa** (kwän′zə), a yearly African American celebration celebrating various African festivals. It lasts from December 26 to January 1. *n.* (*Kwanzaa* is from Swahili *Kwanza,* originally meaning "first (fruits)," which comes from *kuanza,* meaning "to begin.")

Kwanzaa
a family celebrating
Kwanzaa

L

la·crosse (lə krós′), game played on a field with a ball and long-handled, loosely strung rackets by two teams, usually of 10 players each. The players carry the ball in the rackets, trying to send it into the other team's goal. *n.*

la·dy (lā′dē), **1** woman of good family and high social position: *a lady by birth.* **2** a well-bred woman: *I borrowed the lady's umbrella.* **3** a polite term for any woman. "Ladies" is often used in speaking or writing to a group of women: *They went to the ladies' room.* **4** woman who has the rights and authority of a lord. *n., pl.* **la·dies.**

lamb (lam), a young sheep. *n.*

land·form (land′fôrm′), a physical feature of the earth's surface. Plains, plateaus, hills, and mountains are landforms. *n., pl.* **land·forms.**

large (lärj), of more than the usual size, amount, or number; big: *America is a large country. A hundred thousand dollars is a large sum of money.* *adj.,* **larg·er, larg·est.**

la·sa·gna (lə zä′nyə), dish consisting of chopped meat, cheese, and tomato sauce, baked with layers of wide noodles. *n.*

lasagna
lasagna topped with grated cheese

a	hat	ī	ice	u̇	put	ə stands for	
ā	age	o	not	ü	rule	a	in about
ä	far, calm	ō	open	ch	child	e	in taken
âr	care	ȯ	saw	ng	long	i	in pencil
e	let	ô	order	sh	she	o	in lemon
ē	equal	oi	oil	th	thin	u	in circus
ėr	term	ou	out	ᴛʜ	then		
i	it	u	cup	zh	measure		

library (definition 2)
gathering information at
the **library**

late·ly (lāt/lē), a little while ago; not long ago; recently: *He has not been looking well lately. adv.*

lat·i·tude (lat/ə tüd *or* lat/ə tyüd), distance north or south of the equator, measured in degrees. A degree of latitude is about 69 miles (111 kilometers). *n.*

laugh (laf), make the sounds and movements of the face and body that show one is happy or amused: *We all laughed at the joke. v.*, **laughed, laugh·ing.**

lay-up (lā/up/), (in basketball) a shot from close under the basket. *n.*

la·zy (lā/zē), not willing to work or be active: *He lost his job because he was lazy. adj.*, **la·zi·er, la·zi·est.**

lead (lēd), the opening paragraph in a newspaper or magazine article. A lead often summarizes the information in the body of the article. *n.*

lead·er (lē/dər), person who leads, or is well fitted to lead: *an orchestra leader. That girl is a born leader. n., pl.* **lead·ers.**

least (lēst), less than any other; smallest; slightest: *Ten cents is a little money; five cents is less; one cent is least. I have the least work. adj.*

leg (leg), one of the limbs on which people and animals stand and walk. *n.*
on one's last legs, about to fail, collapse, or die.
pull one's leg, INFORMAL. fool, trick, or make fun of one.
shake a leg, hurry up.

length (lengkth *or* length), how long a thing is; what a thing measures from end to end; the longest way a thing can be measured: *the length of a room, an animal eight inches in length. n.*

lens (lenz), **1** a curved piece of glass which brings closer together or sends wider apart the rays of light passing through it. The lens of a camera forms images on film. **2** the part of the eye that focuses light rays upon the retina. *n., pl.* **lens·es.**

let's (lets), let us: *Let's go for a walk.*

let·tuce (let/is), the large, crisp, green leaves of a garden plant, used in salad. *n.*

lev·el (lev/əl), **1** having the same height everywhere; flat; even: *a level floor.* **2** an instrument for showing whether a surface is level. *1 adj., 2 n.*

li·brar·i·an (lī brãr/ē ən), person in charge of a library. *n.*

li·brar·y (lī/brãr/ē), **1** collection of books, magazines, films, recordings, etc. **2** room or building where such a collection is kept for public use and borrowing. *n., pl.* **li·brar·ies.**

limb (lim), a large branch: *They sawed the dead limb off the tree. n.*

line (līn), a set of points continuing without end in both directions. *n.*

li·on (lī/ən), a large, strong, flesh-eating cat, with a dull-yellowish coat, and a loud roar. It is found in Africa and southern Asia. The male has a full, flowing mane of coarse hair. *n.*

liq·uid (lik/wid), **1** substance that is not a solid or a gas; substance that flows freely like water. **2** In the form of a liquid; melted: *liquid soap, butter heated until it is liquid. 1 n., 2 adj.*

lo·cal (lō/kəl), of a place; of a certain place or places: *the local doctor, local self-government, local news. adj.*

lo·cate (lō/kāt), establish in a place: *They located their new store on Second Avenue. v.,* **lo·cat·ed, lo·cat·ing.**

lo·ca·tion (lō kā/shən), position or place: *The camp was in a bad location as there was no water near it. n.*

lock (lok), an enclosed section of a canal or dock in which the level of the water can be changed by letting water in or out, to raise or lower ships. *n., pl.* **locks.**

lon·gi·tude (lon/jə tüd *or* lon/jə tyüd), distance east or west on the earth's surface, measured in degrees from Greenwich, England. *n.*

lion
A **lion** can be 3 feet high at the shoulder.

loose (lüs), **1** not tight: *loose clothing.* **2** not firmly set or fastened in: *a loose tooth.* 1,2 *adj.,* **loos·er, loos·est.**

lose (lüz), **1** not have any longer; have taken away from one by accident, carelessness, parting, death, etc.: *lose a finger, lose a friend, lose one's life.* **2** fail to win: *lose the prize.* v., **lost, los·ing.**

lo·tus (lō′təs), kind of water lily that grows in Egypt, India, and Asia. *n., pl.* **lo·tus·es.**

loud (loud), **1** making a great sound; not quiet or soft: *a loud voice, a loud noise.* **2** in a loud manner: *The hunter called long and loud. adj.*

love (luv), have such a warm liking or deep feeling for: *We love our parents. I love my country. v.,* **loved, lov·ing.**

lux·u·ri·ate (lug zhur′ē āt *or* luk shur′ē āt), **1** indulge in luxury. **2** take great delight: *The campers planned to luxuriate in hot baths when they came home.* **3** grow very abundantly. *v.,* **lux·u·ri·at·ed, lux·u·ri·at·ing.**

M

ma·chine (mə shēn′), arrangement of fixed and moving parts for doing work, each part having some special function: *Sewing machines and washing machines make housework easier. n.*

mag·net (mag′nit), stone or piece of metal that has the property of attracting iron or steel. A lodestone is a natural magnet. *n.*

mag·net·ic field (mag net′ik fēld), space around a magnet or electric current in which its magnetic force is felt.

mag·net·ism (mag′nə tiz′əm), properties or qualities of a magnet; the showing of magnetic properties: *the magnetism of iron and steel. n.*

mar·ble (mär′bəl), **1** a hard rock formed from limestone by heat and pressure. It may be white or colored and can be polished to a smooth gloss. Marble is used for statues and in buildings. **2** made of marble. 1 *n.,* 2 *adj.*

March (märch), the third month of the year. It has 31 days. *n.*

mat·ter (mat′ər), importance; significance: *Let it go since it is of no matter. n.*

maul (mȯl), beat and pull about; handle roughly. *v.,* **mauled, maul·ing.**

max·im (mak′səm), a short rule of conduct; proverb: *"Look before you leap" is a maxim. n.*

may (mā), be permitted or allowed to: *May I have an apple? v., past tense* **might.**

May (mā), the fifth month of the year. It has 31 days. *n.*

mean[1] (mēn), have as a purpose; have in mind. *v.,* **meant, mean·ing.**

mean[2] (mēn), not noble; petty; unkind; small-minded: *It is mean to spread gossip about your friends. adj.*

meant (ment), See **mean**[1]. *She explained what she meant. v.*

meet[1] (mēt), **1** come face to face (with something or someone coming from the other direction): *Our car met another car on a narrow bridge.* **2** fulfill; put an end to; satisfy: *The campers took along enough food to meet their needs for a week.* **3** a meeting; a gathering: *an athletic meet.* 1,2 *v.,* **met, meet·ing;** 3 *n.* —**meet′er,** *n.*

lotus

The **lotus** is the national flower of India.

magnet

A **magnet** attracts iron or steel.

a	hat	**ī**	ice	**u̇**	put	**ə** stands for	
ā	age	**o**	not	**ü**	rule	**a**	in about
ä	far, calm	**ō**	open	**ch**	child	**e**	in taken
âr	care	**ȯ**	saw	**ng**	long	**i**	in pencil
e	let	**ô**	order	**sh**	she	**o**	in lemon
ē	equal	**oi**	oil	**th**	thin	**u**	in circus
ėr	term	**ou**	out	**ᴙH**	then		
i	it	**u**	cup	**zh**	measure		

meet² (mēt), OLD USE. suitable; proper; fitting: *It is meet that you should help your friends. adj.*

Mem·or·i·al Day (mə môr′ē əl dā), holiday for remembering and honoring members of the United States armed services who have died. In most states, it is observed on the last Monday in May.

mem·or·y (mem′ər ē), person, thing, or event that is remembered: *I was so young when we moved that our old house is only a vague memory.* n., pl. **mem·or·ies.**

mem·or·y mi·nus (mem′ər ē mī′nəs), the computer key that enables the user to subtract the display from what is in the memory.

mem·or·y plus (mem′ər ē plus), the computer key that enables the user to add the display to what is in the memory.

mem·or·y re·call (mem′ər ē rē′kȯl′), the computer key that enables the user to display what is in memory.

men·u (men′yü), list of the food served at a meal; bill of fare. n.

me·rid·i·an (mə rid′ē ən), an imaginary circle passing through any place on the earth's surface and through the North and South Poles. Meridians mark longitude. n., pl. **me·rid·i·ans.**

model (definition 1)
painting a **model** of the space shuttle

me·te·o·rol·o·gist (mē′tē ə rol′ə jist), a person who studies weather. n.

me·ter¹ (mē′tər), the basic unit of length in the metric system. A meter is equal to 39.37 inches. n. Also, **metre.**

me·ter² (mē′tər), **1** any kind of poetic rhythm; the arrangement of beats or accents in a line of poetry. **2** musical rhythm; the arrangement of beats in music: *Three-fourths meter is waltz time.* n.

met·ric (met′rik), of the meter or the metric system. adj.

Mich·i·gan (mish′ə gən), **Lake,** one of the five Great Lakes. It lies entirely within the United States. n.

middle ear (mid′l ir), the three tiny bones that carry sound waves from the eardrum to the inner ear.

Middle English (mid′l ing′glish), period in the development of the English language between Old English and Modern English, lasting from 1100 to about 1500.

might (mīt), See **may.** *Mother said that we might play in the barn. v.*

might·'ve (mīt′uv), might have: *He might've been outdoors when you called.*

mis·be·have (mis′bi hāv′), behave badly. v., **mis·be·haved, mis·be·hav·ing.**

mis·for·tune (mis fôr′chən), bad luck; unlucky accident. *She had the misfortune to break her arm. n.*

mis·lead (mis lēd′), cause to go in the wrong direction; lead astray: *Our guide misled us and we got lost.* v., **mis·led, mis·lead·ing.**

mis·led (mis led′), See **mislead.** *We were misled on our hike by a careless guide. v.*

mis·place (mis plās′), put in a place and then forget where it is; mislay: *I have misplaced my pencil.* v., **mis·placed, mis·plac·ing.**

miss (mis), **1** fail to hit: *I swung at the ball and missed it.* **2** fail to catch: *miss the train.* **3** notice the absence of; feel keenly the absence of: *I missed you while you were away.* v. **missed, miss·ing.**

mis·sion (mish′ən), a sending or being sent on some special work; errand. An operation by one or more aircraft against the enemy is called a mission. n.

Mis·sis·sip·pi (mis′ə sip′ē), **1** large river in the United States. It flows south from N Minnesota to the Gulf of Mexico. **2** one of the south central states of the United States. *Abbreviation:* Miss. or MS. *Capital:* Jackson. n.

mis·spell (mis spel′), spell incorrectly. v.

mis·treat (mis trēt′), treat badly. v.

mod·el (mod′l), **1** a small copy: *a model of a ship or an engine.* **2** thing or person to be copied or imitated: *Your mother is a fine person; make her your model. n.*

mois·ture (mois′chər), slight wetness; water or other liquid suspended in drops in the air or spread on a surface. *n.*

mo·lar (mō′lər), tooth with a broad surface for grinding. A person's back teeth are molars. *n.*

mo·ment (mō′mənt), a very short space of time; instant. *n.*

mon·ey (mun′ē), coins of gold, silver, or other metal, or paper notes which represent these metals, issued by a government for use in buying and selling. *n., pl.* **mon·eys** or **mon·ies.**

mon·key (mung′kē), **1** animal of the group most like human beings. **2** person, especially a child, who is full of mischief. *n., pl.* **mon·keys.**

mood (müd), state of mind or feeling: *I am in the mood to play now; I don't want to study. n.*

morn·ing (môr′ning), the early part of the day, ending at noon. *n.*

moth·er (muᴛʜ′ər), a female parent. *I'll have to ask my mother. n.*

mo·tor (mō′tər), an engine, such as a gasoline or diesel engine, that makes a machine go. *n.*

mo·tor·cy·cle (mō′tər sī′kəl), a two-wheeled motor vehicle which resembles a bicycle but is heavier and larger. *n.*

moun·tain (moun′tən), a very high hill. *n.*

mouth (mouth), the opening through which a person or animal takes in food; space containing the tongue and teeth. *n.*
down in the mouth, INFORMAL. in low spirits; discouraged.

move·ment (müv′mənt), **1** act or fact of moving: *We run by movements of the legs.* **2** the moving parts of a machine; special group of connected parts that move together. The movement of a watch consists of many little wheels. *n.*

Mr. or **Mr** (mis′tər), Mister, a title put in front of a man's name or the name of his position: *Mr. Stern, Mr. President. pl.* **Messrs.**

Mrs. or **Mrs** (mis′iz), a title put in front of a married woman's name: *Mrs. Weiss. pl.* **Mmes.**

Ms. (miz), a title put in front of a woman's name: *Ms. Karen Hansen. pl.* **Mses.**

muf·fin (muf′ən), a small, round cake made of wheat flour, corn meal, or the like, often without sugar. *n.*

mul·ti·pli·ca·tion (mul′tə plə kā′shən), operation of multiplying one number by another. *n.*

mu·sic (myü′zik), beautiful, pleasing, or interesting arrangements of sounds. *n.*

music box (myü′zik boks), box or case containing apparatus for producing music mechanically.

music hall (myü′zik hȯl), hall for musical performances.

music vid·e·o (myü′zik vid′ē ō), a short musical film or videotape or videodisc.

mus·tard (mus′tərd), a yellow powder or paste made from the seeds of the mustard plant, used as seasoning. *n.*

must·n't (mus′nt), must not: *You mustn't wake the baby.*

my·self (mī self′), form used instead of *me* or *I* in cases like: *I can cook for myself. I hurt myself. pron.*

mys·ter·y (mis′tər ē), something that is hidden or unknown; secret. *n., pl.* **mys·ter·ies.**

monkey (definition 1)

mountain

a	hat	ī	ice	u̇	put	ə	*stands for*
ā	age	o	not	ü	rule	a	in about
ä	far, calm	ō	open	ch	child	e	in taken
âr	care	ȯ	saw	ng	long	i	in pencil
e	let	ô	order	sh	she	o	in lemon
ē	equal	oi	oil	th	thin	u	in circus
ėr	term	ou	out	ᴛʜ	then		
i	it	u	cup	zh	measure		

N

na·tion (nā′shən), people occupying the same country, united under the same government, and usually speaking the same language. *n.*

na·tion·al (nash′ə nəl), of a nation; belonging to a whole nation: *national laws, a national disaster.* *adj.*

na·tur·al gas (nach′ər əl gas), a combustible gas formed naturally in the earth, consisting primarily of methane. It is used as a fuel.

Nav·a·jo (nav′ə hō), member of a tribe of American Indians living mainly in New Mexico, Arizona, and Utah. *n., pl.* **Nav·a·jos** or **Nav·a·joes.**

nee·dle·leaf (nē′dl lēf′), a type of tree with thin, sharp needles. A pine is a needleleaf tree. *adj.*

neg·a·tive (neg′ə tiv), a photographic image in which the lights and shadows are reversed. Prints are made from it. *n.*

neigh·bor (nā′bər), someone who lives in the next house or nearby. *n.*

neph·ew (nef′yü), son of one's brother or sister; son of one's brother-in-law or sister-in-law. *n.*

nerve (nėrv), **1** mental strength; courage: *nerves of steel.* **2** INFORMAL. rude boldness; impudence. *n.*

net (net), an open fabric made of string, cord, or thread, knotted together in such a way as to leave holes regularly arranged. *n.*

news·cast·er (nüz′kas′tər or nyüz′kas′tər), person or commentator who gives the news on a newscast. *n.*

news·pa·per (nüz′pā′pər or nyüz′pā′pər), a daily or weekly publication printed on large sheets of paper folded together, telling the news, carrying advertisements, and having stories, pictures, articles, and useful information. *n.*

newspaper
We read **newspapers** for information.

nic·o·tine (nik′ə tēn′), poison contained in the leaves, roots, and seeds of tobacco. *n.* (*Nicotine* comes from Jean *Nicot,* about 1530-1600, a Frenchman who introduced tobacco to France in about 1560.)

night (nīt), **1** the time between evening and morning, especially when it is dark. **2** the darkness of night; the dark. *n.*

night crawl·er (nīt krôl′ėr), a large earthworm that comes to the surface of the ground at night.

night·gown (nīt′goun′), a long, loose garment worn by a woman or child in bed. *n.*

night·mare (nīt′mâr or nīt′mar′), a very distressing dream or experience: *The hurricane was a nightmare. n.*

night·time (nīt′tīm′), time between evening and morning. *n.*

non·sense (non′sens), worthless stuff; junk: *a drawer full of useless gadgets and other nonsense. n.*

noon (nün), 12 o'clock in the daytime; middle of the day. *n.*

nose (nōz), the part of the face or head just above the mouth. The nose has openings for breathing and smelling. *n.*
lead by the nose, have complete control over.

No·vem·ber (nō vem′bər), the 11th month of the year. It has 30 days. *n.*

num·ber (num′bər), **1** the count or sum of a group of things or persons; amount: *The number of students in our class is twenty.* **2** figure or mark that stands for a number; numeral. *n.*

num·ber key (num′bər kē), a key on a calculator that shows one of the numbers 0 through 9. *n., pl.* **num·ber keys.**

num·ber sen·tence (num′bər sen′təns), a way to write a relationship between numbers. 18 + 27 = 45 and 9 > 6 are number sentences.

O

oak (ōk), several kinds of trees or shrubs found in most parts of the world, with strong, hard, durable wood and nuts called acorns. *n.*

oc·cur (ə kėr′), take place; happen: *Storms often occur in winter. v.*, **oc·curred, oc·cur·ring.**

o·cean (ō′shən), the great body of salt water that covers almost three-fourths of the earth's surface; the sea. *n.*

o·ce·lot (ō′sə lot *or* os′ə lot), a spotted cat somewhat like a leopard, but smaller, found from Texas through Mexico and into parts of South America. *n.*

o'clock (ə klok′), of the clock; by the clock: *It is one o'clock. adv.*

Oc·to·ber (ok tō′bər), the tenth month of the year. It has 31 days. *n.*

odd (od), strange; peculiar; unusual: *What an odd house; it has no windows. adj.*

of (ov *or* uv; *unstressed* əv), **1** belonging to: *a friend of my childhood, the news of the day, the driver of the car.* **2** in regard to; concerning; about: *think well of somebody. prep.*

off (ȯf), so as to stop or lessen: *Turn the water off. adv.*

of·fer (ȯ′fər), hold out to be taken or refused; present: *offer one's hand. She offered us her help. v.*

of·fice (ȯ′fis), place in which the work of a business or profession is done; room in which to work: *The doctor's office is closed. n.*

of·ten (ȯ′fən), in many cases; many times; frequently: *Blame is often misdirected. We come here often. adv.*

oil (oil), any of several kinds of thick, fatty or greasy liquids that are lighter than water, burn easily, and are soluble in alcohol, but not in water, such as mineral oils, kerosene, vegetable and animal oils, olive oils. *n.*

oil gland (oil gland), gland of the skin that secretes oil.

Old English, period in the history of the English language before 1100.

om·niv·ore (om′nə vôr), a consumer that eats producers and consumers. *n.*

on·ly (ōn′lē), merely; just: *only on weekends. adv.*

On·tar·io (on târ′ē ō), **Lake,** one of the five Great Lakes that borders New York and Canada. The water from Niagara Falls flows from Lake Erie to Lake Ontario. It is the smallest of the five Great Lakes. *n.*

o·pen (ō′pən), **1** not shut; not closed; letting (anyone or anything) in or out: *Open windows let in the fresh air.* **2** make or become open: *He is opening the window. The door opened.* **3** spread out or unfold: *open a book, open a letter.* **1** *adj.,* **2,3** *v.,* **o·pened, o·pen·ing.**

op·er·a·tion (op′ə rā′shən), the way a thing works: *The operation of this machine is simple. n.*

op·er·a·tion key (op′ə rā′shən kē), the key which tells the calculator what to perform. The symbols +, −, ×, and ÷ appear on the operation keys. *n., pl.* **op·er·a·tion keys.**

op·tic (op′tik), of the eye; of the sense of sight. The **optic nerve** goes from the eye to the brain. *adj.*

or·ches·tra (ôr′kə strə), group of musicians playing together on various stringed, wind, and percussion instruments. *n., pl.* **or·ches·tras.**

ocelot
An **ocelot** can be up to 3 feet long without the tail.

a	hat	**ī**	ice	**u̇**	put	**ə**	stands for
ā	age	**o**	not	**ü**	rule	**a**	in about
ä	far, calm	**ō**	open	**ch**	child	**e**	in taken
âr	care	**ȯ**	saw	**ng**	long	**i**	in pencil
e	let	**ô**	order	**sh**	she	**o**	in lemon
ē	equal	**oi**	oil	**th**	thin	**u**	in circus
ėr	term	**ou**	out	**ᴛʜ**	then		
i	it	**u**	cup	**zh**	measure		

parallel (definition 1)
parallel stripes on a piece of fabric

oth·er (uᴛʜ′ər), **1** additional or further: *I have no other place to go.* **2** other person or thing. 1 *adj.*, 2 *pron.*

our (our), of us; belonging to us: *We need our coats now. adj.*

our·selves (our selvz′), form used instead of *we* or *us* in cases like: *We cook for ourselves. pron. pl.*

out·cast (out′kast′), person or animal cast out from home and friends. *n.*

out·er ear (ou′tər ir), the part of the ear outside of the head and the ear canal.

out·look (out′lůk′), way of thinking about things; attitude of mind; point of view: *a cheerful outlook on life. n.*

out·side (out′sīd′), **1** the side or surface that is out; outer part: *polish the outside of a car, the outside of a house.* **2** on or to the outside; outdoors: *Run outside and play.* 1 *n.*, 2 *adv.*

o·ven (uv′ən), an enclosed space, usually in a stove, for baking, roasting, and sometimes broiling food. *n.*

P

pack·age (pak′ij), bundle of things packed or wrapped together; box with things packed in it; parcel. *n.*

pad·dle (pad′l), row (a boat or canoe) with a paddle or paddles. *v.*, **pad·dled, pad·dling.**

pain·ful (pān′fəl), causing pain; unpleasant; hurting: *a painful illness, a painful duty. adj.*

pan·ic (pan′ik), a fear spreading through a multitude of people so that they lose control of themselves; unreasoning fear: *When the theater caught fire, there was a panic. n.*

Parthenon
the ancient **Parthenon** in Greece

par·al·lel (par′ə lel), **1** straight lines or planes, lying or extending alongside of one another, always equidistant, but never meeting. **2** any of the imaginary circles around the earth parallel to the equator, marking degrees of latitude that run east and west. 1 *adj.*, 2 *n.*, *pl.* **par·al·lels.**

par·al·lel cir·cuit (par′ə ləl sèr′kit), a circuit that connects several objects in a way that the current for each object has its own path.

par·ent (pâr′ent *or* par′ənt), father or mother. *n.*, *pl.* **par·ents.**

Par·the·non (pär′thə non), temple of Athena on the Acropolis in Athens, regarded as the finest example of Doric architecture. *n.*

par·tic·i·pate (pär tis′ə pāt), have a share; take part. *v.*, **par·tic·i·pat·ed, par·tic·i·pat·ing.**

pave·ment (pāv′mənt), a covering or surface for streets, sidewalks, etc., made of asphalt, concrete, gravel, stones, etc. *n.*

pay·ment (pā′mənt), amount paid: *a monthly payment of $10. n.*

peace (pēs), freedom from war: *work for world peace. n.*

peace·ful (pēs′fəl), **1** full of peace; quiet; calm: *It was peaceful in the mountains.* **2** free from trouble or disturbance. *adj.*

ped·al (ped′l), **1** lever worked by the foot; the part on which the foot is placed to move any kind of machinery. **2** move by pedals: *He pedaled his bicycle slowly up the hill.* 1 *n.*, 2 *v.*

pe·des·tri·an (pə des′trē ən), person who goes on foot; walker. *n.*, *pl.* **pe·des·tri·ans.**

peep (pēp), **1** the cry of a young bird or chicken; a sound like a chirp or squeak. **2** make such a sound; chirp. 1 *n.*, 2 *v.*

pe·o·ny (pē′ə nē), garden plant with large, showy red, pink, or white flowers. *n.*, *pl.* **pe·o·nies.** (The *peony* was named by the Greeks for Paeon, physician of the gods (because the plant was used in medicine).)

peo·ple (pē′pəl), men, women, and children; persons. *n.*, *pl.* **peo·ple**

per·fect (pèr′fikt), without defect; not spoiled at any point; faultless: *a perfect spelling paper. adj.*

pe·rim·e·ter (pə rim′ə tər), the outer boundary of a figure or area: *the perimeter of a circle, the perimeter of a garden. n.*

per·pen·dic·u·lar (pėr′ pən dik′ yə lər), at right angles to. Perpendicular lines intersect to form right angles. *adj.*

per·son·al (pėr′sə nəl), of a person; individual; private: *a personal letter, a personal matter. adj.*

per·son·al·i·ty (pėr′sə nal′ə tē), pleasing or attractive qualities of a person: *The boy is developing a personality. n., pl.* **per·son·al·i·ties.**

pet·al (pet′l), one of the parts of a flower that are usually colored. A daisy has many petals. *n.*

pho·to (fō′tō), picture made with a camera. A photograph is made by the action of light rays from the thing pictured passing through the lens of the camera onto the film. *n.*

pick·le (pik′əl), cucumber preserved in salt water, vinegar, or other liquid. *n.*

piece (pēs), **1** one of the parts into which a thing is divided or broken; bit. **2** portion; limited part; small quantity: *a piece of bread. n.*

pig·eon (pij′ən), any of a group of birds with thick bodies, short tails and legs, which makes a cooing sound, including doves and many varieties of domestic pigeons. *n.*

pil·grim (pil′grəm), **Pilgrim,** one of the Puritan settlers of Plymouth Colony in 1620. *n. pl.,* **Pil·grims.**

pint (pīnt), unit of measure for liquids and dry things, equal to ½ quart; 2 cups; 16 fluid ounces. *n.*

pis·til (pis′tl), the part of a flower that produces seeds. It consists, when complete, of an ovary, a style, and a stigma. *n.*

pitch·er[1] (pich′ər), container for holding and pouring liquids, with a lip on one side and a handle on the other. *n.*

pitch·er[2] (pich′ər), a baseball player who pitches the ball to the batter. *n.*

piz·za (pēt′sə), a spicy Italian dish made by baking a large flat layer of bread dough covered with cheese, tomato sauce, herbs, etc. *n., pl.* **piz·zas.**

plain (plān), a flat stretch of land; prairie: *Cattle and horses wandered over the plains. n., pl.* **plains.**

pla·teau (pla tō′), plain in the mountains or at a height considerably above sea level; large, high plain. *n.*

plate (plāt), a large section of rock that makes up part of the earth's crust. *n., pl.* **plates.**

play (plā), **1** something done to amuse oneself; fun; sport; recreation: *The children are happy at play.* **2** have fun; do something in sport. *The kitten plays with its tail. He played a joke on his sister.* 1 *n.,* 2 *v.*

pledge (plej), **1** a solemn promise: *they made a pledge to give money to charity.* **2** promise solemnly: *We pledge allegiance to the flag.* 1 *n.,* 2 *v.,* **pledged, pledg·ing.**

pluck·y (pluk′ē), having or showing courage: *a plucky dog. adj.,* **pluck·i·er, pluck·i·est.**

pock·et (pok′it), a small bag or pouch sewed into clothing for carrying money or other small articles. *n.*

pod (pod), a small herd of whales or seals. *n.*

po·et·ry (pō′i trē), poems: *a collection of poetry. n.*

point (point), (in mathematics) something that has position without length or width. *n.*

pitcher[1]
a **pitcher** of milk

a	hat	**ī**	ice	**u̇**	put	**ə** stands for	
ā	age	**o**	not	**ü**	rule	**a**	in about
ä	far, calm	**ō**	open	**ch**	child	**e**	in taken
âr	care	**ȯ**	saw	**ng**	long	**i**	in pencil
e	let	**ô**	order	**sh**	she	**o**	in lemon
ē	equal	**oi**	oil	**th**	thin	**u**	in circus
ėr	term	**ou**	out	**ᴛʜ**	then		
i	it	**u**	cup	**zh**	measure		

polar bear

po·lar bear, (pō′lər ber) a large, white bear of the artic regions.

pole (pōl), either of two parts where opposite forces are strongest. A magnet or battery has both a positive pole and a negative pole. *n., pl.* **poles.**

pol·len (pol′ən), tiny grains that make seeds when combined with a flower's eggs. *n.*

pol·lu·tion (pə lü′shən), anything that dirties the environment, especially waste material: *pollution in the air. n.*

pond (pond), body of still water, smaller than a lake. *n.*

pop (pop), make a short, quick, explosive sound. *v.,* **popped, pop·ping.**

pore (pôr), a very small opening. Sweat comes through the pores in the skin. *n.*

por·trait (pôr′trit *or* pôr′trāt), picture of a person, especially of the face. *n.*

pot·ter·y (pot′ər ē), pots, dishes, vases, etc., made from clay and hardened by heat. *n., pl.* **pot·ter·ies.**

pottery
ancient **pottery** made by North American Indians

pour (pôr), flow or cause to flow in a steady stream: *I poured the milk from the bottle. The rain poured down on the field. v.*

pow·er (pou′ər), **1** strength or force; might. **2** authority; influence; control; right: *Congress has power to declare war. n.*

pow·er·ful (pou′ər fəl), having great power or force; mighty; strong: *a powerful person, a powerful medicine, a powerful argument. adj.*

pred·a·tor (pred′ə tər), a consumer that hunts and eats animals. *n.*

pres·sure (presh′ər), a state of trouble or strain: *working under pressure. n.*

prey (prā), animal hunted and killed for food by another animal: *Mice and birds are the prey of cats. n.*

prime me·rid·i·an (prīm mə rid′ē ən), meridian from which the longitude east and west is measured. It passes through Greenwich, England, and its longitude is 0 degrees.

print (print), **1** photograph produced from a negative. **2** produce a photograph by transmission of light through a negative. 1 *n.,* 2 *v.*

pri·vate (prī′vit), not for the public; for just a few special people or for one: *a private road, a private house. adj.*

prob·a·bly (prob′ə blē), more likely than not. *adv.*

pro·duc·er (prə dü′sər), a living thing that can use sunlight to make sugars. *n., pl.* **pro·duc·ers.**

prod·uct (prod′əkt), **1** that which is produced; result of work or of growth: *factory products, farm products.* **2** number resulting from multiplying two or more numbers together: *40 is the product of 8 and 5. n., pl.* **prod·ucts.**

proud (proud), feeling or thinking well of, showing satisfaction: *I am proud to call him my friend. adj.*

psy·chol·o·gist (sī kol′ə jist), an expert who is trained to help people with feelings, especially troubled feelings that last a long time. *n.*

pud·ding (pud′ing), a soft cooked food, usually sweet: *rice pudding. n.*

pueb·lo (pweb′lō), an Indian village built of adobe and stone. *n., pl.* **pueb·los.**

pun·ish (pun′ish), cause pain, loss, or discomfort to for some fault or offense: *punish criminals for wrongdoing. v.* (Punish is from Old French *puniss-,* a form of *punir,* meaning "punish," which came from Latin *punire,* meaning "penalty.")

pun·ish·ment (pun′ish mənt), pain, suffering, or loss: *Her punishment for stealing was a year in prison. n.*

pup (pup), a young dog; puppy. *n.*

pu·pil[1] (pyü′pel), person who is learning in school or being taught by someone. *n.*

pu·pil[2] (pyü′pel), the opening in the center of the iris of the eye which looks like a black spot and where light can enter the eye. *n.*

pur·suit (per süt′), a chase: *The dog is in pursuit of the cat. n.*

Q

quart (kwôrt), measure of capacity for liquids, equal to one-fourth of a gallon: *a quart of milk. n.*

queen (kwēn), woman who rules a country and its people. *n.*

ques·tion (kwes′chen), thing asked in order to get information; inquiry: *The teacher answered the children's questions. n.*

quick (kwik), fast and sudden; swift: *The cat made a quick jump. Many weeds have a quick growth. adj.*

qui·et (kwī′et), making no sound; with little or no noise: *quiet footsteps, a quiet room. adj.*

quilt (kwilt), cover for a bed, usually made of two pieces of cloth with a soft pad between, held in place by stitching. *n.*

quit (kwit), **1** stop: *They quit work at five.* **2** leave: *quit one's job. v.,* **quit** or **quit·ted, quit·ting.**

quite (kwīt), **1** completely; entirely: *a hat quite out of fashion. I am quite alone.* **2** actually; really; positively: *quite the thing. adv.*

quo·tient (kwō′shent), number arrived at by dividing one number by another. In $26 \div 2 = 13$, 13 is the quotient. *n.*

R

rain gauge (rān gāj), a tool that measures precipitation. *n.*

rat·tle (rat′l), toy, instrument, etc., that makes a noise when it is shaken. *n.*

ray (rā), a set of points that has one endpoint and that extends without end in one direction. *n.*

Rd., Road.

re·act (rē akt′), act in response: *Dogs react to affection. v.*

re·al·ly (rē′e lē), actually; truly; in fact. *adv.*

rea·son (rē′zn), **1** justification; explanation: *What is your reason for being so late?* **2** think logically; think things out: *Most animals can't reason.* 1 *n.,* 2 *v.*

re·bound (rē′bound′), (in basketball) a ball that bounds back off the backboard or the rim of the basket after a shot has been made. *n.*

re·build (rē bild′), build again or anew. *v.,* **re·built, re·build·ing.**

re·call (ri kȯl′), call back to mind; remember: *I can recall stories told to me when I was a small child. v.*

re·ceiv·er (ri sē′ver), thing that receives: *Public telephones have coin receivers for change. n.*

re·cent (rē′snt), done or made not long ago: *recent events. adj.*

re·cess (rē′ses *or* ri ses′), time during which work stops: *There will be a short recess before the next meeting. n.*

rec·og·nize (rek′eg nīz), **1** know again: *You have grown so much that I scarcely recognized you.* **2** identify: *recognize a person from a description. v.,* **rec·og·nized, rec·og·niz·ing.**

quilt
a sampler **quilt**

a	hat	ī	ice	u̇	put	ə	stands for
ā	age	o	not	ü	rule	a	in about
ä	far, calm	ō	open	ch	child	e	in taken
âr	care	ȯ	saw	ng	long	i	in pencil
e	let	ô	order	sh	she	o	in lemon
ē	equal	oi	oil	th	thin	u	in circus
ėr	term	ou	out	ŦH	then		
i	it	u	cup	zh	measure		

re·cord (rek'ərd), a thin, flat disk, usually of vinyl or other plastic, with narrow grooves on its surface, used on a phonograph. *n.*

record

re·cov·er (ri kuv'ər), **1** get back (something lost, taken away, or stolen): *recover one's health, recover a lost purse.* **2** get well; get back to a normal condition: *She is recovering from a cold. v.*

rec·tan·gle (rek'tang'gəl), a four-sided plane figure with four right angles. *n.*

re·cy·cle (rē sī'kəl), to process or treat (something) in order that it may be used again. Paper, aluminum, and glass products are commonly recycled. *v.,* **re·cy·cled, re·cy·cling.**

red (red), the color of blood or of a ruby: *The jewel is redder than the sun at sunset. n., adj.,* **redder, reddest.**

re·flec·tor (ri flek'tər), a piece of glass or metal for reflecting light: *The motorist saw the reflector on the girl's bike and slowed down. n.*

re·late (ri lāt'), **1** give an account of; tell: *The traveler related her adventures.* **2** be connected in any way: *We are interested in what relates to ourselves. v.,* **re·lat·ed, re·lat·ing.**

recycle
children **recycling**
paper, cans, and bottles

rel·a·tive (rel'ə tiv), person who belongs to the same family as another, such as father, brother, aunt, nephew, or cousin. *n., pl.* **rel·a·tives.**

re·lax (ri laks'), loosen up; make or become less stiff or firm: *Relax when you dance. v.*

re·main·der (ri mān'dər), **1** number left over after subtracting one number from another. In 9 − 2, the remainder is 7. **2** number left over after dividing one number by another. In 14 ÷ 3, the quotient is 4 with a remainder of 2. *n.*

re·mem·ber (ri mem'bər), call back to mind: *I can't remember that man's name. v.*

re·mote (ri mōt'), out of the way; secluded. *adj.*

re·place (ri plās'), fill or take the place of: *A substitute replaced our teacher. v.,* **re·placed, re·plac·ing.**

re·ply (ri plī'), answer by words or action; respond: *She replied with a shout. The washing machine replied with a bang. v.,* **re·plied, re·ply·ing.**

rep·re·sent (rep'ri zent'), act in place of; speak and act for: *We chose a committee to represent us. v.*

re·pro·duce (rē'prə düs' *or* rē'prə dyüs'), produce offspring: *Most plants reproduce by seeds. v.,* **re·pro·duced, re·pro·duc·ing.**

re·pub·lic (ri pub'lik), nation or state in which the citizens elect representatives to manage the government, which is usually headed by a president. The United States and Mexico are republics. *n.*

res·cue (res'kyü), a saving or freeing from danger, capture, harm, etc.: *A dog was chasing our cat when your sister came to the rescue. n.*

re·search (ri serch' *or* rē'serch'), **1** a careful hunting for facts or truth; inquiry; investigation: *cancer research.* **2** to hunt for facts or truth; inquire; investigate. 1 *n., pl.* **re·search·es;** 2 *v.*

re·sent (ri zent'), feel injured and angry at; feel indignation at: *I resented being called lazy. v.*

res·er·va·tion (rez'ər vā'shən), land set aside by the government for a special purpose: *an Indian reservation. n.*

re·source (ri sôrs' *or* rē'sôrs), **1** any supply that will meet a need. We have resources of money, of knowledge, of strength, etc. **2 resources,** *pl.* the actual and potential wealth of a country: *natural resources, human resources. n., pl.* **re·sourc·es.**

re·sult (ri zult'), good or useful effect: *The new medicine got results. n.*

ret·i·na (ret'n ə), layer of cells at the back of the eyeball that is sensitive to light and receives the images of things looked at. *n., pl.* **ret·i·nas, ret·i·nae** (ret'n ē').

re·un·ion (rē yü′nyən), a coming together again: *the reunion of parted friends. n.*

re·use (rē yüz′), use again: *reuse the papers. v.*, **re·used, re·us·ing.**

Rhode Is·land (rōd ī′lend), one of the northeastern states of the United States. Rhode Island is the smallest state. *Abbreviation:* R.I. or RI *Capital:* Providence.

Rich·ter scale (rik′tər skāl), a scale for indicating the force or magnitude of earthquakes. On this scale, light tremors register 1.5, while highly destructive earthquakes measure 8.3.

rid·den (rid′n), See **ride.** *I had ridden my horse all day. v.*

ride (rīd), sit on a horse and make it go. *v.*, **rode, rid·den, rid·ing.**

rim (rim), an edge, border, or margin on or around anything: *the rim of a wheel, the rim of a basketball net. n.*

riv·er (riv′ər), **1** a large, natural stream of water that flows into a lake, ocean, etc. **2** any abundant stream or flow: *rivers of lava. n.*

rob (rob), take away from by force or threats; steal from; plunder; pillage: *Bandits robbed the bank of thousands of dollars. v.*, **robbed, robbing.**

rough (ruf), **1** not smooth; not level; not even: *rough boards, the rough bark of an oak tree, a rough, rocky hill.* **2** INFORMAL. unpleasant; hard; severe: *She had a rough time in the hospital. adj.*

run·way (run′wā′), **1** a paved strip at an airport on which aircraft land and take off. **2** way, track, groove, trough, etc., along which something moves, slides, etc. *n.*

S

sad (sad), not happy; full of sorrow: *You feel sad if your best friend goes away. adj.*, **sad·der, sad·dest.**

safe (sāf), free from harm or danger: *Keep money in a safe place. adj.*, —**safe′ly,** *adv.*

sage·brush (sāj′brush′), a grayish shrub that smells like sage, common on the dry plains of western North America. *n.*

said (sed), See **say.** *He said he would come. They had said "No" every time. v.*

salm·on (sam′ən), a large saltwater and freshwater food fish with silvery scales and yellowish-pink flesh. It appears in the northern Atlantic and northern Pacific, and it swims up rivers in order to spawn. *n., pl.* **salm·on.**

say (sā), speak; utter: *What did you say? "Thank you," she said. v.* **said, saying.**

scar·y (sker′ē *or* skâr′ē), INFORMAL. **1** causing fright or alarm: *scary sounds, a scary movie.* **2** easily frightened. *adj.*, **scar·i·er, scar·i·est.**

school¹ (skül), place for teaching and learning. *n.*

school² (skül), a large number of the same kind of fish or water animals swimming together: *a school of mackerel. n.*

scis·sors (siz′ərz), tool or instrument for cutting that has two sharp blades so fastened that their edges slide against each other. *n. pl. or sing.*

scrap·book (skrap′bùk′), book in which pictures or clippings are pasted and kept. *n.*

a	hat	ī	ice	ù	put	ə stands for	
ā	age	o	not	ü	rule	a	in about
ä	far, calm	ō	open	ch	child	e	in taken
âr	care	ò	saw	ng	long	i	in pencil
e	let	ô	order	sh	she	o	in lemon
ē	equal	oi	oil	th	thin	u	in circus
ėr	term	ou	out	ŦH	then		
i	it	u	cup	zh	measure		

scratch (skrach), **1** rub or scrape to relieve itching: *Don't scratch your mosquito bites.* **2** a mark made by scratching: *He had a large scratch on his arm.* 1 *v.,* 2 *n., pl.* **scratches.**
from scratch, with no advantages; without help; without prepackaged ingredients.

scream (skrēm), a loud, sharp, piercing cry. *n.*

screen (skrēn), **1** wire woven together with small openings in between. **2** a glass surface on which television pictures, computer information, radar images, etc., appear. *n.*

seal

Seals usually live in cold areas.

scrub (skrub), **1** rub hard; wash or clean by rubbing: *I scrubbed the floor with a brush and soap.* **2** a scrubbing: *Give your hands a good scrub.* 1 *v.,* **scrubbed, scrub·bing;** 2 *n.*

seal (sēl), a flesh-eating sea mammal with large flippers, living usually in cold regions. *n., pl.* **seals** or **seal.**

sea·son (sē′zn), **1** one of the four periods of the year; spring, summer, autumn, or winter. **2** any period of time marked by something special: *a holiday season, the harvest season. n.*

see (sē), be aware of by using the eyes; look at: *See that black cloud. v.,* **saw, seen, see·ing.**

seed (sēd), the part of a plant from which another plant like it can grow. A seed has an outer skin or coat which encloses the embryo that will become the new plant and a supply of food for its growth. *n., pl.* **seeds** or **seed.**

seen (sēn), See **see.** *Have you seen Father? v.*

seg·ment (seg′mənt), two points and the part of a line between them. *n.*

seismograph

A **seismograph** records sudden movements of the earth's crust.

seis·mo·graph (sīz′mə graf), instrument for recording the direction, strength and length of earthquakes. *n.* (*Seismograph* comes from Greek *seismos,* meaning "earthquake," and the combining form *-graph.*)

sep·a·rate (sep′ə rāt′), **1** keep apart; be between; divide: *The Atlantic Ocean separates America from Europe.* **2** divide into parts or groups: *separate a tangle of yarn. v.,* **sep·a·rat·ed, sep·a·rat·ing.**

sep·a·ra·tion (sep′ə rā′shən), a being apart; being separated: *The friends were glad to meet after so long a separation. n.*

Sep·tem·ber (sep tem′bər), the ninth month of the year. It has 30 days. *n.*

ser·ies cir·cuit (sir′ēz sėr′kit), a circuit that connects several objects one after the other so that the current flows in a single path.

ser·i·ous (sir′ē əs), showing deep thought or purpose; thoughtful; grave: *a serious manner, a serious face. adj.*

serve (sėrv), **1** put (food or drink) on the table. **2** in tennis, a player's turn to start the play by hitting the ball. 1 *v.,* **served, serv·ing;** 2 *n.*

set (set), **1** put in the right place, position, or condition; put in proper order; arrange: *The doctor set my broken leg. Set the clock. Set the table for dinner.* **2** number of things or persons belonging together; group; outfit: *a set of dishes.* 1 *v.,* **set, set·ting;** 2 *n.*

sev·er·al (sev′ər əl), more than two or three but not many; some; a few: *gain several pounds (adj.). Several have given their consent (n.)*

sham·poo (sham pü′), **1** wash (the hair, the scalp, a rug, etc.) with a soapy or oily preparation. **2** a washing of the hair, the scalp, a rug, etc., with such a preparation. **3** the preparation used in this way. 1 *v.,* **sham·pooed, sham·poo·ing;** 2,3 *n., pl.* **sham·poos.**

share (shãr *or* shar), use together; enjoy together; have in common: *The sisters share the same room. v.,* **shared, shar·ing.**

she (shē), anything thought of as female and spoken about or mentioned before: *She was my sister. She was a fine old ship. pron.*

sheep (shēp), mammal with a thick coat and hoofs that chews its cud, and makes a baaing sound. Sheep are related to goats and are raised for wool, meat, and skin. *n., pl.* **sheep.**

she'll (shēl; *unstressed* shil), she will: *She'll help you with your problem.*

shel·ter (shel′tər), **1** something that covers or protects from weather, danger, or attack. **2** protection; refuge. *n.*

sher·iff (sher′if), the most important law-enforcing officer of a county. A sheriff appoints deputies who help to keep order in the county. *n.*

shoot (shüt), **1** send swiftly: *A bow shoots an arrow. She shot question after question at us.* **2** move suddenly and swiftly: *A car shot by us. Flames shot up from the burning house.* **3** take (a picture) with a camera; photograph. **4** send (a ball, puck, marble, etc.) toward the goal, pocket, etc. *v.,* **shot, shoot·ing.**

short (shôrt), not long; of small extent from end to end. *adj.*

should·n't (shùd′nt), should not: *You shouldn't cross the street without looking both ways.*

show (shō), **1** make clear to; explain to: *Show us how to do the problem.* **2** a play, motion picture, etc., or a performance of one of these: *The show starts at 6:00.* **1** *v.,* **showed, shown** or **showed, show·ing; 2** *n.*

show·er (shou′ər), bath in which water pours down on the body from an overhead nozzle. *n.*

shown (shōn), See **show.** *We were shown many tricks by the magician. v.*

shud·der (shud′ər), tremble with horror, fear, cold. *v.*

shut·ter (shut′ər), a movable cover, slide, etc., for closing an opening. The device that opens and closes in front of the lens of a camera is the shutter. *n.*

sign (sīn), **1** write: *Sign your initials here.* **2** an inscribed board, space, etc., serving for advertisement, information, regulations, etc.: *See the sign over the door. The stop sign is used by the crossing guard.* **3** motion or gesture used to mean, represent, or point out something: *talk to a deaf person by signs.* **1** *v.,* **2,3** *n.*

sig·nal (sig′nəl), **1** a sign giving notice, warning, or pointing out something. **2** make a signal or signals to: *She signaled the car to stop by raising her hand.* **1** *n.,* **2** *v.,* —**sig·naled, sig·nal·ing** or **sig·nalled, sig·nal·ling.**

sil·ver (sil′vər), **1** a shiny, white, precious metal. **2** made of silver: *a silver spoon.* **1** *n.,* **2** *adj.*

sim·ple (sim′pəl), easy to do or understand: *a simple problem. adj.,* **sim·pler, sim·plest.**

si·ren (sī′rən), kind of whistle that makes a loud, piercing sound: *We heard the fire engine's siren. n.*

sis (sis), INFORMAL. sister. *n.*

sit (sit), rest on the lower part of the body with the weight off the feet: *She sat in a chair. v.,* **sat, sit·ting.**

skate·board (skāt′bôrd′), **1** a narrow board resembling a surfboard, with roller-skate wheels attached to each end, used for gliding or moving on any hard surface. **2** to ride a skateboard: *The neighborhood children love to skateboard in the summer.* **1** *n.,* **2** *v.*

skate·board·ing (skāt′bôr′ding), the sport of riding a skateboard. *n.*

sheep
a **sheep** and its young

silver
a **silver** table setting

a	hat	**ī**	ice	**ù**	put	**ə** stands for	
ā	age	**o**	not	**ü**	rule	**a**	in about
ä	far, calm	**ō**	open	**ch**	child	**e**	in taken
âr	care	**ò**	saw	**ng**	long	**i**	in pencil
e	let	**ô**	order	**sh**	she	**o**	in lemon
ē	equal	**oi**	oil	**th**	thin	**u**	in circus
ėr	term	**ou**	out	**ᵺ**	then		
i	it	**u**	cup	**zh**	measure		

ski (definition 1)
equipment for snow
skiing

soccer
playing the game of
soccer

ski (skē), 1 one of a pair of long, slender pieces of hard wood, plastic, or metal, that can be fastened to the shoes or boots to enable a person to glide over snow. 2 glide over the snow on skis. 1 n., pl. **skis** or **ski**; 2 v., **skied, ski·ing.**

skirt (skėrt), 1 a woman's or girl's garment that hangs from the waist. 2 something like a skirt: *A skirt covered the legs of the chair. n.*

skulk (skulk), a group of animals that prey on game, as the fox or weasel. *n.*

sky·scrap·er (skī/skrā/pər), a very tall building. *n.*

slam-dunk (slam dungk), (in basketball) a shot made by leaping so that the hands are above the rim of the basket, and throwing the ball down through the netting. *n.*

slap (slap), put, dash, or cast with force. *v.*, **slapped, slap·ping.**

slip (slip), slide suddenly without wanting to: *He slipped on the icy sidewalk. v.*, **slipped, slip·ping.**

slip·per (slip/ər), a light, low shoe that is slipped on easily: *dancing slippers, bedroom slippers. n., pl.* **slip·pers.**

slow (slō), not fast: *Traffic is very slow during rush hour. I walked slowly home. adj.* —**slow/ly,** *adv.*

small (smȯl), 1 not large; little; not large as compared with other things of the same kind: *A cottage is smaller than a house.* 2 not great in amount, value: *The cent is our smallest coin. adj.*, **small·er, small·est.**

smoke (smōk), the mixture of gases and particles of carbon that can be seen rising in a cloud from anything burning. *n.*

smug·gle (smug/əl), bring, take, put, etc., secretly: *I tried to smuggle my puppy into the house. v.*, **smug·gled, smug·gling.**

snack (snak), 1 a light meal, especially one eaten between regular meals. 2 to eat a light meal. *We snacked on fruit after school.* 1 *n.*, 2 *v.*

snail (snāl), a small, soft-bodied animal that crawls very slowly. Most snails have spiral shells on their backs into which they can move for protection. *n.*

snap·shot (snap/shot/), photograph taken quickly with a small camera. *n.*

snore (snôr), a harsh rough sound made in sleeping. *n.*

soc·cer (sok/ər), game played with a round ball between two teams of eleven players each. The players may strike the ball with any part of the body except the hands and arms. Only the goalkeeper may touch the ball with the hands and arms. Players score by knocking the ball into a net cage at either end of the field. *n.*

soft (sȯft), 1 not hard; not stiff; yielding easily to touch: *a soft pillow.* 2 not loud: *a soft voice.* 1,2 *adj.* —**soft/ness,** *n.*

soft·ball (sȯft/bȯl/), 1 a kind of baseball that is played on a smaller field, with a larger and softer ball, and lighter bats. Softball must be pitched underhand. 2 the ball used in this game. *n.*

soft-boiled (sȯft/boild/), (of an egg) boiled only a little so that the yolk is still soft. *adj.*

soft drink (sȯft dringk), drink that does not contain alcohol.

soft·en (sȯf/ən), make or become soft: *Hand lotion softens the skin. Soap softens in water. v.*

soft soap (sȯft sōp), a liquid or semiliquid soap.

some·one (sum/wun), some person; somebody: *Someone is coming. pron.*

some·thing (sum/thing), some thing; a particular thing not named or known: *I'm sure I've forgotten something. n.*

some·times (sum/tīmz), now and then; at times. *adv.*

some·where (sum/hwâr *or* sum/hwar), in or to some place; in or to one place or another: *She lives somewhere in the area. adv.*

source (sôrs), person or place from which anything comes or is obtained: *The newspaper gets news from many sources. Mines are the chief source of diamonds.* n., pl. **sourc·es.**

south·ern (suᴛн′ərn), 1 toward the south: *a southern view.* 2 from the south: *a southern breeze.* adj.

speak (spēk), 1 say words; talk: *speak clearly.* 2 use (a language): *Do you speak French?* v., **spoke, spo·ken, speak·ing.**

spe·cial (spesh′əl), more than ordinary; unusual; exceptional. adj.

speech (spēch), what is said; the words spoken: *We made the usual farewell speeches.* n., pl. **speech·es.**

spi·der (spī′dər), a small animal with eight legs, no wings, and a body divided into two parts. Spiders are arachnids that spin webs to catch insects for food. n.

spider web (web), the delicate, silken threads spun by a spider.

spore (spôr), a single cell capable of growing into a new plant or animal. Spores are produced by plants that do not have flowers, such as ferns or molds. n., pl. **spores.**

spot·less (spot′lis), without a spot: *a spotless white shirt.* adj.

square (skwâr), 1 a plane figure with four equal sides and four right angles. 2 having this shape: *a square box. A block of stone is usually square.* 1 n., 2 adj., **squar·er, squar·est.**

squash (skwosh), press or be pressed until soft or flat; crush: *She squashed the bug. Carry the cream puffs carefully, for they squash easily.* v.

squeak (skwēk), make a short, sharp, shrill sound: *A mouse squeaks.* v.

squeal (skwēl), 1 make a long, sharp, shrill cry: *A pig squeals when it is hurt.* 2 such a cry. 1 v., 2 n.

squeeze (skwēz), 1 press hard; compress: *Don't squeeze the kitten; you'll hurt it.* 2 force out by pressure: *squeeze juice from a lemon.* 3 crush; crowd: *Six people squeezed into the little car.* v., **squeezed, squeez·ing, —squeez′a·ble,** adj.

squirm (skwėrm), turn and twist; writhe: *The restless boy squirmed in his chair.* v.

squir·rel (skwėr′əl), a small, bushy-tailed rodent that usually lives in trees. n.

squirt (skwėrt), force out (liquid) through a narrow opening: *squirt water through a tube, squirt water at the statue.* v.

sta·men (stā′mən), the part of a flower that contains the pollen. The stamens are surrounded by the petals. n., pl. **sta·mens, stam·i·na** (stam′ə ne).

stand (stand), be set upright; be placed; be located: *The box stands over there. Some food stood on the table.* v., **stood, stand·ing.**

state (stāt), of a state: *a state road, state police, state government.* adj.

state·ment (stāt′mənt), something stated; report; account: *Her statement was correct.* n.

sta·tion (stā′shən), a regular stopping place: *She met her at the bus station.* n.

steal (stēl), 1 take (something) that does not belong to one; take dishonestly. 2 move secretly or quietly: *She stole softly out of the house.* 3 (in baseball) run to (second base, third base, or home plate) as the pitcher throws the ball to the catcher. v., **stole, sto·len, steal·ing.**

spider
a crab **spider**

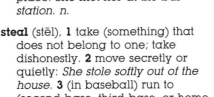

a	hat	**ī**	ice	**u̇**	put	**ə** stands for	
ā	age	**o**	not	**ü**	rule	**a**	in about
ä	far, calm	**ō**	open	**ch**	child	**e**	in taken
âr	care	**ȯ**	saw	**ng**	long	**i**	in pencil
e	let	**ô**	order	**sh**	she	**o**	in lemon
ē	equal	**oi**	oil	**th**	thin	**u**	in circus
ėr	term	**ou**	out	**тн**	then		
i	it	**u**	cup	**zh**	measure		

steam (stēm), give off steam: *The cup of coffee was steaming. v.*

steel (stēl), an alloy of iron and carbon. Steel has greater hardness and flexibility than cast iron and is used for tools and machinery. *n.*

stiff (stif), **1** not easily bent; fixed; rigid. **2** hard to move. *adj.*

St. Law·rence Sea·way (sānt lôr′ens sē′wā′), waterway that links the Great Lakes to the Atlantic Ocean by means of canals and the St. Lawrence River.

stole (stōl), See **steal**. *They stole my car. v.*

stom·ach (stum′ek), the large muscular bag in the body which receives swallowed food, and digests some of it before passing it on to the intestines. *n.*

stood (stùd), See **stand**. *She stood in the corner for five minutes. I had stood in line all morning to buy tickets to the game. v.*

stop (stop), leave off (moving, acting, doing, being, etc.); come to an end; cease: *The baby stopped crying. The rain is stopping. v.,* **stopped, stop·ping.**

storm
a lightning **storm**

storm (stôrm), a strong wind often accompanied by rain, snow, hail, or thunder and lightning. In deserts there are storms of sand. *n.*

St. Pat·rick's Day (sānt pat′riks dā), a holiday celebrated in honor of St. Patrick, who converted Ireland to Christianity; March 17.

strange (strānj), unusual; odd; peculiar: *a strange accident, a strange experience. adj.,* **strang·er, strang·est.**

strat·e·gy (strat′ə jē), plan based on skillful planning: *We need some strategy to win this game. n., pl.* **strat·e·gies.**

straw·ber·ry (strȯ′ber′ē), the small, juicy, red fruit of a plant that grows close to the ground. Strawberries are good to eat. *n., pl.* **straw·ber·ries.**

street (strēt), place or way for automobiles, wagons, etc., to go. *n.*

strength (strengkh), **1** quality of being strong; power; force; vigor. **2** something a person is strong in or can do well. *n.*

strike (strīk), **1** set or be set on fire by hitting or rubbing: *strike a match.* **2** a stopping of work to get better pay, shorter hours, and so on. *The workers were home for six weeks during the strike last year.* **3** baseball pitched through the strike zone and not swung at, any pitch that is swung at and missed, or any pitch that is hit foul. After three strikes, a batter is out. *1 v.,* **struck, struck** or **strick·en, strik·ing;** *2,3 n.*

stroke (strōk), a single complete movement to be made again and again: *He rowed with a strong stroke of the oars. She swims a fast stroke. n.*

stud·y (stud′ē), try to learn: *She studied her spelling lesson for half an hour. I am studying to be a doctor. v.,* **stud·ied, stud·y·ing.**

stuff (stuf), belongings; goods: *What will we do with all this stuff? n.*

suc·cess·ful (sək ses′fəl), having success; ending in success; prosperous; fortunate. *adj.*

sud·den (sud′n), happening without warning or notice; not expected: *a sudden stop, a sudden rainstorm, a sudden rise to power. adj.*

sud·den·ly (sud′n lē), in a sudden manner. *adv.*

suf·fer (suf′ər), **1** have or feel (pain, grief, etc.): *I suffered sunburn from being at the beach all day.* **2** bear with patiently; endure: *I will not suffer such insults. v.*

suf·fix (suf′iks), syllable or syllables put at the end of a word to change its meaning or to make another word, as *-ly* in *badly, -ness* in *goodness,* and *-ful* in *spoonful. n., pl.* **suf·fix·es.**

sug·ar (shùg′ər), a sweet substance obtained chiefly from sugar cane or sugar beets and used extensively in food products; sucrose. *n.*

suit (süt), set of clothes to be worn together. A man's suit consists of a coat, pants, and sometimes a vest. A woman's suit consists of a coat and either a skirt or pants. *n.*

Sun., Sunday.

su·pe·ri·or (sə pir′ē ər), above the average; very good; excellent: *superior work in school. adj.*

Su·pe·ri·or (sə pir′ē ər), **Lake**, the largest of the five Great Lakes. These lakes form the largest group of freshwater lakes in the world. *n.*

sup·per (sup′ər), the evening meal; meal eaten early in the evening. *n.*

sup·ply (sə plī′), **1** provide (what is lacking); furnish: *Many cities supply books for children in school.* **2 supplies,** *pl.* the food, equipment, etc., necessary for an army drive, or the like. 1 *v.*, **sup·plied, sup·ply·ing;** 2 *n., pl.* **sup·plies.**

sup·port (sə pôrt′), **1** give strength or courage to; keep up; help. **2** be in favor of; back; second: *She supports the amendment.* **3** help or assistance: *They need our financial support.* 1,2 *v.*, 3 *n.*

sup·pose (sə pōz′), **1** consider as possible; take for granted; assume. **2** believe, think, or imagine: *I suppose he will come at noon. v.*, **sup·posed, sup·pos·ing.**

sur·prise (sər prīz′), cause to feel surprised; astonish: *The victory surprised us. v.*, **sur·prised, sur·pris·ing.**

sus·pense·ful (sə spens′fəl), characterized by or full of suspense. *adj.*

swarm (swôrm), group of bees settled together in a hive. *n.*

sweat gland (swet gland), gland of the skin that secretes sweat. A sweat gland is connected with the surface of the skin by a tube or duct that ends in a pore.

swim (swim), move along on or in the water by using arms, legs, fins, etc.: *Fish swim. Most boys and girls like swimming in the lake. v.*, **swam, swum, swim·ming.**

sword (sôrd), weapon, usually metal, with a long, sharp blade fixed in a handle or hilt. *n.*

swum (swum) See **swim**. *We have swum in that lake many times. v.*

T

Taj Ma·hal (täj′ mə häl′), a famous white marble mausoleum in northern India, built in the 1600s.

take (tāk), **1** lay hold of; grasp: *I took her hand when we crossed the street.* **2** indulge in: *take a nap, take a vacation. v.*, **took, tak·en, tak·ing.**

tax (taks), money paid by people for the support of the government and services; money regularly collected from citizens by the government. *n., pl.* **tax·es.**

teach·er (tē′chər), person who teaches, especially one who teaches in a school: *We entered the teachers' lounge. n.*

team·mate (tēm′māt′), a fellow member of a team. *n.*

tear (tir), drop of salty liquid coming from the eye. *n., pl.* **tears.**

tem·per·a·ture (tem′pər ə chər), **1** degree of heat or cold. The temperature of freezing water is 32 degrees Fahrenheit (0 degrees Celsius). **2** a body temperature higher than normal; fever: *A sick person may have a temperature. n.*

swim

swimming the backstroke

a	hat	**ī**	ice	**u̇**	put	<u>ə stands for</u>	
ā	age	**o**	not	**ü**	rule	**a**	in about
ä	far, calm	**ō**	open	**ch**	child	**e**	in taken
âr	care	**ȯ**	saw	**ng**	long	**i**	in pencil
e	let	**ô**	order	**sh**	she	**o**	in lemon
ē	equal	**oi**	oil	**th**	thin	**u**	in circus
ėr	term	**ou**	out	**ᵺ**	then		
i	it	**u**	cup	**zh**	measure		

thrill

The roller coaster gave us
a **thrill**.

tiger

The **tiger** is about 9
feet long with the tail.

tem·ple (tem′pəl), building used for
the service or worship of a god or
gods. *n.*

ten·sion (ten′shən), **1** a stretching.
2 mental strain: *Tension may be
brought on by overwork. n.*

Tex·as (tek′səs), one of the
southwestern states of the United
States. *Abbreviation:* Tex. or TX
Capital: Austin. *n.*

than (ᴛʜan; *unstressed* ᴛʜən), **1** in
comparison with. **2** compared to
that which: *You know better than I
do.* 1,2 *conj.,* 1 *prep.*

that's (ᴛʜats), that is: *That's a beautiful
picture.*

their (ᴛʜâr), of them; belonging to
them: *I like their house. adj.*

them (ᴛʜem; *unstressed* ᴛʜəm), the
persons, animals, things, or ideas
spoken about: *The books are new;
take care of them. pron.*

then (ᴛʜen), **1** being at that time;
existing then: *the then President.*
2 soon afterwards. 1 *adj.,* 2 *adv.*

there (ᴛʜâr *or* ᴛʜar; *unstressed* ᴛʜər), in
or at that place: *Finish reading the
page and stop there. adv.*

they (ᴛʜā), the persons, animals,
things, or ideas spoken about: *I
had three books yesterday. Do you
know where they are? They are on
the table. pron. pl.*

they'd (ᴛʜād), **1** they had: *They'd
arrived late.* **2** they would: *They'd
come if they could.*

they'll (ᴛʜāl), they will: *They'll be a
few minutes late.*

they're (ᴛʜâr), they are: *They're going
to be leaving soon.*

thirst·y (thėr′stē), **1** feeling thirst;
having thirst: *The dog is thirsty:
please give it some water.*
2 having a strong desire or
craving; eager. *adj.,* **thirst·i·er,
thirst·i·est.**

thought·ful (thȯt′fəl), full of thought;
thinking: *He was thoughtful for a
while and then replied, "No." adj.*

thou·sand (thou′znd), ten hundred;
1000. *n., adj.*

threat (thret), sign or cause of
possible evil or harm. *n.*

thrill (thril), a shivering, exciting
feeling. *n.*

throat (thrōt), the passage from the
mouth to the stomach or the lungs.
n.

throne (thrōn), chair on which a king,
queen, bishop, or other person of
high rank sits during ceremonies.
n.

through (thrü), **1** from end to end of;
from side to side of; between the
parts of; from beginning to end of:
*march through a town, cut a tunnel
through a mountain.* **2** here and
there in; over; around: *stroll
through the streets of a city. prep.*

throw (thrō), **1** send through the air;
toss; hurl. **2** bring to the ground: *His
horse threw him.* **3** put by force:
throw someone into jail. v., **threw,
thrown, throw·ing.**

thrown (thrōn), See **throw.** *She has
thrown her old toys away. v.*

thumb (thum), the short, thick finger of
the hand. It can be moved against
any of the other four fingers to
grasp things. *n.*

ti·ger (tī′gər), a large, fierce,
flesh-eating mammal of Asia, that
has dull-yellow fur striped with
black. It is related to the cat and
the lion. *n., pl.* **ti·gers.**

ti·tle (tī′tl), **1** the name of a book,
poem, picture, song, etc. **2** name
showing rank, occupation, or
condition in life. King, duke, lord,
majesty, highness, captain, doctor,
and Miss are titles. *n.*

to (tü; *unstressed* tu̇ *or* tə), **1** in the
direction of; toward a destination:
She came to school. **2** *To* is used
with verbs. *I like to play the piano.*
3 on against: *Nail the shelf to the
wall.* **4** *To* is used to show action
toward. *Give the book to me. prep.*

toe (tō), one of the five divisions that
end the foot. *n., pl.* **toes.**

tomb (tüm), grave, vault, mausoleum,
etc., for a dead body, often above
ground. *n.*

to·mor·row (tə môr′ō), **1** the day after today. **2** on the day after today. **1** *n.,* **2** *adv.*

tongue (tung), the movable fleshy organ in the mouth. The tongue is used in tasting and by people, for talking. *n.*

too (tü), **1** in addition; also; besides. **2** beyond what is desirable, proper, or right; more than enough. *adv.*

took (tùk), See **take**. *She took the car an hour ago. v.*

toot (tüt), sound of a horn, whistle, etc. *n.*

tot (tot), a little child. *n.*

touch·down (tuch′doun′), score of six points made in football by putting the ball on the ground behind the opponent's goal line. *n.*

tough (tuf), **1** hard to cut, tear, or chew. **2** strong; hard: *a tough team. adj.*

track (trak), **1** a double, parallel line of metal rails for cars to run on: *railroad tracks.* **2** a course for running or racing. *n.*

trash (trash), **1** broken or torn bits, such as leaves, twigs, husks, etc.: *Rake up the trash in the yard.* **2** worthless stuff; rubbish: *That magazine is trash. n.*

tread (tred), **1** set the foot down; walk; step: *Don't tread on the flower beds. They trod through the meadow.* **2** move the legs and feet as if walking: *Everyone in swimming class treads water for five minutes.* **3** act or sound of treading: *We heard the tread of marching feet.* **1,2** *v.,* **treads, trod, trod·den** or **trod, tread·ing; 3** *n.*

treat (trēt), **1** entertain with food, drink, or amusement: *treat some friends to ice cream.* **2** anything that gives pleasure. **1** *v.,* **2** *n.*

treat·ment (trēt′mənt), way of treating: *This cat has suffered from bad treatment. n.*

tre·men·dous (tri men′dəs), INFORMAL. very great; enormous: *That is a tremendous house for a family of three. adj.*

tri·an·gle (trī′ang′gəl), a plane figure having three sides and three angles. *n.*

trou·ble (trub′əl), **1** cause trouble to; disturb: *The lack of business troubled the grocer.* **2** extra work; bother; effort: *Take the trouble to work.* **1** *v.,* **trou·bled, trou·bling, 2** *n.*

truth·ful (trüth′fəl), telling the truth: *He is a truthful boy and will tell exactly what happened. adj.* —**truth′ful·ly,** *adv.*

tun·dra (tun′drə), a vast, level, treeless plain in the arctic regions. The ground beneath its surface is frozen even in summer. Much of Alaska and northern Canada is tundra. *n.*

two (tü), one more than one; 2. *n., pl.* **twos;** *adj.*

track (definition 2) running on a **track**

U

ug·ly (ug′lē), very unpleasant to look at. *adj.,* **ug·li·er, ug·li·est.**

un·con·test·ed (un′kən test′əd), undisputed; unopposed: *The referee's decision was uncontested. adj.*

un·for·tu·nate (un fôr′chə nit), not lucky; having bad luck. *adj.* —**un·for′tu·nate·ly,** *adv.*

un·friend·ly (un frend′lē), not friendly; hostile. *adj.*

un·heard (un hėrd′), not listened to; not heard: *unheard melodies. adj.*

a	hat	**ī**	ice	**ù**	put	**ə** stands for	
ā	age	**o**	not	**ü**	rule	**a**	in about
ä	far, calm	**ō**	open	**ch**	child	**e**	in taken
âr	care	**ȯ**	saw	**ng**	long	**i**	in pencil
e	let	**ô**	order	**sh**	she	**o**	in lemon
ē	equal	**oi**	oil	**th**	thin	**u**	in circus
ėr	term	**ou**	out	**ŦH**	then		
i	it	**u**	cup	**zh**	measure		

u·ni·verse (yü′nə vėrs′), the whole of existing things; everything there is, including all space and matter; the cosmos. *Our world is but a small part of the universe. n.*

un·known (un nōn′), not known; not familiar; strange. *adj.*

un·til (un til′), up to the time when. *conj.*

un·u·su·al (un yü′zhü əl), not usual; not ordinary; not in common use; uncommon; rare. *adj.*

up·on (ə pȯn′ *or* ə pon′), on. *prep.*

up·set (up′set′), an unexpected defeat: *The hockey team suffered an upset. n.*

up·stairs (up′stârz *or* up′starz′), on or to an upper floor: *She lives upstairs (adv.). He is waiting in an upstairs hall (adj.).*

use·less (yüs′lis), of no use; worthless: *A television set would be useless in a house without electricity. adj.*

u·su·al (yü′zhü əl), commonly seen, found, or happening; ordinary; customary. *adj.*

u·su·al·ly (yü′zhü ə lē), according to what is usual; commonly; ordinarily; customarily; often: *We usually eat dinner at 6. adv.*

walrus
The **walrus** has ivory tusks.

V

va·ca·tion (vā kā′shən), **1** freedom from school, business, or other duties: *There is a vacation from school every summer.* **2** take a vacation. **1** *n.,* **2** *v.*

Val·en·tine's Day (val′ən tīnz dā), a holiday in which cards or small gifts are given to friends and loved ones, February 14.

val·ley (val′ē), low land between hills or mountains. *n., pl.* **val·leys.**

van·ish (van′ish), disappear, especially suddenly: *The sun vanished behind a cloud. v.*

ver·i·fy (vâr′ə fī), test the correctness of; check for accuracy: *You can verify the spelling of a word by looking in a dictionary. v.,* **ver·i·fied, ver·i·fy·ing.**

ver·tex (vėr′teks), the point where two sides of an angle meet. *n.*

vil·lage (vil′ij), group of houses, usually smaller than a town. *n.*

vol·ca·no (vol kā′nō), an opening in the earth's crust through which steam, ashes, and lava are forced out in periods of activity. *n., pl.* **vol·ca·noes** *or* **vol·ca·nos.**

vol·ume (vol′yəm), space occupied: *The storeroom has a volume of 800 cubic feet. n.*

W

waist (wāst), the part of the human body between the ribs and the hips. *n.*

wal·rus (wȯl′rəs *or* wol′rəs), a large sea mammal of the arctic regions, resembling a seal but having long tusks. It is hunted for its hide, tusks, and blubber oil. *n., pl.* **wal·rus·es** *or* **wal·rus.**

want (wont *or* wȯnt), wish for; wish: *We want a new car. I want to become an engineer. v.*

wash (wosh), clean with water or other liquid: *wash one's face, wash clothes, wash dishes. v.,* **washed, wash·ing.**

wash·a·ble (wosh′ə bəl *or* wȯ′shə bəl), able to be washed without damage: *washable silk. adj.*

wash·cloth (wosh′klȯth *or* wȯsh′klȯth′), a small cloth for washing oneself. *n.*

was·n't (woz′nt *or* wuz′nt), was not.

waste (wāst), **1** make poor use of; spend uselessly; fail to get full value or benefit from: *Though I had much work to do, I wasted my time doing nothing.* **2** poor use; useless spending; failure to get the most out of something: *Buying that suit was a waste of money.* **1** *v.* **wast·ed, wast·ing;** **2** *n.*

watch (woch *or* wȯch), **1** look attentively or carefully. **2** device for telling time, small enough to be carried in a pocket or worn on the wrist. **1** *v.,* **2** *n., pl.* **watch·es.**

wa·ter foun·tain (wȯ′tər or wot′ər foun′tən), **1** water flowing or rising into the air in a spray. **2** place to get a drink.

wa·ter·way (wȯ′tər wā′ or wot′ər wā′), river, canal, or other body of water that ships can go on. *n.*

weak·ness (wēk′nis), a weak point; slight fault: *Putting things off is her weakness. n., pl.* **weak·ness·es.**

weave (wēv), make out of thread, strips, or strands of the same material. *v.,* **wove, wo·ven** or **wove, weav·ing.**

we'd (wēd), **1** we had: *We'd left the party early.* **2** we would: *We'd love to see you again.*

Wed., Wednesday.

week·end (wēk′end′), Saturday and Sunday as a time for recreation, visiting, etc. *n.*

week·ly (wēk′lē), of a week; for a week; lasting a week: *a weekly wage of $150. adj.*

weight (wāt), how heavy a thing is: the amount a thing weighs. *n.*

weight·less (wāt′lis), being free from the pull of gravity. *adj.*

weird (wird), **1** unearthly or mysterious; wild; strange: *They were awakened by a weird shriek. It was the weirdest noise I had ever heard.* **2** odd; fantastic; queer: *The robin made a weirder sound than the sparrow. adj.,* **weird·er, weird·est.**

wel·come (wel′kəm), **1** greet kindly; give a friendly reception to: *We always welcome guests at our house.* **2** a kind or friendly reception: *You will always have a welcome here.* **1** *v.,* **wel·comed, wel·com·ing; 2** *n.*

we'll (wēl), we will: *We'll be arriving at about 6:00.*

went (went), See **go.** *I went home promptly after school. v.*

we're (wir), we are: *We're all looking forward to your visit.*

were (wėr), form of the verb **be** used with *you, we, they* or any plural noun to indicate the past tense. *The officer's orders were obeyed. v.*

we've (wēv), we have: *We've had a wonderful time.*

whale (hwāl), mammal shaped like a huge fish and living in the sea. Oil from whales used to be burned in lamps. *n., pl.* **whales** or **whale.**

what·ev·er (hwot ev′ər or hwut ev′ər), anything that: *Do whatever you like. pron.*

what's (hwots or hwuts), **1** what is: *What's the latest news?* **2** what has: *What's been going on here lately?*

wheat (hwēt), the grain of a common cereal grass, used to make flour. *n.*

when (hwen), **1** at what time: *When does school close?* **2** at the time that: *Stand up when your name is called.* **1** *adv.,* **2** *conj.*

when·ev·er (hwen ev′ər), when; at whatever time; at any time that: *Come whenever you wish (conj.). I'll come whenever possible (adv.). conj., adv.*

where (hwâr or hwar), in what place; at what place: *Where do you live? Where is he? adv.*

wher·ev·er (hwâr ev′ər or hwar ev′ər), where; to whatever place; in whatever place: *Sit wherever you like (conj.) Wherever are you going? (adv.). conj., adv.*

whirl (hwėrl), **1** turn or swing round and round; spin: *The leaves whirled in the wind.* **2** move round and round: *whirl a lasso. We whirled about the room. v.*

weave

weaving on a large loom

a	hat	**ī** ice	**u̇** put	**ə** stands for
ā	age	**o** not	**ü** rule	**a** in about
ä	far, calm	**ō** open	**ch** child	**e** in taken
âr	care	**ȯ** saw	**ng** long	**i** in pencil
e	let	**ô** order	**sh** she	**o** in lemon
ē	equal	**oi** oil	**th** thin	**u** in circus
ėr	term	**ou** out	**ᵺ** then	
i	it	**u** cup	**zh** measure	

whole (hōl), **1** having all its proper parts; complete: *whole egg, whole milk.* **2** full; entire: *He ate the whole melon. adj.*

whole milk (hōl milk), milk from which none of the natural elements have been removed.

whole note (hōl nōt), (in music) note to be played four times as long as one quarter note.

whole-wheat (hōl′hwēt′), made from whole-wheat flour: *whole-wheat bread. adj.*

who'll (hül), who will: *Who'll help me wash the dishes?*

who's (hüz), **1** who is: *Who's going with me?* **2** who has: *Who's seen the new wildlife documentary?*

whose (hüz), of whom; of which: *The girl whose work got the prize is very talented. Whose book is this? pron.*

width (width), how wide a thing is; distance across; breadth: *The room is 12 feet in width. n.*

wild (wīld), not in proper control or order: *wild hair. adj.*

will (wil), am going to; is going to; are going to: *We will go to the beach on Saturday. v., past tense* **would.**

win (win), be successful over others; get victory or success in: *We all hope our team will win. v.,* **won, win·ning.**

win·dow (win′dō), an opening to let in light or air set into an outer wall or roof of a building or into a vehicle. *n.*

wind sock (wind sok), device somewhat like a large sock, mounted on a pole and open at one end to catch the wind and show its direction.

wind vane (wind vān), a tool that shows wind direction.

wish·y-wash·y (wish′ē wosh′ē or wish′ē wȯsh′ē), lacking strength of character; indecisive: *a wishy-washy person. adj.*

wisp (wisp), a flock of birds, especially of marsh birds called snipe. *n.*

wrench
A **wrench** holds and turns bolts and nuts.

with (wiᴛʜ *or* with), *With* shows that persons or things are taken together in some way. **1** in the company of: *Come with me.* **2** by means of: *The man cut the meat with a knife. prep.*

with·draw (wiᴛʜ drȯ′ *or* with drȯ′), draw back; draw away. *v.,* **with·drew, with·drawn, with·draw·ing.**

with·hold (with hōld′ *or* wiᴛʜ hōld′), refrain from giving or granting. *v.,* **with·held, with·hold·ing.**

with·stand (with stand′ *or* wiᴛʜ stand′), stand against; hold out against; resist; oppose, especially successfully. *v.,* **with·stood, with·stand·ing.**

wood (wu̇d), trees or parts of trees cut up for use in building houses, making boats and furniture, etc. *n.*

wor·ry (wėr′ē), **1** feel anxious; be uneasy: *Don't worry about little things. They will worry if we are late.* **2** make anxious; trouble: *The problem worried me. v.,* **wor·ried, worry·ing.**

worth·less (wėrth′lis), without worth; good-for-nothing; useless: *Throw those worthless, broken toys away. adj.*

would (wu̇d), See **will.** *Would you help us, please? v.*

would·n't (wu̇d′nt), would not.

would've (wu̇d′uv), would have.

wow (wou), exclamation of surprise, joy, etc. *interj.*

wreath (rēth), a ring of flowers or leaves twisted together. *n., pl.* **wreaths** (rēᴛʜz).

wreck (rek), **1** what is left of anything that has been destroyed or much injured. **2** cause the wreck of; destroy; ruin: *Raccoons wrecked our campsite looking for food.* **1** *n.,* **2** *v.*

wren (ren), a small songbird with a slender bill and a short tail. Wrens often build their nests near houses. *n.*

wrench (rench), tool for turning nuts, bolts, etc. *n., pl.* **wrench·es.**

wres·tler (res′lər), person who wrestles, especially as a sport. *n.*

wrist (rist), the joint connecting hand and arm. *n.*

write (rīt), make letters or words with pen, pencil, or chalk: *You can read and write. v.,* **wrote, writ·ten, writ·ing.**

writ·ing (rī′ting), literary work; a book or other literary production: *the writings of Benjamin Franklin. n.*

writ·ten (rit′n), See **write.** *He has written a letter. v., a written note. adj.*

Y

yes·ter·day (yes′tər dē), the day before today. *n.*

you'd (yüd; *unstressed* yu̇d), **1** you had: *You'd already left.* **2** you would: *You'd love this book.*

young (yung), without much experience or practice. *adj.*

your (yu̇r; *unstressed* yər), belonging to you: *Wash your hands. adj.*

you're (yu̇r, *unstressed* yər), you are: *Tell me where you're going.*

Z

zin·ni·a (zin′ē ə), a garden plant grown for its showy flowers of many colors. *n.* (The *zinnia* was named in honor of Johann G. *Zinn,* 1727-1759, a German botanist.)

wrestler

wrestlers during a match

a	hat	**ī**	ice	**u̇**	put	**ə**	stands for
ā	age	**o**	not	**ü**	rule	**a**	in about
ä	far, calm	**ō**	open	**ch**	child	**e**	in taken
âr	care	**ȯ**	saw	**ng**	long	**i**	in pencil
e	let	**ô**	order	**sh**	she	**o**	in lemon
ē	equal	**oi**	oil	**th**	thin	**u**	in circus
ėr	term	**ou**	out	**ᴛʜ**	then		
i	it	**u**	cup	**zh**	measure		